FRINGE-DWELLERS AND WELFARE

Jeff Collmann completed degrees at Lehigh University, Pennsylvania in 1971 and the University of Manchester, England, in 1975. He took up a research position at the University of Adelaide, South Australia, in 1974 and taught in the Department of Anthropology from 1978–82. He was awarded a Ph.D. in 1980.

FRINGE-DWELLERS AND WELFARE

THE ABORIGINAL RESPONSE TO BUREAUCRACY

Jeff Collmann

University of Queensland Press

ST LUCIA • LONDON • NEW YORK

First published 1988 by University of Queensland Press
Box 42, St Lucia, Queensland, Australia

Typeset by University of Queensland Press
Printed in Australia by The Book Printer, Melbourne

Distributed in the UK and Europe by University of Queensland Press
Dunhams Lane, Letchworth, Herts. SG6 1LF England

Distributed in the USA and Canada by University of Queensland Press
250 Commercial Street, Manchester, NH 03101 USA

Cataloguing in Publication Data

National Library of Australia

Collmann, Jeff, 1949–   .
   Fringe-dwellers and welfare.

Bibliography.
Includes index.
   1. Aborigines, Australian – Northern Territory – Alice Springs –
Government relations. 2. Aborigines, Australian – Northern Territory – Alice
Springs – Public welfare. 3. Aborigines, Australian – Northern Territory –
Alice Springs – Urban residence. I. Title.

305.8'9915'094291

British Library (data available)

Library of Congress

Collmann, Jeff, 1949–   .
   Fringe-dwellers and welfare.

Bibliography: p.
Includes index.

1. Australia aborigines – Australia – Alice Springs (N.T.)
2. Australian aborigines – Social conditions.
3. Australia – Native races.
4. Squatter settlements – Australia – Alice Springs (N.T.) I. Title.

GN667.N6C646   1987   306'.0899915   86-27216

ISBN 0 7022 2067 1

To my parents

Contents

List of Tables   *ix*
List of Figures   *xi*
Acknowledgments   *xiii*

Introduction   *1*
1. Aboriginal Secrets and White Brokers   *14*
2. The Politics of Detribalization   *39*
3. Living in the Fringe-Camps   *73*
4. Urban Aboriginal Women and Welfare   *105*
5. Finding Work in the Central Australian Cattle
    Industry   *126*
6. The Gift of the Spirit: A Theory of Drinking   *149*
7. Violence, Debt and the Negotiation of Exchange   *169*
8. Burning Mt Kelly   *205*
9. Epilogue: The Bureaucratic Expropriation of Aboriginal
    Culture   *223*

Appendix 1: The Central Australian Cattle Industry   *237*
Appendix 2: Work Careers of Mt Kelly Adults   *258*
Bibliography   *259*
Index   *269*

List of Tables

1. Rural links of fringe-camp dwellers in Alice Springs, 1976   97
2. Violent encounters at Mt Kelly, April 1975 to June 1976   *176*
3. Average station area and percentage distribution of stations   *238*
4. Average herd size per station   *239*
5. Percentage distribution of stations by herd size   *239*
6. Percentage distribution of stations by ownership type   *240*
7. Percentage distribution of stations by management type   *240*
8. Structural improvements − station average by district   *252*
9. Annual number of employees and average duration of employment − station average by district   *253*
10. Road transport of cattle in Northern Territory: 1958–59 to 1964–65   *255*
11. Capital structure − station average by district   *256*
12. Gross annual investment − station average by district   *256*
13. Net income structure − station average by district   *257*

List of Figures

1. Map showing location of *Tjuritja* camp in the 1930s   *89*
2. Map showing direction of Amoonguna   *92*
3. Case One: Extended family tree   *179*
4. Northern Territory cattle numbers, 1910 to 1973   *242*

Acknowledgments

Unquestionably this book is the product of the joint work of many people. I am foremost in the debt of Lilliam and Kristina Collmann who stayed with me throughout the fieldwork and writing up, often at great inconvenience and personal cost. Their loyalty and support were absolutely necessary for all my work. They tolerated not only their own personal discomfort, but also what I myself contributed to a sometimes difficult enough situation. They were not always happy during the years of work, yet they, and now Justin, always supported me and made the entire exercise worthwhile. I could not have done it alone.

People in Alice Springs often commented to me that anthropologists were unwelcome in the region. I never encountered any hostility in this regard. The people of Mt Kelly, the fringe-camp in which I lived, were particularly gracious and tolerant. There is no doubt in my mind that they are responsible for what little insight I have gained into the affairs of Central Australia. They permitted me to observe, and instructed me in, aspects of their lives which, all things considered, they might rather have wished to keep to themselves. In this book I have tried to portray their social world as I understand they perceive it. Only in this way can I explain some aspects of their lives which most outsiders condemn. I hope that I have not misrepresented them or failed in this endeavour. If I have succeeded in any sense, I will have accomplished my primary aim.

There were many other people in Alice Springs who helped me and my family. I cannot enumerate them all. I want to express our special gratitude to our friends, the Little Sisters of Jesus, who never failed to grant the warmth of their home to us. Mrs

Betty McKay and Mr and Mrs Geoff Eames were also very good to us throughout our fieldwork. In general, I owe the people of Alice Springs a great debt.

It is impossible to assess the debt one owes great teachers. I cannot adequately thank the men who, by introducing me to anthropology, changed my world view many times. Professor Bruce Kapferer was my supervisor and counsellor for over nine years. In that time he supported me when I did not consider myself worth supporting. He constantly encouraged me and pressured me to make the most of my material. He frequently referred me to just the book or article I needed to develop a nascent idea which, I am quite sure, he understood better than I. He suggested I go to Alice Springs. I only hope that the end product of all his work somewhat measures up to his expectations.

Dr Lee Sackett and Dr Kingsley Garbett also supervised my work in Alice Springs. Dr Sackett's knowledge of Aborigines and the relevant anthropological literature was very helpful. I began to make major progress in my work during my period as a tutor under Dr Garbett. He gave unsparingly of his time and enthusiasm listening to the often hare-brained ideas which his lectures and courses stimulated in my mind. He also had the thankless task of minding this book in thesis form through the administrative procedures at the end.

The Department of Anthropology at the University of Adelaide was a very stimulating and demanding place in which to write. The quality of criticism and helpful insight characteristic of my fellow postgraduates, in particular, disciplined me and developed my imagination more than I can know. Among the staff, Tom Ernst, Roy Fitzhenry and Adrian Peace were very helpful. David Mearns and Mike Muetzelfeldt shared the problems of being a postgraduate student. Their own work has been a critical standard to which I have always had to measure up.

I benefited from the extensive assistance of scholars outside Adelaide. Dr Don Handelman, Professor Mervyn Meggitt, Professor Anselm Strauss, and Dr J. Clyde Mitchell all read portions of my work at various stages and made extremely valuable comments. As should also be apparent from my work, I have drawn great profit from their own published works. Dr Thomas Hood provided indispensable support in the United States and made my return there much easier. Dr Don Dougall gave the right measure of help at just the right time.

I must also thank the University of Adelaide. My fieldwork

and early writing-up periods were financed by a University Research Grant from the University of Adelaide. The university, through departmental grants, also provided me with a vehicle, money to run it and other material assistance which made my work easier. I could never have gone to Alice Springs without the university's support.

Mrs Jacqui Gray and Mrs Ray Mulvihill typed this book in thesis form. Mrs Pam Story typed the final manuscript. I want to thank them for their diligence, their critical comments on all aspects of the manuscript and their perpetual good humour. Dr Don Lighter and the Department of Pediatrics, University of Tennessee Hospital, graciously allowed me to type the final manuscript on the department's computer.

The editors of *Social Analysis, Ethnology*, and the *Journal of Anthropological Research* permitted me to reprint all or part of chapters one, three, four and six from earlier publications of mine in their journals. I had two teachers early in my academic career who have remained great sources of inspiration: Professor Carl Strauch introduced me to meaningful scholarship and Mr James Snodgrass first stimulated my interest in the social sciences. I want to thank them both very much.

Dr and Mrs Reid Collmann made my whole academic career possible. Without them I would have never gone anywhere or done anything. I can say nothing to thank my parents. My debt to them is ineradicable and a joy to bear.

Acknowledgment is also made to the Australian Government Publishing Service for permission to reproduce ten tables from *Northern Territory Beef Cattle Industry: An economic survey 1942–43 and 1964–65* (Department of Primary Industry, 1968); to the Australian Institute of Aboriginal Studies for permission to quote from R.M. Berndt, *Aborigines and Change: Australia in the Seventies* (1977); to the *Centralian Advocate* for permission to quote from "Hit with Flagon Claim", 12 December 1974; and to Jim Downing, Institute of Aboriginal Development, Alice Springs, Northern Territory, for the reference from "Aboriginal Dreamings and Town Plans" (1974).

Introduction

There is a tendency to analyse the social situation of contemporary Australian Aborigines as if they had fallen from a state of grace, the state of traditional Aboriginal society. The very terms of analysis (detribalization, dehumanization) conjure images of people lost and disoriented in a secular purgatory. A derivative tendency is to assess living Aborigines according to the extent of their damnation. According to this analysis there are a few, increasingly insignificant, "traditionally oriented" people who have not yet succumbed to the temptations of culture contact. However, the vast majority of Aborigines have been lured or dragged away from their natural state and prospects are dim for the remaining minority. Eulogies for the lost have been written. Grave exhortations to salvage the remnants of the traditional state have been enunciated. A sense of gloom as if at the end of an era hangs over all this gnashing of intellectual teeth.

At one level this is harmless enough, a latter-day hankering after images of the analysts' own lost past. When nostalgia repudiates the authenticity of the experiences of the damned and casts them in the role of deviant, however, sentimentality has overcome analysis and clouds judgment. Evidence that this has happened comes from a recent attempt to portray the damned as if they did indeed have something genuinely worth experiencing. In the introduction to *Aborigines and Change: Australia in the '70s*, Berndt (1977, 5) notes:

> The hard facts of socialization within the traditional system per se are the only processes which are available for knowledge and feeling to be transmitted in that respect. Nevertheless, it is possible to have a particular perspective based on what is assumed to be an Aboriginal

way of life — that is, to have an idea or vision of it. Whether we think of this as a "mirage" or not is really beside the point. Certainly it is a mirage in relation to traditional Aboriginal life as it existed in the past or continues to exist today in some regions. But as a viable view, believed in by those who wish to believe in it, it has a reality of its own.

Berndt seems to be directing his attention primarily to those Aborigines who, although not socialized in the "traditional system per se", none the less try to legitimate their identity as Aborigines in terms of their privileged access to Aboriginal culture. Such people are now often found speaking for Aborigines in the context of bureaucratic politics — a context in which few whites recognize the validity of their Aboriginal identity. Berndt appears only just to grant them the right to speak on the basis of their experiences. He unequivocably denies the relevance of their experiences to traditional society and sets them apart from that once "living reality". He thereby leaves them "insecure — unsure of themselves as persons and as members of a group (or groups)" (Berndt 1977, 7). In line with an age-old tradition, Berndt identifies drinking, prostitution, venereal disease, etc. as the symptoms of this declining "Aboriginality" (Berndt and Berndt 1977, 505). Berndt makes his condemnation of this process explicit by saying that change for its own sake (particularly if encouraged by outside bureau-cracies) leads to dehumanization, that is, "a subordination of human values in contrast to purely materialistic and economic ones . . . manifested in social and political agitation" (Berndt 1977, x).

One must question any analysis which denies either that material and economic values are "human" or that people have the right to agitate to secure their well-being. Yet, the fundamental problem with patronizing analyses of this type is that they refer all aspects of contemporary Aboriginal society back to images of the archaic past or some latter-day remnant of it. There is no attempt to comprehend current issues in terms of the con-temporary situation of Aborigines. From this perspective the only meaning of the life of contemporary Aborigines is as an in-dex of the decline of "those features that were distinctively Aboriginal as contrasted with everything else" (Berndt 1977, xii). By themselves, contemporary Aborigines and their social situ-ation are meaningless and of no real interest. This judgment about the authenticity and intrinsic importance of what Aborigines now experience is invidious as a means both of discrediting Aborigines in political conflict and of relegating the understanding of "non-tribal" Aborigines to the intellectual sidelines. Yet, the central thesis of this book is that the "non-tribal" Aborigines, particularly the so-called "fringe-dwellers", are absolutely critical to the understanding of how all Aborigines have responded and adapted to the coming of whites to Central Australia and to their subordination to white power. More generally, the point is that the recent development of Aboriginal society must be analysed in the context of white colonization.

There is perhaps no category of Aborigines who has received the opprobrium of observers more than the fringe-dwellers. Living in self-constructed shacks on the edges of towns throughout Australia, they are usually considered the very embodiment of the process of detribalization. As threats to the public and bureaucratic order, fringe-dwellers represent what most analysts (anthropological and otherwise) would like to avoid in the development of Aboriginal social life. Yet, few analysts have tried to describe how fringe-dwellers perceive their social world or to analyse them in terms of their relationship to the wider setting.[1] Stanner mentions that fringe-dwellers resisted being institutionalized (Stanner 1974, 46). Yet, neither he nor anybody else has tried to relate systematically the emergence of fringe-camps to the development of Aboriginal administrations. This is important because I will argue below that fringe-camps, properly so-called, have developed as part of how Aborigines have attempted to control the effects of the increased power and involvement of various social welfare agencies in their everyday life. Indeed, to assert that fringe-dwellers are simply detribalized people is to transform an important political act into a symptom of individual affliction and group decay. This approach treats fringe-dwellers as misshapen objects instead of thinking, responsive human beings. In the wider context it legitimates ever greater elaboration of the conditions which initially generated the fringe-camps, that is, the impingement of white power (particularly, social welfare agencies of various types) on everyday Aboriginal social life.

In this book I attempt to provide a systematic alternative to the detribalization argument primarily by examining everyday social life in the fringe-camps around Alice Springs and the role of social welfare agencies in it. This study is not simply an analysis of Aborigines: it is an analysis of the community of people (Aborigines and whites) who are involved in making and remaking Aboriginal social life. I base my analysis on the fundamental points made about urban Africans on the Copperbelt by Gluckman (1958, 1971), Mitchell (1956, 1966, 1974), Epstein (1958), Kapferer (1972) and other members of the Manchester School of urban anthropology. The arguments of these analysts are well known, yet two points are worth emphasizing with respect to Aborigines. First, the norms and values based in the context of tribal affairs neither inhibit the adaptation of Aborigines (in this case) to new kinds of situations that emerge from different conditions nor necessarily influence how Aborigines adapt to new settings. The relevance of traditional customs as well as the emergence of new patterns of social life are matters of empirical investigation. Second, whatever patterns of social life are discovered, they must be interpreted situationally, that is, as aspects of how Aborigines actively interpret and respond to the conditions of their daily lives as they define them. Nobody is a blind slave to custom, unable to face new settings and manage them. This perspective does not deny that Aboriginal custom might remain relevant to Aborigines (or, indeed, to whites). Rather, it suggests that the relevance or meaning of traditional custom to Aborigines cannot be interpreted as surviving from the pre-colonial past. Customs maintain themselves insofar as they remain meaningful to contemporary Aborigines. Similarly, Aborigines who have adopted new ways of life in the face of new circumstances cannot be simply dismissed as deviant, detribalized, or somehow less than full members of the community.

One of Gluckman's most important contributions to the analysis of black–white relations in southern and central Africa is that one must examine and understand the impact of white administrators and more generally white power upon local black communities. Indeed, in a much-criticized choice of words, he argues that white administrators are as much a part of black communities as the local black people themselves (Gluckman 1958, 1968, 1971). His point, as well as his choice of words, is entirely appropriate to the understanding of contemporary Aboriginal communities. Not only are whites regular, interacting parts of Aboriginal communities, but also they maintain and control most avowedly "Aboriginal" communities (such as missions and goverment settlements) which they established. Yet, in a manner entirely typical of the white administrators and government analysts of central and southern Africa, little notice has been taken of this fact. As in Africa, the official language speaks of detribalization and stresses the importance of maintaining social control by means of "traditional" norms and sanctions. In Australia this idea has been the critical principle of white administration since the very earliest days and remains the guiding ideal of much contemporary thought and practice; nor have any social analysts questioned the basic assumptions upon which the administrators' ideas rest.

The urban Africans studied by Gluckman and his colleagues were primarily industrial labourers of various types and the analysts' critiques were directed primarily at the whites who were trying to regulate and manage African industrial problems. Perhaps the biggest difference between Africans on the Copperbelt and Central Australian Aborigines is that relatively few Aborigines can find regular work. Although the official statistics are not very accurate, the 1971 census suggests that a range of between 60 and 80 per cent of Aboriginal men (depending upon the community) is unemployed in Central Australia (Australian Bureau of Statistics 1971). Moreover, the opportunities for work have been declining in the last decade and show no signs of increasing in the immediate future.

This has important consequences for relations between Aborigines and social welfare agencies. On the one hand, the welfare agencies are charged with providing Aborigines with basic subsistence resources, rather than simply managing consumer items that Aborigines purchase with resources they have earned or produced. On the other hand, Aborigines in Central Australia have very few opportunities outside the welfare apparatus for gaining a living. Those Aborigines who do have jobs outside the welfare structure or otherwise earn their own living are rare and constitute special cases. Consequently, much of Aboriginal daily life is concerned with managing the welfare agencies who control the basic resources they need to survive. With respect to Gluckman's arguments, it means that the attitudes and administrative procedures of the white bureaucrats working in, or concerned with, Central Australia are very much more important to Aborigines than they were to urban Africans on the Copperbelt. Indeed, that Aborigines must take the ideas of white administrators into account in the course of even their most intimate domestic affairs is perhaps the single most important fact of their lives and the key to many of the social changes which have developed in Aboriginal life in recent years. The elaboration of the welfare apparatus responsible for Aborigines in Central Australia is the critical social process reorganizing Aboriginal social life, not processes of industrial development.

Given the administrators' view on Aboriginal culture and detribalization, these circumstances have had some striking results. Most notably, they have produced the very ways of life they were officially supposed to prevent, that is, those under-stood as "detribalized" ways of life. The most obvious phenomena of this type are the fringe-camps around the major urban centres in the Northern Territory. The fringe-camps around Alice Springs, particularly a camp I will call Mt Kelly, are the focus of this book. The term "fringe-camp" refers in Australia to an encampment of people (usually Aborigines, but often including a few white men) living in rudimentary shacks they constructed themselves on the edges of town.[2] These camps usually lack running water, electricity, and conventional sewerage systems. Although many of their residents spend most of their lives in the fringe-camps, many (particularly the men) must often also leave the camps to find work. This coming and going of some fringe-camp residents gives many outsiders the impression that the camps are impermanent and their residents shiftless. This general impression of social decay is heightened by what many outsiders consider to be abnormally high amounts of alcohol consumption, violence, disease, and other apparent signs of disorganization. Given that the majority of fringe-camp residents are Aborigines, the camps seem at first glance to pro-vide the most unequivocable documentation of the validity of the detribalization thesis. Indeed, as I suggested earlier, the fringe-camps are usually interpreted as precisely the develop-ments all social welfare agencies and perhaps the Australian public as a whole would like to avoid.

It is curious, therefore, to discover that from the fringe-camp residents' point of view the camps are as much about controlling the power of social welfare agencies as they are about anything else. Moreover, some of the phenomena the welfare bureaucrats find most objectionable (for example, drinking) emerged as part of the fringe-campers' attempts to manage the effects of white power, particularly the power of social welfare agencies. The implication of these points is that one cannot understand fringe-camps without reference to the whites who try to control them. Nor can one completely understand white welfare policies with-out reference to the actions Aborigines take in response to the welfare apparatus itself. Aboriginal clients and welfare agents interact with and affect each other.

These points provide only a partial description of the problems for analysis. It is impossible to understand Aboriginal–white relationships without reference to relationships among whites and among Aborigines. On the one hand, processes of conflict and competition among whites have historically compelled one white agency after another to impinge upon Central Australian Aboriginal groups. Indeed, the detribalization thesis has been most important in the context of the competition of whites for Aboriginal clients. Aboriginal "problems" (as summarized in the detribalization thesis) have been major resources for white groups of all political persuasions in their efforts to maintain or acquire local power since the earlist days of white settlement in the Northern Territory. On the other hand, in their efforts to manage whites, Aborigines both cooperate and compete among themselves. Because whites monopolize the basic resources in Central Australia, all Aborigines must gain access to white agents who will provide them with what they need to survive. Given the high rate of unemployment among Aboriginal adults and their general class position, the competition among Aborigines for the available scarce resources is fierce, and, in general, it fragments Aboriginal communities. None the less, Aborigines do and, indeed, must cooperate with one another if they are to gain access to whites; and they must cooperate with whites if they are to maintain access to other Aborigines. In short, nothing less than a community study of whites, Aborigines, and their various interrelationships is sufficient to understand contemporary developments in Central Australia.

These points establish the basic goals of my analysis. In the course of developing arguments about the particular problems of my work, other people have raised some important general issues. Among the most important perhaps are the related questions of the significance of culture to fringe-dwellers and the problem of choice or strategizing. In general, transactional analyses similar to mine have been criticized for being insensitive to cultural constraints and for reducing all social behaviour to an expression of the urge to maximize. Kapferer, for example, although a transactionalist himself, has argued that the promise of transactionalism will go unfulfilled if the cultural meaning of particular social practices is ignored or dismissed as irrelevant to the conduct of everyday affairs (Kapferer 1976). There is a clear sense in which I see the fringe-campers as strategizing. However, I do not see this sense of strategizing as inconsistent with my attempts to understand the fringe-campers' definition of their situation, norms, and values, that is, with those things I understand loosely as culture. On the contrary, I have tried to explain how new cultural practices (for example, new marriage and kin-naming types) have emerged as part of the fringe-dwellers' studied efforts to manage their social situation. I think that Klockars's notion of ingenuity perhaps best expresses my general view on this issue (Klockars 1974).

According to Klockars (1974, 185), "ingenuity" springs from an actor's intimate knowledge of the "norms, conventions, participants, practices, and procedures" in his social environment and underlies his capacity to take advantage of the opportunities it offers. The particular types of knowledge necessary to establish ingenuity vary with the social context, and, to that extent, any socially competent actor has a degree of ingenuity. What distinguishes the ingenuity of fringe-dwellers from anybody acting in his own social world are the general conditions under which they must live. Unlike the professional fence Klockars analyses, the fringe-campers are not criminals. None the less, Aborigines in Central Australia generally, and fringe-campers particularly, have been historically classed as deviants and have been the objects of overt techniques of therapy, social engineering and punishment. Consequently, they have developed both a keen sense of how whites (particularly social welfare agents) can affect their lives and clear strategies for handling them.

The basis of Aboriginal ingenuity with respect to whites is a battery of techniques whereby they gain access to white-controlled resources but seek to minimize their debt to, and involvement with, white agencies. This idea is a recurring theme throughout this book and will become clearer as the argument develops. For the moment, let me examine what this idea implies about culture and strategizing. First, Aborigines have developed a working knowledge of white society insofar as it affects them. They have not necessarily learned the details of the various social welfare ordinances which have been used to control them over the years.[3] However, they have learned the law's consequences. During the regime of the Welfare Branch, for example, the Mt Kelly people learned that white welfare officers had the power to confine Aborigines to settlements and, equally as important, they learned the limits of the welfare agents' power. Running away from settlements was a reasonable response to those conditions and an expression of ingenuity. Second, Aborigines have learned what whites expect of them and the consequences of fulfilling or ignoring their expectations. The fact that whites have developed fairly explicit programmes and ideological descriptions of what they expect from Aborigines has helped this process, but Aborigines did not require such statements to learn what whites wanted. Moreover, they learned that whites wanted more than what they presented in their public statements and that not all aspects of the programme were mutually consistent. Quite to the contrary, the explicit programmes and unstated demands were usually predicated upon basic inconsistencies. Third, Aborigines have adapted their own conventions, norms, values, and typical understandings in an effort to manage the demands of white agencies. I will detail repeated examples of this process throughout the book. A notable example, however, is that new types of marriage have developed among Aborigines in Alice Springs. Although Aborigines have names for these new types of marriage (firestick, kangaroo, and proper) and recognize them as types, they none the less also manipulate their use of these terms in their dealings with each other and, critically, with the welfare agents. To a welfare agent, a kangaroo marriage warrants supporting mother's pensions, rent subsidies and general support. A proper marriage, on the other hand, warrants court action and the removal of children from their natal domestic group. Finally, Aborigines know that there is often a conflict between how whites perceive them and how they perceive themselves. Managing this conflict is a regular part of daily life, particularly for fringe-dwellers. The implication of these four points is that Aboriginal fringe-dwellers have developed cultural understanding about how to manage their relationships with white people.

Mt Kelly

Mt Kelly, the camp in which I lived and gathered most of my information, raises some interesting questions in the light of previous points.[4] As I said, outsiders typically think that fringe-camps are impermanent and that fringe-campers are shiftless people who never live anywhere for long. Most Mt Kelly people had lived in the camp's immediate environs for over twenty years at the time of my fieldwork. Some people had lived there

since the end of the Second World War. All the young residents
under the age of thirty were born in Mt Kelly or on a cattle station to which their parents had gone to work from Mt Kelly. The
people did tend to come and go primarily in response to the demand for labour on the cattle stations. Yet, it was to Mt Kelly
that they regularly returned and that their regular employers
journeyed when looking for workers.

It looked like any other fringe-camp around Alice Springs.
There were a couple of tents. Most people lived in shacks (locally
known as "humpies") which they had constructed themselves
from corrugated iron, wood and, occasionally, canvas. Everybody cooked and warmed themselves with a woodburning fire-
bucket. Unlike most fringe-camps, Mt Kelly had running water
from three cold taps and two cold showers. Since the earliest
days of the camp's settlement, the people dug privies and constructed their own privie sheds. These aspects of the camp's
material culture are typically interpreted as indices of the people's
poverty and social degradation. It is interesting, therefore, to discover that the Mt Kelly people deny that they are poor, spend
large amounts of money on items such as alcohol which they
might well have used to rent better housing, and present their
living conditions as marks of their independence and sense of
personal responsibility. I frequently heard people speak proudly
of welfare houses in Alice Springs which they had either refused
to accept or had destroyed. The Mt Kelly people explicitly say
that by living in the fringe-camps and tolerating unconventional
housing, they escape the controlling efforts of the welfare apparatus. Stories of how they ran away from welfare settlements
or otherwise resisted the welfare officers' attempts to control
them are critical parts of individual life histories and of the
fringe-campers' total self-perception. As I will detail below, the
fringe-camps really emerged as such in Alice Springs as the
Welfare Branch began to increase its power and efforts to control
Aborigines throughout the region. Mt Kelly has been involved in
this process from the very beginning.

There is little doubt that the Mt Kelly people do not enjoy a
standard of living equivalent to the average middle-class
Australian. It is equally true that their low standard of living is
principally the result of their working-class position and
macrosociological processes beyond their control. However,
relative to what is available to them, the Mt Kelly people live less
well than they could because they restrict their demand for

material goods, particularly those controlled by welfare officials.

By the same token, the people appear poor, but live well in comparison to many other Aborigines, particularly those living on the missions or settlements. The Mt Kelly people were fortunate because several pastoralists recruited almost all their labour from the camp and had done so for many years. Many pastoralists bypassed settlements, missions, or large station communities to recruit men from the camp. The Mt Kelly men were mostly part-Aborigines and had wide reputations as reliable, skilled cattleworkers. Occasionally, Mt Kelly people also worked in Alice Springs. Most women, for example, had worked as domestics in Alice Springs. Many in the camp held urban jobs during their careers. The fringe-camps are distinctive precisely because they offer this diverse range of employment opportunities.

The basis of the Mt Kelly economy, however, was the social security pension, of various kinds. In contrast to the money earned from cattleworking or urban employment, the pension money was regular. Although relatively small in amount, it was not subject to the ebbs and flows of earned money. A critical aspect of camp life and of my argument is that women substantially controlled pension incomes while men usually had to work. Moreover, men had to depend upon women's income during their own periods of unemployment. This is the key both to the consumption of liquor and to the patterns of interpersonal violence in the camp. The point I wish to emphasize now is that the combination of small, regular incomes and relatively large but irregular incomes is the basis of the Mt Kelly people's image of themselves as affluent. They restrict their demands for material goods to what they can usually afford on the basis of pension incomes. They splurge the irregular income derived from work on "luxuries", principally liquor. What outsiders interpret as degenerate self-destructive behaviour, the Mt Kelly people interpret as the foremost manifestation of their wealth, independence, and self-control.

The General Administrative Context

There were many different types of white people interacting with the Mt Kelly people and other Central Australian Aborigines during my fieldwork. Lawyers, doctors, politicians, social welfare workers, pastoralists, tourists, stockmen and many other white people either worked with or were in some way directly associated with Aborigines. In this book I shall try to analyse as much of the field of black–white interaction as possible. The main focus of my argument, none the less, will be the dynamics of interaction between Aborigines and the various social welfare agencies working in Central Australia, particularly the Department of the Northern Territory, Welfare Branch (1951 to 1972) and the Department of Aboriginal Affairs (from 1972). Not only were these agencies the source of most operating funds during their respective regimes, but they were also officially responsible for the welfare of Aborigines and constituted the major administrative fields within which most bureaucratic and political negotiations about Aboriginal welfare occurred.

My fieldwork was undertaken during a period of major administrative reorganization and transition. The old regime of the Welfare Branch was collapsing and the new regime of the Department of Aboriginal Affairs was being constructed. Consequently, the competition for Aboriginal clients which is a basic structural aspect of the local, regional, and Commonwealth administration emerged overtly in a series of major crises and minor scandals. Indeed, crises and scandals about Aboriginal "problems" became major political resources in everyday administrative life, and I devote much attention to these processes. Very little of contemporary Aboriginal life in Alice Springs or in the outlying missions, settlements and cattle stations can be understood without reference to the administrative structure itself or the competition among its various agencies for Aboriginal support.

It is equally important to realize that the role and importance of the welfare administration in the everyday life of Aborigines has increased dramatically in the last thirty years. The inauguration of the Welfare Branch in the early 1950s was a watershed in this respect. Prior to that time the Commonwealth tried to administer Aboriginal welfare through non-government agencies (such as missions and pastoralists) or through government agencies (such as the police or Department of Public Health) whose resonsibilities lay primarily elsewhere. The modern history of Aboriginal affairs in the Northern Territory begins with the Welfare Branch and the substantial increase in Commonwealth power over Aboriginal daily life it embodied.

This structural development occurred simultaneously with,

and was developed through, a wide range of laws, ordinances and regulations which have officially tried to control Aboriginal life. In some cases these laws denied Aborigines basic rights (such as the right to vote, the right to move as one wishes, the right to marry whom one pleases and the right to drink intoxicating beverages) which other Australians have long enjoyed and taken for granted. Few of these laws remained in force during my fieldwork and Aborigines enjoyed much greater constitutional control over themselves than in the past. None the less, the welfare administration controlled the basic resources Aborigines needed to survive more completely during my fieldwork than ever before. This was true in spite of (and, perhaps, even because of) the official ideology of "self-determination". More generally, the structural conditions of Central Australia life have substantially limited and, in some cases, vitiated the effect of the constitutional reforms. How this has occurred is a major problem for analysis and political consideration.

Notes

1. The most notable exception is Jeremy Beckett (see Beckett 1964).
2. Charles Mullard (1974) has made some trenchant criticisms of the term "fringe-camp", saying that it reflects the antagonistic, sometimes racist views of most observers of fringe-camp life. While I agree most observers have a distorted and usually hostile view of fringe-camp life, I retain the term "fringe-camp" primarily because it reflects how the Mt Kelly people themselves perceived its significance. I examine this in detail in chapter 3.
3. Klockars points out that fences are not successful because they know all the laws on burglary and receiving stolen goods. Specialized fences may know the laws covering the type of goods they handle. All fences must know the convention of their business environment, the characteristics of their products, and how to handle the law-enforcing agencies responsible for fences so as not to go to gaol (Klockars 1974).
4. My fieldwork in Alice Springs extended from September 1974 to June 1976. My family and I lived in Mt Kelly from April 1975 to June 1976.

1

Aboriginal Secrets
and White Brokers

Throughout the last century Aborigines across the Australian continent have become increasingly subject to various numbers and types of welfare agencies. In many regions of Australia Aboriginal dependence upon welfare resources initially emerged because of the expropriation of the land and the ensuing collapse of the hunting and gathering economy. In other areas, however, missionaries, police, public health officials and various other governmental welfare agencies invaded the Aboriginal scene in advance of the strictly economic frontier of colonial occupation. The indirect link between the economic exploitation of Australia and the rise of the field of Aboriginal care was the emergence and elaboration of the political issue of Aboriginal welfare. Whether cleaning up after the damage was done (known as "smoothing the dying pillow") or crossing the frontier in antici-pation of economic expansion, social welfare agencies have described their activities as safeguarding Aborigines from the in-evitable and destructive consequences of white colonization. By so arguing they legitimated their involvement with Aborigines and helped establish the autonomy of welfare administration in the colonization process as a whole.

Historically the field of Aboriginal welfare has been relatively fragmented in Australia. The Commonwealth, state, and local governments initially devolved most responsibility for Aboriginal welfare on to non-government agencies (for example, missions and cattle stations) or on to government agencies which were only tangentially concerned with welfare issues as a whole (Rowley 1974; Barwick 1974). During this period there was rela-tively little effort made to plan or implement an Aboriginal welfare policy as such. The local agencies were left to manage in the ways they thought best.

After the Second World War, however, the Commonwealth and state governments began to create and control more centralized administrations charged with responsibility for Aboriginal welfare. The various governments committed more money to Aboriginal programmes and established new welfare agencies under their own control. They also began to subsidize and try to direct the activities of earlier workers in the field. In addition, this concentration of Aboriginal administration in government hands occurred under the aegis of a new, more coordinated welfare orientation, widely known as the "assimilation policy".

These new initiatives developed in the context of continuing conflict about Aboriginal welfare. On the one hand, the government was trying to respond to public critiques of earlier workers and their efforts. Increased national and international awareness of spectacular incidents (for example, massacres in the Northern Territory) and of the general condition of Aborigines throughout the continent provoked recurrent demands for reform. On the other hand, the government's efforts to assume command of Aboriginal affairs generated competition and conflict among workers in the field as well as interested outsiders. The key point is that by taking these new initiatives the Commonwealth and state governments tried to bring conflict over the issue of Aboriginal welfare into their own domains. As Aboriginal welfare became a manifest political issue, the governments tried to make their own welfare administrations the ground upon which contention occurred.

A fundamental premise of welfare administration since the earliest days has been that ontological differences divide Aborigines and other Australians. Although variously conceived as cultural, ethnic or normative differences, they constitute an organic boundary between Aborigines and Europeans (Collmann 1981) which substantially isolates them from one another. This boundary has an absolute quality in the sense that violations of it necessarily produce disorder. On the one hand, Aborigines may not easily adapt to white-imposed circumstances. Rather, they must either remain oriented to their own values or completely assimilate white norms. Any partial assimilation generates symptoms of personal and group decay (alcoholism, prostitution, and so on). On the other hand, the introduction of nonassimilated Aborigines into white society generates cross-cultural conflict and racial tension.

The relevance of these ideas to the legitimation of assimilationist policies is clear enough. It is less clear but more significant that the organic boundary assumption makes bureaucratic intervention *per se* absolutely necessary in Aboriginal affairs irrespective of administrative policy. This is because the call for the administrative regulation of cross-boundary relationships is implicit in the assumption of the organic boundary's existence. The welfare apparatus has systematically tried to impose itself on Aborigines and supplant any relations between them and non-administrative agencies. In other words, the Aboriginal welfare apparatus is predatory and expansive (see Sahlins 1961). Moreover, the assumption that administratively uncontrolled relations between whites and Aborigines are impossible has been critical in the welfare bureaucracy's attempts legitimately to monopolize those relations (Stein 1964; Whyte 1955). What the welfare apparatus has portrayed as a boundary between two societies (Aboriginal and European) is in fact a constituted boundary *within* the field of the welfare apparatus itself.

These points have some important consequences for understanding the social situation of whites who work with Aborigines. In particular, we must understand that such whites are boundary riders and must act as brokers;[1] that is to say, if they are either to recruit Aboriginal clients or to receive support from Commonwealth agencies, they must maintain access to, and legitimate their identities within, both Aboriginal communities and the Commonwealth administration. This point is generally significant for several reasons. First, it emphasizes the extent to which Aboriginal and white interpretations of Aboriginal social life are resources in administrative politics. Second, it suggests that, irrespective of their ideological positions, white administrators must actively impinge upon Aborigines. Third, Aborigines must develop means to control how white administrators impinge upon them. These conditions indicate generally that the analysis either of Aboriginal administration or of Aboriginal social life is incomplete without reference to the dynamics of relationships between Aborgines and whites.

Major changes occurred in the administration of Aboriginal welfare during my fieldwork. As a result of the Australian Labor Party's success in the 1972 federal election, a new regime was developing in the Northern Territory. The new government disbanded the Welfare Branch which administered Aboriginal affairs from 1951 to 1972 and redistributed its responsibilities to other Commonwealth agencies. In addition, it created the Department of Aboriginal Affairs and began to implement its new "self-determination" policy. Although many white agents who worked under the Welfare Branch maintained their relationships with local Aborigines, new agencies and new people entered the field. Consequently, the conditions which enabled any particular white agency to play the broker's role were unsettled and everyday administration was full of ambiguities. In particular, the increase in white agencies working with Aborigines meant that no single agency could count upon the full support of its Aboriginal clients. On the contrary, there was tremendous competition among local whites for Aboriginal support and Aborigines themselves were exploring the opportunities the new agencies made available.

These local conditions influenced the practical implementation of the federally constituted self-determination policy. The self-determination policy was supposed to have been a nationally coordinated, comprehensive effort. Yet, because of the patterns of competition and interdependence among local administrators and Aborigines, the self-determination policy ultimately legitimated, and even encouraged, the fragmentation of Aboriginal administration in Central Australia.

A Case: The Department of Aboriginal Affairs

Upon taking power in December 1972, Gough Whitlam's Labor government established the Department of Aboriginal Affairs (DAA). In so doing, it endorsed and consummated three trends which had been developing in the administration of Aboriginal welfare during the preceding several years. First, it founded a Commonwealth administration whose chief responsiblity was to plan and implement a *national* programme for all Australian Aborigines. Under the previous regime, which dated from the end of the Second World War, each state government administered its own Aboriginal welfare programme. In spite of the fact that all states shared a general orientation to Aboriginal affairs (known as the assimilation policy), there were great differences in actual policy and practice from state to state (Rowley

1974). The Labor government presented its new mode of administration as fulfilling the demands of the 1967 Commonwealth referendum in which Australian voters endorsed the idea
that Aboriginal affairs be managed by the Commonwealth, not
the states. The DAA was the vehicle for reorganizing Aboriginal
administration in conformity with this broad premise.

Second, the Whitlam government inaugurated the Aboriginal
self-determination policy which explicitly coopted Aborigines
into the new administration as planners, welfare workers and
administrators (Collmann 1981). The self-determination policy
was presented as a radical departure from the earlier assimilation policy. Aborigines were supposed to participate directly in
the welfare programmes designed to help them. Aboriginal ideas
about social well-being were to be the basis for planning, not
those of white welfare workers. Specifically, the policy was
supposed to enable Aborigines to follow their own customary
ways of life if they so chose. There were to be no explicit
attempts to make them conform to conventional, middle-class
Australian norms.

Finally the new administration officially disavowed the
relevance of the distinction between part-Aborigines and
Aborigines. For the purpose of its programmes, anyone who
claimed Aboriginal descent was considered an Aborigine and
was eligible to participate or receive benefits.

In order to begin the implementation of its programme the
DAA took a number of steps very quickly. It established the
National Aboriginal Consultative Committee in order to implement its pledge to involve Aborigines in policy planning at the
national level. Parliament passed a bill outlawing racial
discrimination. The DAA funded special works projects in order
to help establish jobs for Aboriginal people and expanded the
number of jobs on settlements. It paid all workers in these projects at the appropriate award rate. The DAA also purchased and
subsidized cattle stations and agricultural projects in South
Australia, Western Australia and the Northern Territory. It
made loans available for Aboriginal people to start private
businesses. In the field of education, the DAA supported a
number of research projects, special grant schemes, and programmes for adult education. The DAA also made broad efforts
to improve the amount and quality of adequate housing for
Aboriginal people throughout Australia through grants to states,
housing associations and other agencies. Mr Justice A.E. Wood-

ward was commissioned to examine the question of land rights for Aboriginal people in the Northern Territory on 9 February, 1973. In order to advance its aims to improve Aboriginal health and position before the white Australian law, the DAA also established and subsidized Aboriginal legal aid services and medical centres. The DAA also initiated and supported a wide range of legislative proposals, commissions of inquiry, research projects, and community organizations throughout the nation in its efforts to meet the goals established by ALP policy.

It is important to understand that the DAA considered most of its programmes served two purposes: to relieve or eliminate some particular need in social welfare (for example, poor housing) and to encourage the processes of "self-determination". Indeed, in the early period of its history, the DAA was willing to subsidize unprofitable or technically inefficient programmes which promised to train Aboriginal people in essential technical and managerial skills or otherwise establish themselves in a lifestyle they preferred. Moreover, the DAA and its public supporters expressed the view that only by soliciting actively the felt needs of Aboriginal clients in a manner consistent with their own modes of decision making could the social welfare programmes be successful (Coombs 1972a, 5).

Although the DAA documented its stance on this issue in many areas, the dual purpose of social relief and self-determination emerged most clearly in its health, legal aid and housing programmes. The DAA channelled most of its support for these types of programme through locally based "Aboriginal organizations". Aboriginal organizations were local bodies established for the benefit of, and managed by, Aboriginal people.[2] Most Aboriginal organizations maintained their own management committees and were function-specific. For example, although some health and legal services were jointly associated with one overarching Aboriginal community centre, all Aboriginal legal services were organizationally autonomous and independently funded by the DAA. The management committees were supposed to recruit local Aboriginal leaders, reflect the local community's authority structure and, therefore, be able to express the needs of the organization's clientele. Moreover, each group was supposed to decide upon its leaders according to its own customary procedure.

The Aboriginal Legal Service (ALS) programme was perhaps the showpiece of the self-determination policy. Not only did the legal services address a vital and pressing problem in Aboriginal social welfare (defence of Aborigines in court), they were also models of Aboriginal self-determination. Each service was controlled by a council composed entirely of Aborigines, which was responsible for all activities of each agency. According to the policy of self-determination, the officials of the DAA had no formal right to interfere in the daily operations of the ALS agencies. Moreover, the ALS's legal programme was the basis for a broad frontal attack upon many aspects of Aborginal welfare not conventionally understood as narrowly "legal" in nature. The legal services addressed themselves to basic issues such as Aboriginal land rights, the relationship between conventional Australian and Aboriginal customary law, prisoner rehabilitation, consumer protection, anti-discrimination laws and similar things. In these capacities the legal services interpreted court work and legal representation as only the foundation for a general advocate's role in the communities where Aborigines lived (Collmann 1981). As general advocates and active practitioners of self-determination, the ALS personnel regarded themselves as the vanguard of the DAA's programme and were often dedicated, highly committed activists.

In practice, the principle of "self-determination" did not always relate unambiguously to other aspects of organizational life. In particular, there was great uncertainty about the relationship between local autonomy in actual decision making and the fact that the DAA provided most operating funds. Although a few Aboriginal organizations existed prior to 1972, the DAA none the less established and provided the money necessary to run most of them. For example, prior to 1973, the Commonwealth government provided no money for the provision of legal services designed for Aboriginal people. By June 1976, it had invested the following amounts: 1972–73, $715,000; 1973–74, $1,190,000; 1974–75, $2,582,000; 1975–76, $3,746,000 (DAA 1974, 59; 1976, 53). This money financed eight legal services operating in all the states and the Northern Territory. In spite of this large investment, the legal services frequently complained that they had insufficient money to meet their clients' demands. Most services felt they needed more staff of all kinds and more equipment. They argued that because of staff shortages they had to refer many clients to private legal practitioners, a procedure which cost more than augmenting their own staff. Some services, particularly those working among rural Aborigines in the outback, complained that because they had too little equipment and money, whole sections of their potential clientele were left unaided.

Officially, the DAA placed high priority on the provision of adequate legal services for Aborigines and considered the legal services one of its most successful programmes. However, it also argued that money was limited and that the legal services were only one part of the total programme. The legal services had to consider their particular interests in the context of the well-being of the whole programme. The DAA also insisted that the legal services spend their money wisely and charged some services with being irresponsible.

The pressures from the DAA often meant that individual legal services did not receive the amounts of money they considered necessary to expand properly. In response they often argued that, although the DAA provided the funds, it should not question either how much money the legal services demanded or how they used it. Rather, it should simply supply the money required and permit the local services to decide for themselves how to spend it. As self-determining bodies, the legal services should have complete control over such issues. In particular, the DAA should not dictate what types of problems (legal, political or otherwise) the legal services should choose to prosecute. The problem was to decide in practice the scope and meaning of the legal services' local discretion in the management of their own affairs. Throughout, the discussion was developed in terms of the self-determination policy.

As I will describe in detail below, we must locate these disputes between the DAA and local ALS agencies in their wider social context. As brokers in the field of Aboriginal administration, the ALS agencies were competing with each other, with other new DAA agencies and, most particularly, with white agencies already established in the field. They depended heavily upon DAA resources to infiltrate their client areas and provide the services necessary to recruit their support. Not only did referring Aboriginal clients to private lawyers cost more money, for example, it turned away clients whose patronage the ALS needed in order to carve out their niches on the boundary between the administration and the Aborigines in the welfare context.

Culture and the Ideology of Self-determination

It was widely accepted that earlier government policy had created at least two culturally distinct groups of Aboriginal people. On the one hand, there were "tribal" people who had been institutionalized or spent their lives on missions and settlements. These people were said to follow Aboriginal customary law and to understand little of white Australian culture. At the other end of the spectrum were the completely "detribalized" or "urban" people who no longer knew or followed traditional norms. Some of these people had "blended in" with the white community and were indistinguishable from it. Others had adopted white norms but retained a sense of their Aboriginal origins. For the most part these people lived in the large southern cities. A number lived in small country towns. In between these two poles of the cultural continuum were an unlimited number of variations. For convenience, they were often lumped into two groups: people resident on cattle stations and "fringe-dwellers" on the edges of towns. The cattle station people were often described as "semi-tribal" in that they followed many customary laws but in a context dominated by white influences. The "fringe-dwellers" were described as people who had lost most of their tribal ways and not yet completely learned white norms. It was argued that they were caught between the two cultural groups and had no true culture of their own.[3]

DAA policy asserted that all these people had the right to call themselves "Aborigines" and to participate in its programmes. It explicitly denied the old criteria of racial origins which had separated the "full-bloods" from the "half-castes", or part-Aborigines, and had created different life chances for the two groups. Officially, it wanted to give all people who identified themselves as Aborigines an equal chance to benefit from the resources it had available. However, it accepted the proposition that the different cultural backgrounds of particular groups created differences in local desires and basic needs. It took Stanner's view as axiomatic (1969, 54).

> There is no one "aboriginal problem" and much of the talk about the "aborigines" is misleading. We are looking at a spectrum that is almost indefinitely divisible. A problem, such as housing, at one end is not identical with what may seem to be the problem at the other end.

The policy of self-determination allowed for cultural diversity by letting people use the DAA's programmes in the light of local needs. Although the DAA recognized that most Aborigines lacked basic goods and services, its policy officially accepted that some groups might place more emphasis on the integrity of their cultural life than upon acquiring the material goods of white culture. Indeed, the DAA took as a matter of policy the obligation actively to help "tribal" communities restructure their social lives around traditional concerns if they so wished. The idea was to permit each group to act upon its own priorities (DAA 1974, 7).

This approach generated serious administrative problems particularly in the context of "tribal" communities. On the one hand, many Aboriginal people (mostly notably, the tribal people) lived in squalor and suffered tremendously as a result. One important way of relieving their suffering was to provide adequate housing. On the other hand, the DAA's official consideration for the cultural traditions of Aboriginal people prevented it from developing a single approach to the problem. Indeed, it forced them to adopt a piecemeal, group-by-group approach which was quite expensive and slowed progress. Had the DAA not been publicly accountable for both the delivery of adequate housing and the processes of self-determination, it might have been able to rationalize its approach. The self-determination policy, however, generated a politically potent critique which insisted that "imposed solutions" for the social welfare problems of Aborigines would only exacerbate local difficulties.

For example, in an article entitled "Aboriginal 'Dreamings' and Town Plans", the Reverend J. Downing, a social worker among Central Australian Aborigines, argued that, however imaginative, town plans which did not reflect local Aboriginal peoples' ideas about camp layouts imprisoned their thinking in white structures, weakened customary tradition, and ruptured their sense of community.

> . . . the layout of Pitjantjara camps was an unconscious reminder to people of their law, and the whole proper order of things. A man got up in the morning, rubbed his eyes and gazed around, and was immediately reminded who he was – for example, a person of the malu or papa dreaming – and of the location of his sacred country, of the nature of his relationships and his proper behaviour towards the people immediately around him, and to the other groups scattered around. Camp layout undergirded and strengthened the whole fabric of his society.
>
> We Europeans entered the historical scene, and with varying degrees of ignorance and arrogance proceeded in most situations to shatter this structure.

In its place we put barren and unimaginative town plans. The results of this were the loss of the re-enforcement of law, and of social structure, the breaking up of extended family groupings, and increase in social pressures and a consequent worsening of community health (Downing n.d.).

Downing argued that proper consultation between local groups and architects in order to elicit the traditional residential patterns "liberated" Aboriginal thinking and strengthened Aboriginal community life. Frequently this was a slow process and could not bend to the demands of impatient bureaucracies.

Although Downing applied his ideas specifically to the question of housing, his argument was relevant to the DAA's total programme. The main thrust of his line was that questions of cultural life, community organization and techniques for the provision of basic social services were inextricably interdependent. Administrative programmes that did not take cognizance of local cultural and community life risked undermining their own efforts. In this basic respect, he echoed Coombs's statement (1972, 5).

> A study of our own efforts and those of welfare programmes abroad like the "War on Poverty" and the programmes for American Indians in the United States shows that apparently well-conceived programmes designed by social scientists and administrators have failed because their clients, the Aborigines, the Indians, or the poor, have been involved only as passive recipients – at most invited to endorse programmes already approved. Our failures will continue until the goals the Aborigines are assisted to achieve are those they freely chose themselves and until they themselves plan and largely administer the means by which they are to be helped.

The key point to observe, however, is that this ideological line legitimated the role of brokers and created the need for Aboriginal spokesmen in Aboriginal administration. Indeed, it placed a premium on the insight of those local (usually white) men who could communicate with tribal spokesmen and articulate their needs for national administrators. The full implications of this are examined below. The general point is that because of these conditions the DAA's policy, in conjunction with the significance of brokers in Central Australia, legitimated and even encouraged the fragmentation of Aboriginal administration. What was intended as a national policy ended up being a multitude of local policies funded by national resources.

Central Australia

The establishment of the Department of Aboriginal Affairs in 1972 signalled the beginning of major changes in the administration of Aboriginal affairs in the Northern Territory. In particular, it marked the dismantling of the Welfare Branch and the official repudiation of the assimilation policy (or the integration policy as it was then labelled). These changes had important effects on the structure of the local bureaucratic apparatus responsible for Aborigines, the rhetoric of local debate about Aboriginal affairs, and the transactions between Aborigines and local administrators. In general these changes proliferated the number and types of bureaucratic agencies which included Aborigines among their clients. Moreover, all agencies had to seek ways to coopt Aborigines into their overt, publicly visible decision-making processes.

A key point is that the new regime was established against the background of, and often with the personnel of, the previous administration. When the DAA was established, it wholly incorporated the staff and responsibilities of the Welfare Branch.[4] Of the initial 957 original staff members of the DAA nationwide, 897 were from the Northern Territory Division. By June 1973 the transfer of staff and administrative responsibility in the areas of health, education, labour, community welfare, funding and Aboriginal research to other Commonwealth agencies had reduced the Northern Territory Division's non-industrial staff to 358. Although the DAA expanded its Canberra staff and introduced some new personnel in the Northern Territory, the Northern Territory Division still employed just over 40 per cent of the DAA's non-industrial staff and 100 per cent (372) of its industrial staff in June 1976 (DAA 1976, 62). In addition, many welfare officers who were transferred to new Commonwealth departments still continued to work with their previous Aboriginal clients. The new programmes and new agencies did not enter an administrative vacuum. On the contrary, they had to compete for the attention and support of local Aborigines and whites who were already involved in long-standing, multiplex relationships with one another.

In addition to establishing housing associations, local Aboriginal councils and other new social welfare programmes, the DAA subsidized several new Aboriginal organizations in Central Australia. In September 1974 the largest of these was the

Central Australian Aboriginal Legal Aid Service (CAALAS).[5] It
employed a staff of five including a senior and a junior lawyer,
administrative assistant, secretary and two field officers.
CAALAS was a model Aboriginal organization in that it was
formally governed by a council composed entirely of Aborigines
recruited from many Aboriginal communities throughout the
region. Moreover, the lawyers who worked for CAALAS in
September 1974 vigorously supported the self-determination
policy, took special care to encourage the Aboriginal councillors
to consider all of CAALAS's administrative problems and
honoured their decisions.

CAALAS's staff also tried to work closely with the Aboriginal
councillors in the various rural communities they serviced; for
example, CAALAS appeared for Aboriginal defendants in the
court of summary jurisdiction at Yuendumu, an Aboriginal
settlement approximately 300 kilometres northwest of Alice
Springs. Prior to appearing in court the CAALAS lawyers held
meetings with the Aboriginal councillors to discuss the cases and
decide upon pleas. CAALAS almost always entered the plea the
concillors favoured even if the client did not agree. CAALAS also
encouraged the councillors to raise other issues such as housing
problems, pensions, land rights and problems with local white
administrators.

The service also actively campaigned against local practices it
thought discriminated against Aborigines or increased their
subordination to whites. For example, it frequently criticized the
police for harassing Aborigines in a manner in which they would
not treat whites. It pressured local businesses that discriminated
against Aborigines, and particularly tried to stop some used-car
dealers from selling Aborigines defective cars at high prices.
CAALAS also criticized politicians or other local whites who
made public comments or supported policies it considered
racist. It kept its office open and staff available for Aborigines to
drop in and seek help as they needed it. In particular, it
employed field officers (who were all Aborigines) to attend to
any social welfare or individual problems of clients. CAALAS
regarded, and encouraged Aborigines to regard, its legal role as
simply the foundation for a general advocate's role which could
potentially embrace any and all problems Aborigines faced.

CAALAS's views assume a particular sociological significance
in light of the organization's position in the contemporary
bureaucratic context: it was trying to establish itself as a broker

in a social field already inhabited by powerful brokers. On the one hand, its capacity to recruit Aborigines as clients determined its capacity to gain the support of the DAA. On the other hand, its capacity to elicit the support of the DAA conditioned its ability to serve its Aboriginal clients and compete successfully for their attention with the other local brokers. From this perspective, CAALAS's services as a legal aid welfare organization (as well as its emphasis on self-determination) were basic resources in its attempts to recruit clients, meet whatever needs they expressed and survive as an organization in a highly competitive environment.

CAALAS faced a particularly difficult situation in Central Australia because it was competing with missions and settlements which maintained long-standing, multiplex relationships with their Aboriginal clients and enjoyed highly respected identities with agencies of the Commonwealth government and the public at large. Under the Welfare Branch, these agencies had divided up the field and substantially minimized the competititon among themselves for the support of particular Aboriginal groups. Most had also tried to satisfy all their clients' needs from within their own organizational resources. Hence, although most of the money originally came from the Commonwealth, there developed extensive duplication of welfare services for Aborigines.

When the DAA initiated its new policies, the field within which whites had to negotiate for Aboriginal support opened up tremendously. New agencies moved into the field and old agencies could no longer take for granted either the division of the field or the support of their Aboriginal clients. It became more difficult for anyone (new or old agencies alike) to play the broker's role, and the competition for clients became overt. None the less, the established agencies did enjoy major advantages; in particular, they serviced settled, resident populations, each of which had social welfare problems. In spite of the fact that the DAA established new central welfare agencies to meet specific needs, the duplication of welfare services characteristic of the earlier regime persisted and, indeed, with the tremendous increase in available funds, proliferated. For example, the DAA funded Aboriginal Hostels to recondition old homes and build new ones to provide temporary and permanent housing for Aborigines in Alice Springs; however, it is also granted money to two missions and a local church-related organization to build hostels in Alice Springs. In the wider context of inter-agency competition, therefore, social services were basic means whereby white agencies marshalled their Aboriginal clients and kept them inside the organization.

Handelman has shown how transactions in short-term, case-specific aid, such as social work, hostels, legal aid, and health care, can generate social relationships between agencies and their clients over an extended period (Handelman 1976, 224). His points are even more valid in the context of missions and settlements that service encapsulated, resident communities. However much they worked to provide case-specific aid, the new organizations such as CAALAS could not initially rely on the long-term consequences of many contacts to make inroads into the local population or establish firm relationships with their clients. Rather, its organizational context demanded that CAALAS engage in particular types of transactions with key Aborigines which by themselves could create commitments. Land rights and the transactions associated with land rights claims were crucial for CAALAS in this respect. Unlike court work, pension claims, or consumer protection work, land rights legitimated CAALAS's continuing involvement in local Aboriginal communities and, quite significantly, generated relationships with Aborigines whose social identities were highly valued in local politics – the so-called "tribal elders".

Although the DAA did not orginally appoint CAALAS as the Central Land Council's legal adviser, it became involved in land rights very early in its history. At least one Aboriginal group approached CAALAS to help lodge a claim for its homeland on a cattle station prior to January 1974. By the time I entered the field, Judge Woodward had submitted both of his reports, legislation was being drafted, and local pressure to introduce a land rights bill into Parliament was growing (Woodward 1974, iii).[6] With the exception of Woodward's reluctance to guarantee Aborigines resident on cattle stations the same land rights as settlement and mission people, CAALAS supported the Woodward Report. Indeed, CAALAS came to the conclusion that land rights was the most important issue to all Aborigines throughout Central Australia and basic to the solution of all other problems. Its commitment to land rights was, in many respects, the fullest expression of its demand for major political change in relationships between Aborigines and whites.

The procedure Woodward recommended for the preparation of land claims encouraged the development of social relationships between Aborigines and the white processors of the land claims. On the basis of anthropological evidence and local common sense Woodward accepted the idea that Aborigines' access to particular tracts of land was legitimated by their religious relationship to local sacred sites. He also accepted the idea that tribal elders, as the traditional religious experts, knew the myths that described the links to the sacred places, cared for the sacred materials and ruled local groups; accordingly, he recommended that recruits for land trusts be drawn from among them (1974, 71). Preparing a land claim, therefore, involved discovering the identity of local tribal elders (the men who "really knew"), recording the sacred stories and mapping the information for presentation at the land claim hearings. The cultural significance of sacred material, however, compounded the merely technical aspects of this procedure and transformed it into a very powerful mechanism for generating relationships between Aborigines and white administrators. Indeed, it appears that land rights and this particular means of legitimating land claims were manifestations of a more general, quite long-standing type of transaction between Aborigines and whites.

The sacred material Woodward required for land claims is generally understood to be "secret". According to customary law, women and uninitiated boys are not allowed to hear, see or in some instances even approach certain kinds of sacred songs, objects and places. In Central Australia it is widely argued that Aboriginal elders have extended these restrictions to white people and, in general, do not permit whites to see any secret material. On the other hand, it is widely known that Aborigines sometimes give particular white men access to sacred material. Aborigines tell "special" whites sacred stories, show them sacred objects and, in some very special cases, initiate them into tribal manhood. Yet, even as they display this sacred material, Aborigines insist that whites keep the rule of secrecy and tell no one else (particularly other whites) the details of what they observe.

Simmel suggests that the analysis of secrecy is part of the sociology of the way encapsulated and often oppressed social groups protect themselves from the demands of the wider society. Secrecy defines and guards the boundaries of such groups, in particular of those groups which stress their own self-sufficiency with respect to the outside world (for example, secret societies) (Simmel 1964, 345, 362). Simmel's remarks are of general importance. In the course of this book it will be argued that although Aborigines do not form a secret society in Simmel's sense, they none the less withdraw from white society and try to be self-sufficient. However, because whites monopolize all resources necessary to survive in Central Australia, Aborigines must interact with them to some extent. The rule of secrecy is one aspect of how Aborigines relate to, but withdraw from, whites. Those whites who are shown sacred material are thrust into the role of what Simmel calls "the middler". As the term indicates, a "middler" occupies a role between the encapsulated group and the outside world. The middler is not often a fully initiated member of the group, but usually a type of novice who has the "dual function" of connecting and separating – mediating the transition from the outside world to the innermost sanctuaries of the group. In Simmel's terms the middler establishes a "graduated secrecy" which "produces an elastic sphere of protection . . . around its innermost essence" (Simmel 1964, 367).

In light of this argument, the rule of secrecy points to an important conjunction of interests between Aborigines and white agencies such as CAALAS. On the one hand, as brokers, white agencies must insert themselves between Aborigines and the larger bureaucratic edifice if they are to survive. Aborigines, on the other hand, must recruit and control whites who will feed them the resources they need to survive. They must make some whites middlers, who will be part of, but separate from, Aboriginal groups. The exchange of sacred material and the rules of secrecy are well adapted to generate this kind of relationship and are of major political significance.

The key to the significance of transactions in sacred material and the rules of secrecy is their exclusive nature. In Simmel's terms they are a recruiting device whereby particular members from a category which is otherwise excluded from the inner group are explicitly included within it (Simmel 1954, 369). When Aborigines show sacred material to a white, they often flatter him by saying that he is a special white man who understands Aborigines. As a token of their respect for his special sensitivities, they show him their most sacred lore and, perhaps initiate him into the esoterica of their most sacred rituals and mythology. They suggest to him that with this transaction they set him apart from other white men and establish a special, often unique relationship between him and the local group. In exchange for this privileged access to Aboriginal experience, the white man must obey the laws of Aboriginal custom. Most particularly, he must honour the customary laws of reciprocity and the authority of the elders. He must keep the laws of secrecy and, in general, not question the basis of the elders' claims. Because Aborigines have suspended the relevance of a favoured white man's ethnic identity by showing him sacred material, he must cease to act as a white man and behave as an Aborigine; that is to say, the rules Aborigines impose make their demands upon white associates non-negotiable.

The exclusive function of this transaction distinguishes Aborigines as well as whites. When a white man accepts sacred material, he recognizes the unique identity both of the gifting group and, most particularly, its tribal elders. He accepts obligations to a particular group, not to Aborigines in general. This is important for the analysis of secrecy. Aborigines usually preface displays of sacred material with the note that they are the knowledgeable men who control this particular information. Other Aborigines who may claim such knowledge are, in fact, imposters or, at best, inadequately informed, not truly knowledgeable. Indeed, some might be mere "boys" (that is, uninitiated) and therefore totally unqualified to speak on the matter. By imposing the rule of secrecy Aborigines prevent their white man (insofar as he obeys "the law") from checking the validity of such claims and thereby discrediting the identity of his giftors. By the same token Aborigines do not hesitate to debunk the claims of rival Aborigines. Indeed, Aborigines often extend access to their sacred material in the context of efforts to ridicule the claims they know other Aborigines have made to whites they are trying to recruit. Taken as a whole, transactions in sacred material and the rule of secrecy are means whereby Aborigines distinguish themselves from rival groups and coopt powerful whites in the service of local interests. As the basic resources in the competition among Aborigines for white resources, transactions in sacred material measurably contribute to the further fragmentation of Aboriginal administration and local Aboriginal communities.

In the context of political negotiations among whites, these transactions and rules acquire further significance. In particular, whites use their access to sacred material and the rules of secrecy as unequivocally authentic, non-negotiable documentation of their relationships with local Aborigines. Indeed, it is often in this form that Aborigines become political resources for

whites. The policy of self-determination emphasized this use of
white interpretation of Aboriginal culture. Yet, the use of sacred
material by whites in this way antedated the new policy and
highlights a more general problem. The basic premise upon
which social welfare agencies operate is intervention. In order to
work they must involve themselves in the everyday life of their
clients and must be accepted by the wider society as acting
legitimately in that process. When such agencies cross ethnic,
cultural and class boundaries, the legitimacy of their intervention is questionable. If the client population seems to accept or
even welcome intervention, social welfare agencies can present
themselves as major forces in orderly social evolution and,
perhaps, of intergroup peace. The existence of white agents who
have been shown Aboriginal sacred material constitutes
evidence that both the individuals themselves and the welfare
edifice as a whole have been accepted by Aborigines. If white
brokers can present themselves to the wider white Australian
community as "trusted", they document that in their relationships with Aborigines the racial, cultural and class barriers
which divide Central Australia are irrelevant and even overcome.

This analysis suggests that the land rights issue and the policy
of self-determination as a whole are radical generalizations of
the transactions in sacred material and, in Simmel's terms, of the
principle of exclusivity. On the one hand, self-determination
means that white intervention in contemporary Aboriginal life
must occur according to the rules of Aboriginal society. On the
other hand, because only a minority of favoured whites know
these rules, the policy restricts the number of personnel to, and
channels administration through, a few select, locally based
whites. The point about secrecy in this context is that it makes
the rules, as well as the way they are applied, unavailable for
public inspection. Not only is administration channelled through
a restricted number of whites, but their decision-making processes also are rendered unaccountable and their results non-
negotiable. Whites who are outside the privileged circle cannot
question the basis of their authority or their decisions. As a
device for insulating Aborigines and favoured whites from
public accountability, secrecy (particularly if glossed as an intrinsic aspect of traditional Aboriginal society) is quite powerful.

These conditions make transactions in sacred material and the
rules of secrecy crucial aspects of the broker's role in Central

Australia. In general, whites who project and authenticate identities as knowledgeable about and favoured by Aborigines are focal points in the administration of Aboriginal affairs. Once an individual or group can say that it has been entrusted with sacred information, other whites and Aborigines try to recruit its attention. On the one hand, national politicians and administrators look to favoured whites to establish contact with local communities. On the other hand, local whites who lack special access to Aborigines depend upon favoured whites for guidance and, more importantly, for legitimacy in the local arena. Finally, because they understand the channelling effect of the broker's role, Aborigines seek out favoured whites who appear to control access to key resources.

These features of the situation establish the condition for the relative expansion or contraction of secrecy. For example, if a white agent is to establish himself in the region independent of favoured whites or to introduce alternative views about Aboriginal affairs (that is, become a broker), he must recruit Aborigines who will show him sacred material, impose the rule of secrecy and, in general, make him a middler. Otherwise, he is politically dependent upon other whites and can speak with no authority in local affairs. By the same token, Aborigines must incorporate potent white brokers if they are to control the forces which impinge upon them in any way. Hence, the institution of secrecy should expand during periods of major administrative change and contract as the points of administrative power become clear. The proliferation of white agencies operating in Aboriginal affairs during my fieldwork generated great uncertainty and overt inter-agency competition concerning who controlled access to what kinds of resources. The emergence of many new would-be white brokers encouraged Aborigines to extend sacred material to, and make middlers of, more whites. Because the new regime generated such uncertainty and competition, the value of sacred material and the middler's role increased for whites. Consequently, transactions in sacred material and secrecy expanded. The history of CAALAS provides evidence for these propositions.

When CAALAS first started work in Central Australia, it discovered that the established white agencies (missions and government bodies alike) legitimated themselves by displaying their access to secret information and the support of tribal elders. Because CAALAS was new it was not so privileged. On the contrary, CAALAS intitially worked primarily among urban Aborigines around Alice Springs. Moreover, although it included several tribal councillors on its management committee, its most public spokesmen were also urban Aborigines. The DAA and CAALAS officially denied the relevance of the distinction between tribal (full-blood) and urban, non-tribal (part-Aboriginal) Aborigines for their administration and programmes. Yet, most white people (particularly in Alice Springs) denied that urban Aborigines knew much about customary Aboriginal culture or retained close ties with sacred religious sites. Consequently, they did not accept urban Aborigines as legitimate spokesmen for tribal Aborigines. Both the DAA and CAALAS had to come to terms politically with this fact in spite of their ideological commitment to the contrary. In practice, they had to put a premium upon tribal people. Hence, although CAALAS had many clients and was ostensibly an Aboriginal organization, the identities of the Aborigines with whom it initially associated were not strong political resources either in the context of local politics or in its relationships with the DAA; some were distinct liabilities. In order to establish itself as a legitimate spokesman for Aboriginal interests, CAALAS had to play down the significance of its urban, non-tribal constituents and actively recruit the support of "tribal" Aborigines, particularly of elders.

In September 1974 when I began my fieldwork, CAALAS represented Aborigines in the courts of summary jurisdiction in Alice Springs, Yuendumu and Tennant Creek. Throughout the early months of my fieldwork, the CAALAS lawyers busily travelled in the bush around Alice Springs contacting new Aboriginal communities and encouraging them to send representatives to its management committee meetings. Although they had an ideological commitment to Aboriginal land rights, the CAALAS lawyers only began to emphasize it as the key to their work as they made their increasingly extensive bush trips. Their overt commitment to land rights grew as Aborigines began to show them the sacred material which validated their local land claims. Aborigines told them sacred stories, showed them *tjuringas*, and swore them to secrecy. CAALAS was to tell the government what it needed to know in order to accept the local peoples' land claims but, otherwise, it was to keep the information secret. By May 1975 Aboriginal groups (in particular, Walbiri groups) began to contact CAALAS directly, offering to make known their land claims and pass on the sacred information necessary to legitimate them. By September 1975 groups as far northeast as Booroloola, as far northwest as Wattie Creek, and as far north as the Darwin fringe-camps had asked CAALAS to handle their land rights work. Indeed, CAALAS represented the Gurrindji in their final negotiations with Vestey's and attended the ceremony in which they finally regained their land at Wattie Creek. In other words, the passing of secret information and the lodging of land ·claims became a formal means for recruiting CAALAS's support for local groups. This process was the mechanism for the greatest period of CAALAS's expansion and marked the shift from an emphasis on non-tribal to tribal Aborigines.

It is also crucial to understand that as CAALAS expanded and did more work in land rights, the level of the DAA's support for its activities increased. The DAA finally agreed (after several months of delay) to lease an adequate office, house the CAALAS lawyers, purchase new equipment and expand the CAALAS staff. Most significantly, the DAA decided to transfer official responsibility for the preliminary organization of land rights and the Central Lands Council to CAALAS. Hence, as CAALAS received sacred information, prepared land claims and expanded its support among tribal Aborigines, the uncertainty characteristic of its early position in the DAA bureaucracy faded and its overall capacity to play a broker's role became greater.

Of special interst, however, is the fact that as CAALAS expanded, it began to conflict seriously with the established local brokers and the wider interests (white and Aboriginal) they represented – a question that is considered at length in the next chapter on the significance of racial tension crises. For the moment, it is appropriate to emphasize that, as CAALAS expanded its base among "tribal elders" and began to legitimate its new ideas about Aboriginal administration in terms of their support, other local brokers began to criticize them. A key element in their critique was that CAALAS did not represent the opinions of "true" tribal elders. Indeed, it was claimed that their major spokesmen earlier in their lives had forsaken the opportunity to become fully knowledgeable, had broken the sacred trust of their kinsmen and tribes and were disgraced identities. They could no more speak for Aboriginal opinion than the average white man. Because CAALAS based its view of the situation upon their word, CAALAS was misguided, misrepresented local opinion and should have no power in local affairs. The most outspoken critics of CAALAS from this perspective were the staff and associates of Hermansburg mission, the longest-standing white broker in Central Australia.

Conclusion

In conclusion I wish to consider a phenomenon which has generated great interest in the circles of Aboriginal administration: the outstation movement. In recent years, Aborigines have been moving away from the central communities of settlements and missions out to areas they claim are part of their traditional countries. This movement is commonly explained as the resurgence of Aboriginal elders' customary concern to protect their sacred sites, maintain the vitality of their ancient religious customs (particularly with the young), and thereby reassert their traditional authority (Wallace 1977; Downing, unpublished manuscript, n.d.). Gray has added that Aborigines are also trying to protect their land from mining interests, indicate their "feelings about their own land" for land rights purposes, escape the control of the local land owners or institutionalized communities and, in general, realize their own ideas about where and how to live (Gray 1977, 115–17). In general, these approaches interpret the outstation movement as an indigenous, often tribally motivated reaction against institutional life and the detribalization processes it encouraged. Most whites who offer this analysis also suggest that the decentralization process should be encouraged so as to permit Aborigines to stop the detribalization process and express fully their efforts to revitalize tribal life. Indeed, support of the outstation movement is taken as a key aspect of the full implementation of the self-determination policy.

Without necessarily denying that some Aborigines worry about the effects of settlement life upon their customary religious beliefs and culture, I suggest that the outstation movement can be more fully understood if set in the context of Aborigines' relationships with white administrators; in particular, the outstation movement is the fullest manifestation of the fragmentary tendencies I have been arguing are critical aspects of contemporary administrative practice and ideology. By moving out on to their "traditional land", Aborigines identify their local groups, assert the uniqueness of their particular interests, and thereby legitimate administrative support of their own needs independent of the competing demands of other Aboriginal groups. The proliferation of local groups and their special interests also encourages, and makes room for, increased action by white brokers. Hence, although white brokers might themselves genuinely share the concern of some tribal elders for traditional custom, by supporting the outstation movement they legitimate their own continued presence between local groups and the wider administrative world.

The outstation movement only makes sense in the context of Aboriginal dependence upon white resources. At one level, it is certainly a reaction to the conditions of settlement life, yet it does not necessarily mark a return to the life Aborigines led prior to the coming of white men. On the contrary, because the outstation movement is a means whereby Aborigines maintain access to, but withdraw from, white resources, it commits them to the wider administrative apparatus in which they are now encapsulated. Moreover, it fragments Aboriginal communities, binds them to white administrators, and thereby inhibits the development of a sense of common interest among Aborigines at the local level.

Notes

1. I have adopted Blok's use of the term "broker" for my analysis (Blok 1974: 7).
2. Although there were no legal restrictions on the membership of Aboriginal organizations, it was generally accepted that the majority of benefactors and decision-makers should be Aborigines. The only exception to this was the law prohibiting anyone not of Aboriginal descent from belonging to an Aboriginal housing association. The actual number of Aborigines on management committees varied from majorities of one to informal exclusion of all non-Aborigines. Aboriginal organizations sometimes helped non-Aborigines, particularly if they lived with Aborigines. Yet, the idea was to meet the needs of Aborigines and rely on general community agencies to help other people.
3. For a critique of this approach, see chapter 3 below.
4. In 1972 the title of the Welfare Branch was officially the Welfare Division of the Northern Territory Administration. In order to be consistent, I will refer to it always as the Welfare Branch, its original title.
5. The Central Australian Aboriginal Congress (CAAC), Aboriginal Hostels Ltd, and the Central Lands Council (CLC) all officially existed. None were well established in 1974. All expanded tremendously during my fieldwork.
6. As noted above, the Labor government's Aboriginal policy included a clause promising to grant land rights to Aborigines and Torres Strait Islanders who retained "a strong tribal structure" or who demonstrated "a potential for corporate action in regard to land at present reserved for the use of Aboriginals"

(DAA 1974). On February 8, 1973, Justice A.E. Woodward was commissioned to inquire into and report upon how to recognize and grant such land rights in the Northern Territory. He held public and private hearings throughout the Northern Territory and received written submissions from all over Australia. He submitted his first, preliminary report on July 19, 1973, and a second, final report on May 3, 1974. These reports were the basis of discussion about land rights during my fieldwork and eventually of the Aboriginal Land Rights Bill. The Central Lands Council was established to coordinate the land claims for groups in the administrative area around Alice Springs, including the northern parts of South Australia.

7. The DAA had previously employed two solicitors (one from Adelaide and one from Melbourne) to represent the Central Lands Council. Because they came to Central Australia only for Central Lands Council meetings, they could not receive the information or process the claims efficiently. In general, they could not be brokers and inhibited the full development of the land rights issue as a political resource.

2

The Politics of Detribalization

Ever since the Commonwealth government assumed control of the Northern Territory in 1911, various experts have been called in to examine problems in the administration of Aborigines and propose solutions for them (Spencer 1913, 36–52; Bleakley 1928, 3–40; Rowley 1974, 305–40). A major source of concern during that entire period has been the so-called "breakdown" of Aboriginal society in the face of white contact or aggression. When Baldwin Spencer conducted his tour at the beginning of the century he found that many Aborigines were being "corrupted" by opium (Spencer 1913, 42). Almost twenty years later Bleakley expressed great concern at the prevalence of "gin sprees" and the general prostitution of Aboriginal women on cattle stations and in the towns (Bleakley 1928, 9). Both experts believed that these kinds of problems were expressions of, and measurably contributed to, the disintegration of the fabric of Aboriginal society and culture that followed white contact. Although the larger ideological pictures of which these particular judgments were part have changed many times over the years, the image of cultural decay and demoralization so characteristic of early opinion has continued to the present day. Indeed, the spectre of detribalization still haunts much official policy, commonsense thinking and anthropological discussion about Aborigines in the Northern Territory.

Throughout all these years pronouncements about detribalization have legitimated increases in the power and effectiveness of the Commonwealth's administration of Aborigines. As is well known, the early measures (in particular, the establishment of large reserves) were designed to protect Aborigines and to keep them away from contact with white society. Little was done for those "detribalized" Aborigines who had already suffered with the coming of whites. Although there was some official response to the reports of Spencer and Bleakley, these early efforts were relatively meagre. The inauguration of the assimilation policy after the Second World War, however, marked a profoundly important increase in the role of the administration in Aboriginal life — a process that receives considerable attention below. For the moment I wish to emphasize that the assimilation policy was also intended to avoid detribalization. The major idea was to guide and control the entrance of Aborigines into white society in order that they did not become disoriented or exceed their ability to adapt. In the same way the Labor party's self-determintion policy and its later analogues have been presented as the primary means for avoiding the disintegration of the tribal authority structure and the further decay of Aboriginal society. In principle these policies have given Aborigines the chance to decide for themselves how much of the white cultural repertoire they want. Yet, in order to implement this policy, the power of the white administration had to be increased again. In other words, the detribalization thesis has in the broadest sense legitimated the long-term, systematic encapsulation of Aborigines in an increasingly powerful social welfare administration. As a result, Aborigines are more politically and economically dependent upon whites than ever before. This is so in spite of the fact that all white efforts to administer Aborigines have been justified as efforts to help them solve their "problems".

The link between the detribalization argument and the expansion of the social welfare administration suggests that Aboriginal "problems" are resources in political struggles among whites (part of this process was analysed in the preceding chapter). Although white bureaucrats and politicians have made special use of Aboriginal problems, they often escape the power of the social welfare administration and emerge outside its domain in the community at large. Under these circumstances, Aboriginal problems become resources for actors outside the administration and become the basis of major critiques of the Aboriginal administration itself. In recent years, local people in Central Australia have come to interpret such developments as crises of "racial tension".[1] All the images of detribalization are mobilized, the system is declared to have failed and demands are made for major changes in the bureaucratic order. Indeed, "racial tension" is often interpreted as one of the most important and unpleasant consequences of detribalization.

This chapter will analyse a period of racial tension that I observed in February and March 1975. The main point is that although perceived as a crisis between Aborigines and whites, this period was in fact emergent from major political conflicts among white groups within Alice Springs and between Alice Springs and the Commonwealth government. I do not deny that there are major conflicts between Aborigines and whites in Central Australia. The point is, however, that racial tension crises mark the mobilization of Aborigines and their problems as resources in conflicts among groups which are essentially controlled by whites. None the less, because racial tension crises legitimate increases in the power of the social welfare administration to intervene in everyday Aboriginal social life, they are crucially related to how the wider structure of relationships between Aborigines and whites is elaborated and reproduced.

The Context of Racial Tension in Alice Springs

The racial tension crisis I observed in 1975 occurred in the context of major political and administrative changes in Central Australia and the Northern Territory. Although the Commonwealth government has controlled the Northern Territory since 1911, in recent years successive federal governments have gradually decentralized responsibility for the Territory's government to local politicians and administrators. This process was taken one step further by the Labor government in 1974 when the Legislative Council was upgraded to the Legislative Assembly and made a purely elective body. At the same time, the Labor government under Gough Whitlam was initiating new policies in Aboriginal affairs promised during the 1972 election. As described in the preceding chapter, the government had established the DAA and had officially begun to implement the policy of self-determination. Both of these processes were making new kinds of political and economic resources available to local people throughout the Northern Territory. The implications of these new opportunities for relationships within and between the various levels of government were quite uncertain.

Many local politicians (mainly but not exclusively members of the opposition Country Liberal Party (CLP) of the Northern Territory) criticized the Labor government for hindering the steady development of local government in the Northern Territory. The CLP's critique was part of their wider assault on Labor's new federalism policy. The federalism policy was designed to encourage closer cooperation between state and federal governments on projects of regional and national importance. Although the policy allowed for Commonwealth responsibility for some areas, it officially encouraged regional planning and the development of local projects funded by Commonwealth money. The Country and Liberal parties criticized this programme for being "centralist" and for undermining the rights and powers of the state governments. During the November 1975 election campaign for seats in the first Legislative Assembly of the Northern Territory, for example, the local CLP argued that the key issue was who controlled local goverment. The CLP supported "a free and independent Northern Territory" with autonomous powers. Although the CLP made this issue the centre of its campaign platform, discontent with the ALP's progress on this issue was not restricted to it. On the contrary, important local leaders who did not offically espouse any particular political persuasion were also concerned about the meaning of the Legislative Assembly. The mayor of Alice Springs, for example, urged people to cast informal votes at the election because the Commonwealth government had not made the powers of the Legislative Assembly clear. He suggested that because their votes and the election itself meant nothing, people should cast votes expressing their concern. They should not elect members to the Legislative Assembly until they knew what power they could effectively wield.

The administration of Aboriginal affairs was a critical area that documented for many people the Labor government's duplicity in this matter. Whereas decentralization and self-government implied that local people controlled local affairs, Labor's new policies for Aborigines (in particular, its land rights policy) appeared to be a vehicle for Commonwealth control of a major local issue. Local leaders were particularly concerned about comments attributed to Senator J. Cavanaugh, the then minister for Aboriginal Affairs. During the first week of October 1974, Senator Cavanaugh was quoted as having said that the Commonwealth government would not permit a CLP majority in the Legislative Assembly to block its policies on Aboriginal affairs. He allegedly favoured passing federal legislation to override any

Assembly efforts to obstruct the national policies on Aboriginal affairs. Many local leaders interpreted Cavanaugh's comments as clear evidence that both the minister himself and the Labor government were genuinely unwilling to delegate effective power over local issues to Northern Territory leaders.

Local leaders were not only worried about the Commonwealth retaining control of Northern Territory affairs in Canberra. They were equally concerned that the Labor government was implementing policies, particularly in Aboriginal affairs, that were inimical to the Northern Territory's general welfare. The CLP was notably worried that the Aboriginal Land Rights bill would discourage the development of the Northern Territory's mineral wealth. Many pastoralists were also concerned that their interests would be subordinated to those of the Aborigines. More generally, many people felt that the Labor government unnecessarily and illegitimately supported Aborigines at the expense of whites. Hence, many local politicians wanted to change the type of policies the government pursued as well as increase their local power.

In contrast to this body of opinion, there were other people (for example, CAALAS and other local supporters of Labor's policy on Aboriginal affairs) who depended upon Commonwealth control of Aboriginal affairs to insulate themselves and their Aboriginal clients from the power of local officials. They publicly criticized the CLP and argued that the move towards self-government worked against the interests of Aborigines. They were quite worried that a CLP-dominated Legislative Assembly would try to block the full development of the self-determination policy and, in particular, the implementation of land rights legislation. As outspoken representatives of Labor's policy, they were also fully aware that their own capacity to survive in the district was threatened by any substantial gain in the power of local whites to dictate Aboriginal policy.

The CLP's overwhelming victory in the November 1974 election contributed to increased conflict among local white leaders and to increased pressure on the Commonwealth. On the one hand, the CLP interpreted its success as a sign that Labor's policies were unpopular in the Northern Territory and mounted an even more sustained critique of them. Indeed, the Northern Territory election was one of the events that eventually led to Labor's national defeat in 1976. On the other hand, local groups such as CAALAS became more dependent upon Commonwealth support and, anticipating Labor's defeat, demanded the DAA act more swiftly to implement its programmes and secure their local position.

The major antagonists in these broad political processes were also the most visible participants in the racial tension crisis of February 1975. Indeed, the racial crisis was one context within which many of these key political questions were expressed. As a declaration that the local administrative system had broken down, the racial crisis articulated these conflicts about policy and the relative distribution of power between and within the local and national levels of government. But to stress these aspects alone ignores the fact that many people who had no direct political or economic interests in the administration of Aboriginal affairs were also worried. What matters worried them and why?

Drunkenness, Public Safety and the Problem of Social Order

Very soon after having first arrived in Alice Springs, I became aware that many local people felt that the town was becoming an unsafe place in which to live. People expressed the greatest concern about drunken Aborigines, particularly Aboriginal fringe-dwellers who lived in the Todd River. They were worried that in recent months the level of drunkenness in the fringe-camps had led to a radical and unsatisfactory increase in the level of crime in Alice Springs. People often discussed the problem among themselves, exchanging stories about assaults, near assaults, and otherwise frightening events. The Todd River was itself considered a dangerous place, particularly the area near the Bankside, a local pub heavily patronized by Aborigines. The Bankside was situated at the western end of the causeway which crossed the Todd leading to the suburbs on the east side of Alice Springs. Although most white people feared to pause by the Bankside, the residents of this eastern suburb developed a sense of isolation and special danger because they had to cross this causeway in order to come and go. I heard one white resident of the eastern suburbs tell his wife to floor the accelerator should an Aborigine stand threateningly in front of her car as she tried to come home.

I heard vivid tales of drunken Aborigines appearing out of the

Todd and looming before oncoming cars. The most public expression of these fears, however, appeared in the *Centralian Advocate*, the local Alice Springs newspaper. Between 10 October ,1974 and 6 February, 1975, the *Centralian Advocate* printed thirty-one articles related to Aboriginal drunkenness and violence, including eleven court reports, four Letters to the Editor, six articles reporting local demands for action on the problem and ten reports of alleged violence by Aborigines against people or property. The court reports and articles about local calls for action were specific accounts of particular people and their activities. The Letters to the Editor and the articles on the violent incidents, however, were usually highly abstract caricatures and resembled the stories circulating in the private quarters of Alice Springs. A classic example appeared on 12 December, 1974, (*Centralian Advocate*, 12 December 1974, 2).

Hit with Flagon Claim

A man was allegedly attacked by two Aborigines as he left the Memorial Club last Friday night but he claimed police failed to act when he reported the incident to them.

One of the Aborigines had smashed a flagon on the man's head causing a number of cuts to the head.

The man, who prefers to stay anonymous, said the attack took place at about 7.10 p.m. in the car park opposite the Memorial Club.

He told the Advocate that two Aboriginal men had approached from the direction of the toilets on the hospital lawns.

The man said he paid little attention to them and was opening his car door when one of them suddenly hit him on the head with a flagon.

The flagon smashed and caused several cuts to the man's head.

The man said he had kneed one of the Aborigines in the groin and then "got stuck into the other".

Both of the Aborigines had run off in the direction of the Todd River.

The man said he thought the Aborigines were "probably trying to roll me for a bit of money".

He said he went to the police station to report the incident.

When he told police that the Aborigines had gone into the Todd River he was told "there wasn't much they could do about it".

He said the police said they "wouldn't go down the creek" to look for the Aborigines.

The man later told the *Advocate* he "was not very pleased" and believed the police should have acted. He said he thought that more innocent people were going to get hurt unless police acted.

A check with police this week revealed that the incident was not recorded at the station, but inquiries are being made into the man's allegations.

This account would have been highly significant to anyone familiar with Alice Springs at the time. The first sentence presents the overall importance of the article: a man was attacked by Aborigines but could not enlist the aid of the police. Although the article does not mention it, Senator Lionel Murphy, then federal attorney-general, disallowed arrest for mere drunkenness in the Northern Territory in July 1974. This first sentence could be interpreted as an oblique reference to the fact that many people thought Murphy's decision had undermined the power of the police to maintain local law and order. Indeed, many people dated the contemporary decline in public safety from Murphy's act. The "Memorial Club" refers to the Alice Springs Memorial Club, a predominantly white social club. Most of the town's social, political and business elite belonged to the club and used its services. Of particular importance was the fact that, unlike most other drinking facilities in Alice Springs, the club had a "family atmosphere". Men often took their wives there for a congenial night on the town, particularly on Fridays. It included among its facilities a bowling green with lights which was packed every night during the summer. In general, the Alice Springs Memorial Club represented some of the most civilized aspects of white Australian culture. Furthermore, the Memorial Club was located between the Todd River and the lawn of the Alice Springs hospital. On any day of the week, Aborigines could be seen drinking on this lawn. Coming when and where it did, this attack might be interpreted, therefore, as an index of how Alice Springs citizens were defenceless in the face of an ever-present danger to their personal well-being and their civilized way of life.

There was perhaps no more vivid symbol of Aboriginal drunkenness than the flagon. The flagon was conventionally associated with invalid port, the drink said to be most popular among Aborginal drinkers.[2] Flagon bottles constituted most of the litter drinkers allegedly scattered around the town and about which local citizens complained so bitterly. Empty flagons were also typically known to be hand weapons in drunken brawls.

The significance of the Todd as a dangerous and invulnerable haven for drunks emerges clearly in this account. Most articles of this type simply said that the offending Aborigines "disappeared" into the Todd. Although the Memorial Club was on the western bank of the Todd, the site of this incident was approximately two hundred metres from the river. Hence, the

Aborigines merely ran off in the "direction" of the Todd. The Todd's danger is clearly linked to the impotence of the police. Whatever prevented the police from going "down the creek" to look for the culprits, the river was the preserve of Aborigines. Consequently, "innocent people" were vulnerable and forced to resort to violence to protect themselves. Finally, the moral of the story was clear: unless something was done, more innocent people would be hurt and the violence would spread.

These images of public danger constituted a definition of the situation which was independent of, but relevant to, the political controversies between local and national leaders. On the one hand, many people, irrespective of political affiliation, were concerned about how dangerous life had become in Alice Springs. Indeed, it was quite clear that Aborigines threatened the social order most whites took for granted. This was as true for people who considered themselves "sympathetic" to the Aborigines as for others. None the less, the way most people understood the public safety issue had clear political implications. Of particular importance was the fact that Senator Murphy had disallowed arrest for mere drunkenness. Indeed, the significance of drunkenness provides the key both to the wider understandings and the political importance of the public safety issue.

For many Alice Springs people drunkenness was a general symbol of disorder, particularly with respect to Aborigines who were so often drunk in "public". Yet, the critical point is that drunkenness marked a kind of intermediate state between being orderly and being disorderly. Drunks were not necessarily disorderly but could easily become so and commit serious crimes if not properly contained. It was important, therefore, that drunks be controlled so as not to permit them to become lawless. What forces contained drunks? There was a clear sense in which many Alice Springs people considered private drinking and drunkenness (for example, in one's private social club or home) as contained and relatively harmless. Public drunkenness (for example, in the street, vacant lots, or the river), however, was potentially uncontained and dangerous. Only agents responsible for maintaining public order (that is, the police) could possibly control public drunkenness and prevent it from leading to more disorder.

From the point of view of many Alice Springs people, Aborigines had no private contexts that could effectively control their drinking. On the contrary, they lived in substandard, "public" places and the social controls that had earlier contained them had broken down. From this perspective, drinking was a major index of the breakdown of traditional means of Aboriginal social control. As a result of these facts, Aborigines had to be controlled by outside agents responsible for public order: the police. However, as a result of Murphy's directive, the police could not arrest drunks merely for being drunk. Hence, there were no controls upon public drunkenness and the possibility of public violence was very real. Indeed, the decline in public safety indicated that the effects of Murphy's act were already emerging.

This analysis suggests an explanation of the full meaning of the Todd River and the fringe-dwellers. According to most white people, the Todd River was a public place. No one owned it. It was supposedly administered by a state agency. Yet, Aborigines had transformed it into their own private domain: they lived there and they used the Todd as a sanctuary. Moreover, the type of Aborigine who lived there was subject to no controls. He was detribalized, and the police could not apprehend him. Hence, the Todd was a source of grave danger from within the boundaries of the Alice Springs community itself. As the most manifest expression of the collapse of the local social order, the Todd River fringe-dwellers embodied the white community's worst fears.

The key to the racial tension crisis I witnessed in February 1975 was that local politicians blamed Commonwealth ministers (in particular, Senator Murphy) for the contemporary problems with drunkenness. The drunkenness issue was a classic example of how the Labor government had ignored the wishes and advice of local people and thereby threatened the well-being of Central Australia as a whole. No single issue more dramatically documented the need for a change in government policy and a more rapid move to local control of the Northern Territory's government.

The Period of "Racial Tension"

In the early hours of 10 February, 1975, a group of young Aboriginal men allegedly raped a white woman in Alice Springs. According to many Alice Springs citizens, this event culminated the recent period of increasing public violence and indicated that the situation had become critical. Some sections of the community raised a great public outcry. A group of publicans petitioned the Legislative Assembly protesting the damage they had experienced at the hands of drunks. The *Centralian Advocate* ran front page stories about the alleged rape, violence on a local Aboriginal settlement, and other disruptions to local peace. The headlines read: "Plea to act on violence" and "Women afraid to walk in streets". The most significant expression of this response, however, was a petition sent on 17 February to various national politicians (including Senator Cavanaugh) by twelve Alice Springs citizens, namely, the mayor, the federal member for the Northern Territory, four Central Australian members of the Legislative Assembly, two Alice Springs aldermen, and three Aborigines.

The petitioners expressed their concern that the abolition of drunkenness as a crime "without adequate safeguards to the consequences" had contributed significantly to a major increase in disorderly behaviour and crime in Alice Springs. They noted that because most offenders were Aborigines, the current problems encouraged the deterioration of relationships between blacks and whites in town and damaged the reputation of Aborigines throughout the region. Although government had acted in "good faith", they argued, it had improperly assessed the "best means of helping Aboriginal people and of avoiding the possibility of social conflict". They made the following recommendations:

that the Legislative Assembly reintroduce drunkenness as an offence until the establishment of detoxification centres;

that the police firmly enforce the laws on sale of liquor to underage persons, disorderly behaviour, and drinking in a public place;

that the number of police stationed in Alice Springs be increased;

that the Legislative Assembly fix minimum penalites for drink-related offences and, if necessary, introduce amending legislation;

that licensees consider the desirability of selling flagons to Aborigines;

that adequate camping facilities be provided for people currently living in Alice Springs fringe-camps in order to end "indiscriminate camping" around the town.

The petitioners asked the national leaders to visit Alice Springs to talk with local leaders themselves. They concluded by observing that unless something was done there would soon be a "complete breakdown in race relations in this area to the detriment of everyone concerned" (Milhouse et al. 1975, 1-2).

CAALAS issued a rebuttal to the petition on 19 February and sent copies to the Melbourne *Age*, the *Centralian Advocate* and the local office of the Australian Broadcasting Commission. CAALAS argued that if tougher laws against drunkenness were adopted and selectively supplied against Aborigines, tensions would worsen. Aborigines were fully aware of discriminatory practices and resented the way people inevitably treated Aboriginal drinkers more harshly than whites.

> We are greatly concerned that a "lynch mob" at atmosphere is developing among the white community. In the last month we have been staggered by the number of acts of violence by policemen against Aborigines. Even more staggering is the sense that the European community is shortsightedly supporting such aggression. The violence is spreading to other Europeans. In one such incident last weekend a harmless Aborigine was whitewashed by white louts. Such episodes can only endanger the already fragile fabric of law and order in this town (CAALAS 1975, 1).

CAALAS made the following recommendations.

1. If drunkenness is again made an offence, whites should be subject to arrest as well as Aborigines.
2. The supporters of stronger action should call for passage of the Racial Discrimination Bill currently before Parliament.
3. Wet canteens should be installed on settlements and controlled by Aboriginal Councils.
4. Land rights claims should be supported.
5. Aboriginal defendants should be tried in the presence of their tribal councils. The Stipendiary Magistrates should respect and follow the Council's opinions (CAALAS 1975, 1-2).

In summary, CAALAS observed that such measures would encourage Aborigines to think that "the real causes of their despair" were being considered and would create a setting within which detoxification centres and other programmes might succeed (CAALAS 1975, 2).

It is important to note that the drunkenness petition and the CAALAS statement, although widely interpreted as expressions of antagonistic definitions of the local situation, shared the view that relations between Aborigines and whites were deteriorating and required some kind of intervention. The problem was to determine what kind of action was necessary and who should be responsible for it.

The petition may be specifically interpreted as an attempt to revoke Murphy's decriminalization of drunkenness and to establish the means to deal with the problems it caused. Insofar as it suggested only a temporary return to the previous approach, however, it might be more generally interpreted as one approach to the underlying problem of social order. In particular, the petition seems to address problems of order in the private and the public domains. The petitioners wanted to reintroduce drunkenness as an offence and upgrade the means for policing public drunkenness but they also urged action upon the conditions under which Aborigines led their private domestic lives. They demanded the Commonwealth provide "adequate camping facilities" and back-up detoxification centres, anticipating that these programmes would prevent drunkenness and its disruptive effects from erupting into the public domain. By glossing the stricter public controls as contingent upon creating detoxification centres, they argued that adequate private controls of drunkenness would make public controls unnecessary.

Although the petitioners recognized the effect drunkenness was having upon race relations, they also perceived the "racial" dimension of the conflict as a contingency. The underlying problem in their eyes was the maintenance of social order, not of strife between Aborigines and whites as racial groups. This has crucial implications for the petititoners' ideas about who should have the power and responsibility for correcting the problem. They recommended that the Legislative Assembly enact the laws necessary to deal with the general problem of order and restricted the Commonwealth's intervention to providing camping facilities and detoxification centres. In other words, they granted the Commonwealth a limited warrant to intervene on behalf of one small segment of the Aboriginal population – a segment which posed as many problems for non-drunken Aborigines as for whites. Otherwise, they argued, responsibility for the problem should lie in local hands. Insofar as they glossed the issue in terms of social order, they legitimated local control.

CAALAS's basic ideological and political position differed markedly from the petitioners'. Although it agreed that interracial violence was imminent, it disagreed about the nature of the underlying problem and who should have the responsibility for handling it. For CAALAS, the problem was not the maintenance of social order but the existence of a social order that oppressed Aborigines. From its perspective, violence was a consequence of white bigotry and the more important violence was from whites against Aborigines. Insofar as this was true, CAALAS argued that local leaders should have little to say about the administration of Aboriginal affairs. They should support efforts to return local power to Aborigines and to pass national laws preventing racial discrimination.

These views were consistent with CAALAS's support of the self-determination policy in Aboriginal affairs, yet, they also related intimately to CAALAS's position in the local arena. In the weeks immediately prior to the racial crisis, CAALAS had been investigating reports of violence between Aborigines and white police in various parts of Central Australia, including Finke, Alice Springs and Hooker Creek. At Finke police allegedly beat several Aboriginal prisoners after a major misunderstanding. One Aborigine took offence at the policeman's behaviour and drew his spear. The policeman called for reinforcements from Kulgera and Alice Springs and eventually several local Aborigines were arrested. It was charged that they beat their prisoners on the way to the Alice Springs gaol. There were also reports of a similar incident between white police and a group of Alice Springs Aboriginal teenagers. At Hooker Creek one Aborigine was allegedly beaten so badly he sustained a broken leg. During the week just prior to the rape, CAALAS sent several telegrams to Senator Murphy and Senator Cavanaugh reporting these incidents.

CAALAS relied heavily upon its officers' personal and political links with Commonwealth officials (including Senator Murphy) for support in its local activities. In the opinion of CAALAS only Murphy's tough policy as attorney-general controlled the hostility of the local police against Aborigines and protected CAALAS's own activism. The problem was, however, that Senator Murphy was elevated to the Supreme Court on 13 February, 1975, five days before the petition and right in the middle of CAALAS's investigation of the alleged beatings. CAALAS suspected that the violence petition was directly linked to Murphy's elevation and was an attempt to pressure the new attorney-general, Kep Enderby. When the petition was released, CAALAS was investigating major cases involving relationships among

Aborigines, the police, and its own organization without the benefit of one of its most critical allies.

CAALAS's definition of the situation in terms of the racist structure of Central Australia legitimated broad Commonwealth intervention in local affairs. In this respect, it was a counter to the petitioners' efforts, a response to the specific difficulties of its own immediate situation and a reaffirmation of its commitment to the DAA's national policy. With Murphy's elevation, one of CAALAS's chief supporters vanished and a major obstacle to the power of local officials was removed. Consequently, CAALAS had to pressure those other Commonwealth agencies upon whom it could legitimately call. Without their support its capacity to survive as an organization and continue its work was seriously threatened.

The crisis was precipitated initially by local leaders concerned about the decline in public safety. This issue articulated broad concerns in the whole Alice Springs community and exemplified the particular political problems local leaders were having with Commonwealth officials. The petititoners wanted local control of what they defined as local issues. The implications of this line threatened the positions of other groups in Alice Springs, most notably, the new Aboriginal organizations such as CAALAS. These groups depended upon the Commonwealth's control of Aboriginal affairs to protect themselves from the attacks of local leaders. As a matter of survival, they had to resist, and legitimate resisting, any calls for the devolution of Commonwealth responsibility in this area of concern.

Gouldner has suggested that the analysis of conflict in government bureaucracies might profit from the study of how latent identities and roles (in particular, those of "cosmopolitan" and "local") affect the performance and public expectations of manifest roles (Gouldner 1958, 467). Gouldner argues that manifest identities are identities which actors customarily consider relevant in a particular setting. Latent identities, on the other hand, are those which actors consider irrelevant for the prescribed performance of a role. He notes that although both sociologists and people in their everyday life often officially deny it, latent roles occasionally intrude upon and affect manifest role behaviour. Furthermore, he implies that there is an important connection between the exercise of power, the allocation of official responsibility and the determination of the relevance or irrelevance of particular social identities in given

situations; in particular, although people may publicly legitimate
the allocation of power and responsibility in terms of manifest
role identities, unprescribed, latent identities may actually guide
their behaviour. Insofar as the concept of latent roles focuses
attention upon how unprescribed expections impinge upon the
manifest system, it is important for understanding how people
actually interact and ultimately, how they threaten and change
the "equilibrium of the manifest role system" (Gouldner 1958,
284–86).

Gouldner tried to show that latent identities affect manifest
role performance and to correlate particular behaviour patterns
with particular latent identities. Gouldner fails to note, however,
that in their everyday life actors themselves do not always invoke the manifest role system to explain overt behaviour. Indeed, the extent to which actors account for behaviour in terms
of the manifest or latent role system is variable, negotiable, and
often critical to the development of particular political processes. From this perspective, the question is not whether latent
roles actually account for behaviour but whether actors interpret
behaviour as if it were motivated by manifest or latent identities.
This points ultimately to how people either legitimate or question the right of others to participate in particular social
processes.

I suggest that in Alice Springs a basic criterion for legitimacy is
that an actor be interpreted as acting in good faith; in other
words, everyone recognizes that the actor's problems are authentic and that the person is committed to finding a non-sectarian,
consensual solution to them. Moreover, I suggest that a basic
condition for political negotiations is that all parties to a dispute
recognize that they are each acting in good faith. People may
attempt to dismiss opponents from negotiations by calling their
good faith into question. Alternatively, people might withdraw
from negotiations if they perceive their own good faith as
unambiguously questioned or they perceive others as acting in
bad faith. In other words, good faith is an important ground rule
that conditions the possibility of interaction. The relevance or
irrelevance of identities is related to how they affect the question
of good faith. Although a group might document its good faith in
terms of the manifest role system, for example, other groups
might question its good faith by pointing to latent identities that
are inconsistent with the manifest system. If these inconsistencies can be publicly affirmed, they constitute grounds for

dismissing the particular group and its problems from legitimate participation in the negotiations at hand. Conversely, people may use latent identities which document their good faith to legitimate such participation.

These observations suggest three propositions about the development of the racial crisis in Alice Springs:

1. Latent identities were implicit in, and helped structure, the early debate.

2. As the conflict developed, the Alice Springs people used their interpretations of these identities to debunk the good faith of their opponents.

3. By debunking their opponents' good faith, they tried to disqualify them from participation in negotiations about, and to dismiss their issues as irrelevant to, the administration of Aboriginal affairs in Central Australia.

The racial crisis in Alice Springs did involve a local version of Gouldner's distinction between "locals" and "cosmopolitans" (Gouldner 1958, 290). Most notably, the petitioners appear to be locals in that they expressed loyalty to the Nothern Territory (in particular, the town of Alice Springs), expressed concern about policy only as it affected the town's well-being, and legitimated their proposals in terms of the town's values. CAALAS's spokesmen were cosmopolitans in that they expressed loyalty to a Commonwealth agency, were committed to that agency's national policy and legitimated their actions in terms of the values of the national policy. An important point, however, is that the local people themselves had commonsense, named images of this distinction which were related to how they interpreted their relationships with each other and the outside world. On the one hand, the people who focused on the drunkenness issue (the locals) perceived themselves as "responsible citizens" in contrast to outside "radicals". Groups such as CAALAS (the cosmopolitans) considered themselves equalitarian progressives and considered many local Alice Springs people "racists".

Two interrelated dimensions constituted the "locals" categorization of their political universe. First, they distinguished between people who knew about, and expressed sympathy for, their local problems and those who did not. Second, they distinguished between people who worked to ensure the well-being of the whole community (Aboriginal and white) and those who were sectarian. People who knew about the local problems (primarily because they lived in, and were committed to, Alice Springs) and who proposed non-violent solutions which benefited everybody were "responsible citizens". "Radicals" were misinformed, malicious people who merely wanted to manipulate certain segments of the local population for their own political ends. Because such people were usually outsiders from the urban areas in the southern parts of Australia, they often earned the title "southern stirrers". Behind these distinctions between responsible citizen and stirrer was an image of "normal" relations among the various segments of the Alice Springs community. According to this image, Aborigines and local whites (who understood Aboriginal culture and mentality) lived in harmony if left alone. Racial problems only emerged if outside, unknowledgeable agencies interfered with local customs and upset the Aborigines. As the most manifest threat to local law and order, Aboriginal drunkenness was a particularly serious consequence of radical meddling in local affairs.

These points were generally significant to most Alice Springs people. In the first place, Alice Springs had a national reputation as a particularly troublesome place with respect to race relations. Most local people knew and resented the fact that outsiders as a whole perceived local whites as unnecessarily harsh to Aborigines. They particularly resented the way in which the press portrayed the living conditions of Aborigines and consistently criticized local authorities. Moreover, they despised "experts" who flew into Alice Springs for whirlwind visits, flew out again, and denigrated the town on the basis of superficial impressions. In the second place, Alice Springs was heavily populated by public servants, many of whom considered the town a "hardship" post and stayed only so long as necessary. According to people like the petitioners, these public servants did not live in Alice Springs by choice nor intended to commit their whole lives to the town. However, they were often the very people making the crucial decisions about its well-being. Although few locals considered these public servants malicious, they did think that they were often misinformed and sometimes unsympathetic, and inadvertently made decisions which hurt the long-time, committed residents. In general, the town's people considered themselves at the mercy of outsiders who intentionally or otherwise were gradually undermining the local way of life, particularly in the area of Aboriginal affairs.

These points help explain how many people interpreted

CAALAS. Few people questioned the need for Aborigines to have competent legal representation in court. Insofar as CAALAS restricted its role to legal issues, therefore, most people considered it legitimate. When the senior solicitor of CAALAS arrived in Alice Springs in September 1974, he adopted a relatively low public profile. In contrast to his immediate predecessor who had been quite flamboyant and publicly antagonistic to local views, the new incumbent confined his public statements to the courtroom. Indeed, CAALAS and the Central Australian Aboriginal Congress (CAAC) agreed that the CAAC should be the overtly "political" agency and release under its name any statements their leaders felt were necessary. Although CAALAS often helped draft these statements, the CAAC was the object of the adverse public criticism they elicited, not CAALAS. The local police considered CAALAS a hostile force, yet many local leaders prior to the racial crisis thought the new solicitor a responsible man who had realigned the organization along appropriate paths. CAALAS's public statements during the racial crisis, however, marked the first steps in what became its increasingly critical public role as a general advocate for Aborigines. As CAALAS began to assume its broader advocate's role in Central Australia, it also began to realize its potential as an "imposed" agency and to threaten the local definition of the situation. Because the DAA began to support CAALAS more firmly, many local people came to consider it the most radical and irresponsible agency in the region. And, like the Todd River, CAALAS posed special dangers because it dwelt within the community.

CAALAS legitimated broad Commonwealth intervention in local affairs by explaining the racial tension crisis in terms of the racist structure of Central Australian society. This general description also offered ready labels for particular actors or their proposals. The label "southern stirrer" ascribed hostile motives to outsiders. The label "racist" suggests not only that particular people have a local orientation but that they are motivated by discriminatory attitudes which, in this case, favoured whites at the expense of Aborigines. The general point is that the labels "southern stirrer" and "racist" denied the good faith of the groups to which they were applied. They suggested that in contrast to responsible citizens or egalitarian progressives, neither stirrers nor racists expressed concern for authentic problems or were committed to finding non-sectarian solutions to them.

When the petitioners voiced their concern, they did so in terms of their manifest roles as local leaders. Moreover, they were careful not to question the good faith of the Commonwealth government. Indeed, they granted the Commonwealth's good faith and explained its actions on drunkenness as the result of bad judgment. For its part CAALAS, in its statement, did not directly question the petitioners' good faith, but pointed out that a few "shortsighted" Europeans were causing trouble in Alice Springs and challenged the petitioners to disassociate themselves from such groups by supporting anti-discrimination legislation. The key to the rest of the racial crisis, however, was that Commonwealth officials (most notably, Senator Cavanaugh, the Minister of Aboriginal Affairs) and the national media responded to the crisis in a manner which, to the petitioners at least, denied the good faith of the people who were worried about drunkenness and public safety. Because Cavanaugh's first public response to the situation in Alice Springs was to commence an investigation into the bashing claims, he appeared to respond exclusively to CAALAS's statement and to ignore the drunkenness petition completely. Indeed, Cavanaugh seemed to dismiss the petitioners as "racists". These facts suggested to the petitioners that Cavanaugh himself was not acting in good faith. Most of the racial crisis was concerned thereafter with the petitioners' attempts to reassert the salience of the public safety issue and to deny the relevance of the charge of racism.

The publication of the petition, CAALAS's statement and Cavanaugh's response were crucial in ratifying the existence of a racial tension crisis and in establishing its major issues. In the month that followed, people talked of little else. The local newspaper and radio stations emphasized news items related to the breakdown of public order and highlighted the comments of local, regional and national leaders on the crisis as a whole. The daily schedules of many people (particularly those directly associated with local government and the administration of Aboriginal affairs) were seriously disrupted by special meetings, conferences and extended discussions about the local situation. Much normal work was suspended as people tried to define what was happening, develop plans to meet it and enlist local and national support for their particular approaches. In general, the scope of public participation in the racial crisis expanded extensively.

The member of the Legislative Assembly for Alice Springs, one of the original petitioners, responded first to Cavanaugh's early actions. In the news he stated that he was appalled that the issue of police brutality was being used to "smother" the drunkenness issue and denied that the petition was racist. The petitioners received a further vote of support from the first meeting of what later became the Alice Springs Citizen's Association. Although the meeting's organizers claimed over one hundred people attended, it was not public. They claimed to have invited all the prominent figures from among the town's responsible citizens, including three of the petitioners. According to my informants, people expressed a wide range of opinions about the causes of the racial tension crisis, but the meeting unanimously passed a motion supporting the original petition; it was suggested that another petition be circulated which asked the Legislative Assembly to reintroduce the charge of drunkenness. There were no motions calling for investigations into the charge of police brutality.

During the meeting another Member of the Legislative Assembly made an important and very telling suggestion. He suggested that Cavanaugh and other officials visit the town unannounced so that they might see Alice Springs "the way the people knew it – not cleaned up as it has been for such visits in the past" (ASCA Minutes 1975, 1, unpublished manuscript). The implication was that certain unnamed groups were being deceitful with respect to the drunkenness issue: because they opposed the local definition of the problem in terms of drunkenness, they shipped Aboriginal drunks to outlying regions whenever any Canberra officials visited Alice Springs. Consequently, the Canberra officials had an inadequate picture of how serious a problem drunks posed for the local citizens. The unannounced visit was supposed to prevent such tactics. Cavanaugh agreed to come but announced his date of arrival (Saturday 2 March, 1975).

The demand for the unannounced visit expressed many peoples' sense that the anti-petition lobby was acting in bad faith. In his speech to a public meeting of the Cross-Culture Group, a local organization of Aborigines and whites dedicated to improving communication and intercultural understanding, the mayor of Alice Springs expressed how he thought local citizens (in particular, the town council) had tried to act responsibly and in good faith in the past. He noted that the town council was inadequately equipped to understand the underlying problems that had produced bad relations between Aborigines and whites. The Commonwealth government had assumed responsibility for that kind of problem and had the expertise, the money and the power to act upon it. None the less, the town council had consistently supported local groups and had sponsored programmes designed to relieve the situation. It had supported Aboriginal Hostels' attempts to change the town plan and establish new housing areas for Aborigines; it had conducted its own inquiry into the fringe-dwellers and presented it to Cavanaugh during his last visit to Alice Springs; it had supported the Frontiers Conference, a colloquium on Aboriginal–white relations held in Alice Springs in July 1974; and it had supported the petition calling for the temporary reinstatement of drunkenness as an offence. The problem was that all of this work had produced no results. The Commonwealth government had not responded appropriately.

The mayor stressed that in all of its efforts, the town council tried to reflect the whole community's interests and to lessen dissension. The drunkenness issue, however, had proved quite tough and most devisive. The problem was that current legislation allowed people to get so drunk that serious violence was inevitable. The town needed a measure to encourage drunks to sober up before they became dangerous, until such time as detoxification centres were established. The town council therefore supported the reintroduction of drunkenness as an offence until the reasons for drinking were identified and appropriate steps taken to cure it. Otherwise, it had to rely on higher levels of government and could only try to engender a cooperative atmosphere around the town.

Although the pro-petition lobby assumed that Cavanaugh favoured CAALAS, CAALAS itself took no particular comfort in his public statements. The service had been pressing Cavanaugh for several months to increase its budget, rent houses for its lawyers and increase the government's general support for its programmes. Up to the time of the racial crisis, the DAA had been reticent. Indeed, part of the reason CAALAS made its critique of the original petition through the newspapers was that neither Cavanaugh nor his most important administrators had responded to CAALAS's entreaties vigorously enough in the past. By going to the press, CAALAS hoped to pressure Cavanaugh as well as attack the local politicians.

CAALAS believed that only a royal commission into police–Aboriginal relations had any hope of addressing the fundamental problems in the justice system in the Northern Territory. In particular, CAALAS wanted a thorough examination of police administration and training, relations between Aboriginal and white Australian law, the role of Aboriginal law, and the role of Aboriginal self-determination in the prosecution of criminal justice. Cavanaugh's promises of an inquiry into the bashings fell short of a royal commission and ignored the wider issues. CAALAS interpreted his public statements as an attempt merely to respond to the most spectacular issues and do a "cosmetic job".

CAALAS's own suspicions were confirmed, in its view, when, the day after the press release was issued, it received a call from the DAA official responsible for all the Aboriginal legal services throughout Australia. He noted that CAALAS was not supposed to be involved in politics and suggested it remember who provided its money. Although the DAA had agreed to provide CAALAS with a third lawyer in early February, three days after the DAA official called CAALAS received word that the national budget for Aboriginal legal services had been cut and there was no money for a third lawyer. CAALAS also tried to arrange a private meeting with Cavanaugh during his "inspection tour" of the town, but the attempt was unsuccessful. CAALAS, too, felt it had no real support at the national level of the DAA. In conjunction with Murphy's elevation, the DAA's cool stance discouraged CAALAS and made it feel highly vulnerable to local attack.

In the week prior to his visit on 2 March, Cavanaugh approved funds for a number of social welfare programmes designed to help the local situation. In particular, he approved the CAAC's submission for a pick-up service and night shelter for drunks. The idea was for Aboriginal field officers to drive around Alice Springs offering drunken people a ride either home or to a temporary "sobering up" shelter. The CAAC hoped in this way to clear drunken people off the streets before they became rowdy, caused damage or were arrested by the police. He approved funds for Aboriginal Hostels to purchase two hundred army tents for temporary rental to fringe-dwellers and four houses in Alice Springs. He also initiated talks with the Department of Health about establishing a detoxification centre there. Although he had decided most of these things by 24 February, his decisions were not widely known. Indeed, Cavanaugh made public comments which far outshadowed the significance of his direct actions.

In interviews with the press Cavanaugh made four comments

about the local racial situation. In one interview he compared the troubles in Alice Springs to a similar situation in Redfern, a Sydney suburb with a high proportion of Aboriginal residents. He suggested that level-headed consultation between police and Aborigines in Redfern had reduced tensions, lowered the rate of arrest and almost ended damage in the local hotels. The same progress he felt could be made in Alice Springs. The day before he was due to arrive there, however, he also said that the town was on the verge of racial warfare, that blacks and whites walked on opposite footpaths and that whenever groups of one race found members of another alone there were bashings. The possible inconsistencies in Cavanaugh's appraisals of the local situation were less important to many local people than what they considered to be the underlying, discrediting similarities. In particular, they resented his comparison of Alice Springs with Redfern and the remark that the town was on the verge of racial warfare. Although it may well have been true (as the minister was later to claim) that the local people themselves had painted as gloomy a picture of the situation as Cavanaugh had, many people interpreted his remarks as insults to the town's good name.

By the time Cavanaugh arrived, local people were questioning his value and reliability as a patron for local interests. There were widely repeated rumours that a "clean-up" was in progress; some people specifically suggested that the DAA, CAALAS and the CAAC were conducting it. Cavanaugh had disappointed CAALAS and confirmed his earlier reputation with many town leaders as an irresponsible outsider who would do anything to oppose local opinion. In general, many people concluded that he was not acting in good faith. Insofar as the capacity to enlist the support of powerful national leaders was crucial for roles people played in the local arena, the questions about Cavanaugh's good faith were vital aspects of local struggles for power, not merely epiphenomenal manifestations of them.

Cavanaugh scheduled a meeting for Saturday afternoon, 2 March. He was intended to have met only the town's leaders in a closed session but in the event many people "gatecrashed" the meeting, which effectively became public. As Cavanaugh stated several times, he hoped to use the meeting to establish a local consultative committee of Aborigines and whites. He expected it to function as a forum for the dialogue he thought would solve local troubles. The meeting focused neither upon the committee nor its brief: most people concentrated on Cavanaugh's role as minister and the relevance of his remarks about the town. They restated what they had been saying to each other in the previous weeks about the central issues of the racial crisis. Throughout the meeting, people legitimated their right to speak in terms of their good faith and knowledge about the town and its problems.

The mayor of Alice Springs opened the meeting.

> Mr Minister, Sir, the statement we prepared on February 17 related to the excessive consumption of alcohol. That statement was prepared only after a broad consultation by responsible people, and was designed to draw attention to specific matters which could be readily defined as tension points between black and white. It is not the first time such statements have been expressed and it was made clear that we were speaking of irresponsible minorities. We sought to have enforced existing laws governing the supply of liquor [and] to reintroduce drunkenness as an offense until such time as proper remedial centres were established. We sought proper camping sites for itinerant Aboriginals in particular, a matter first suggested by this community five years ago. We invited those responsible for determining policies to implement it and meet with us . . .
> . . . It is regrettable, Sir, that in the intervening period you have seen fit to make a series of public statements slandering this whole community, black and white. Your emotive references to the imminent outbreak of racial warfare and statements that black and white people walk on opposite footpaths and that whenever one racial group has another in its midst that other is bashed are untrue and inflammatory. Your comparison between Redfern and Alice Springs demonstrates a complete lack of understanding of the real position. For what purpose and upon what advice you've seen fit to malign this community . . . I do not know. But I tell you those utterances have only served to exacerbate tension. [Cries of "Hear, hear" from the audience.] I regret I feel constrained to say that the community no longer has faith in you. Unless you withdraw your allegation and apologize to the town, I see no useful purpose in taking further part in this discussion. [Further cries of "Hear, hear" and applause from the audience.]

After the applause died down, Senator Cavanaugh responded.

> Mr Mayor, I thank you for opening the meeting although I can't say I'm excited about the message you've brought. I am here today at the request of a number of local citizens . . . If I drew any conclusions on the racial tension in Alice Springs it was from the petition which was sent to myself, the Prime Minister, and a number of other officials in Canberra. And, therefore, I am pleased to hear . . . there is [no] racial tension. But, don't make me the one who brought this about. Every press statement [I] made was a reply to some local allegation. And . . . a series of incidents . . . caused great worry.

Cavanaugh continued that someone in the town shared his views because when he agreed to come during the parliamentary recess (six weeks away), they telegrammed saying he did not care about the local troubles and demanded he come earlier. He said further that he had indeed found trouble here and acted to correct it. He had only just approved funds for a night shelter and set machinery in motion to take more action.

Cavanaugh expanded his remarks with a discussion about what he considered the proper general approach to Aborigines and drinking.

> While I recognize that drink has caused problems in all Aboriginal communities . . . Aborigines have been given equality with white people, an equality which they will maintain, which they *have* to maintain under our international obligations. There is no question of taking the right to drink from Aborigines. Society has moved . . . to a state [which recognizes] that crimes without victims should not be punished. [Emphasis in original text.]

He noted that Senator Murphy had instructed the Northern Territory police not to arrest for drunkenness alone as a result of Cavanaugh's own discussion of the problem at Melbourne University in 1974. Although any citizen could be arrested for other breaches of law, drunkenness was not an offence. Finally, he summarized his decisions about the pick-up service, the detoxification centre and the property purchases. He closed his remarks by suggesting that a biracial committee be established to examine the situation and advise the DAA. The problems in Alice Springs, he said,

> cannot be solved by finance. They cannot be solved by restrictions on individuals. They cannot be solved by attack on one or another. They are questions which must be solved by greater communication and cooperation between . . . all those concerned.

The mayor responded that, although Cavanaugh had addressed the problems which originally provoked the drunkenness petition, he had not apologized to the town. Without an apology, the mayor saw no point in continuing the discussions. Cavanaugh tried to justify his comments about racial warfare by invoking the opinion of a "visiting anthropologist" from an overseas university who had only just left Alice Springs. Cavanaugh's efforts to explain the basis of his remarks were interrupted several times by shouts that he should examine the situation for himself on unannounced visits and rely upon the advice of local senior officers, not "idiot anthropologists who

travel all over the world and know nothing about the place".
The mayor remained unsatisfied with Cavanaugh's remarks.

> Senator, I'm afraid to say that your remarks confirm my general im-
> pression already expressed. I regrettably feel that you lack general
> understanding of the local situation, making broad general
> statements where we've tried to detail all those issues of real concern,
> that you've not displayed any real sense of sensibility and objectivity
> towards this community, black and white, and the whole question of
> the difficulties facing this town. It seems to me that to make broad
> sweeping statements about racism and the type of things you're
> reported to have said in the last few days [is] slanderous of the people
> of this town. You've not accepted my invitation to withdraw that
> statement. I invite others who feel as I do to join me, although I
> appreciate public servants may find themselves in difficulty.

He then left the meeting. Fourteen people accompanied him, in-
cluding at least three of the petitioners, two Aborigines, a local
Lutheran pastor and the president of the Northern Territory
Country Liberal Party.

The mayor walked out because Cavanaugh broke and refused
to reaffirm the rule of good faith. Like the rules of face, the rule
of good faith is normally a condition, not an objective of interaction (Goffman 1967, 12). However, under some circumstances,
the problematic nature of good faith becomes the object of
actors' attention and must itself be negotiated. If efforts to re-
establish good faith fail (such as when a necessary apology is not
forthcoming), interaction fails and negotiations stop. The
walkout culminated a period in which the good faith of the
petitioners, CAALAS and Cavanaugh all came under question.
Because Cavanaugh was the man ultimately responsible for taking the actions most local leaders thought necessry, he was
crucial in determining how this process developed. Although he
certainly took action on the drunkenness issue, he did not pay
sufficient deference to the authenticity of the general problem as
the people perceived it or to the goodwill of the people themselves. The mayor made an explicit recognition of those points
(namely, the apology), a necessary condition for further discussion. When he did not receive it, he broke off negotiations.

Although many people in the audience agreed with the mayor,
most stayed at the meeting, which lasted for over three hours. In
addition to responding to individual speakers, Cavanaugh
reiterated his desire to establish a biracial committee of local
leaders to discuss the problems and advise the DAA. The
meeting was otherwise interesting as a context within which

Cavanaugh and the local people debated the kinds of problems for which the DAA and the Commonwealth more generally had to assume responsibility. In the light of the dispute between the mayor and Cavanaugh, it is interesting to note that most people who spoke for any length introduced themselves as bona fide residents of the community. In particular, they consistently asserted their familiarity with local problems and their interest in the community as a whole; they denied they were racist. The two most important speakers were the chairman of the Alice Springs Tourist Promotions Board (the ASTPB) and a social worker from the Institute of Aboriginal Development (IAD).

The ASPTB chairman engaged Cavanaugh in the longest discussion of the afternoon. He was a prominent local business identity and close friend of many of the petitioners, including the mayor. It was commonly assumed by many Alice Springs people that he was a key figure "behind the scenes" in Central Australian politics. In his address he restated the petitioners' case, focusing in particular upon the fringe-campers in the Todd River. He presented himself as a representative of those people who (unlike most public servants) genuinely wanted to live in Alice Springs and were committed to the town. On that basis he claimed to make authoritative judgments about its well-being and questioned the understanding of outside government officials.

> Senator, I can't withdraw because I wasn't invited. I really gate-crashed here because I thought there were a few things I really should bring up. I [have] lived here for over twenty-eight years, not because I have to but . . . out of choice. I hope that I leave here by choice and not because I have to. In this [twenty-eight years] . . . the position of the Aboriginal has deteriorated. The government, not only your government, seemed to think that . . . money . . . [was] the answer to everything . . . But, why is not something being done about the campers in the Todd? . . . We have a situation in which right in the middle of Alice Springs, there are up to six hundred people camped without any facilities whatsoever – no toilets, no shelter. At least fifty percent of the people in the Todd are alcoholics. Now, instead of being able to dry out, they can actually drink themselves to death.

He rhetorically conceded Cavanaugh's point that drunkenness was not a crime, but argued that crime inevitably followed from drunkenness, irrespective of race.

> Okay, drunkenness is not a crime. But, it does lead to other crimes . . . I don't think it's racial discrimination . . . That's just a matter of crime in this community . . . It doesn't matter whether they are black or white or whatever. When they are drunk, they fight. It's no good saying there won't be because there will be fights and rapes.

Finally, he suggested that the fringe-dwellers be moved downstream out of town or out to Amoonguna, the local Aboriginal settlement. He recommended the government fund a free bus to transport drunken people and staff it with a police officer. In this way, he thought people might drink less, mothers could bring up their children "reasonably well" and the drunken people could fight out of sight among themselves.

Cavanaugh refused to recognize the premises of this argument. He stated that everyone had to recognize that Aborigines lived in Alice Springs and would continue to do so in ever-increasing numbers. However, because they had no jobs and little housing, they began far behind the whites, who lived in the town by choice and had jobs. Hence, although the town might not be racist, there were inequalities which kept Aborigines down. He accepted that the government had not done everything possible to help them, but it was also true that the local authorities had not always cooperated with Commonwealth efforts. In particular, people had to realize that Aborigines had the right to live wherever they wished and could not be arbitrarily moved. In summary, Cavanaugh no more accepted the ASTPB chairman's views than he had the original petitioners.

Cavanaugh's response to the ASTPB chairman contrasts with his reaction to the speech of the IAD social worker. The IAD social worker was a prominent local and national spokesman on Aboriginal affairs. Indeed, he maintained close personal and working relationships with powerful men in the Labor government and the DAA, whom he often advised or consulted about local issues. When he stood up to speak, he rose as a visible and highly respected identity in the context of the Commonwealth's new programme for the administration of Aboriginal affairs, and as one with many opponents in Alice Springs.

The social worker did not overtly play upon his well-established identity. He, too, documented his right to speak in terms of his fairmindedness and his intimate knowledge of Aborigines. He explained that he had worked with Aborigines for over fourteen years, five and a half years in Redfern and over nine years in Central Australia. He was well known among local Aborigines. He also knew the problems the town faced, having often had drunken Aborigines in his home and experienced personally the problems they posed. By the same token, he continued, the townspeople had to be fair about the situation. Although the town might perhaps not be "racist", he doubted the "sincerity" of some, such as those who called Aborigines "animals" (a reference to a remark earlier in the meeting), taxi drivers who ran illegal grog, publicans who served drunks and children, local white people who approved of violence against Aborigines, and police who abused their powers and applied the law selectively. If the town was to solve its problems, it had to support the police in the fair application of the laws right across the board and ensure strict enforcement of licensing laws.

The social worker observed that people recognized there was a local drinking problem. It was not, however, limited either to Aborigines or to Alice Springs. On the contrary, there were many white people throughout Australia who, suffering from the pressures of today's lifestyle, had alcohol problems. Excessive drinking was a major nationwide social problem, but Aborigines had special problems. As a result of white Australian society's refusal to understand Aboriginal culture and to communicate on its terms, the authority structure of Aboriginal society had collapsed. Of particular significance in this respect was the way previous and contemporary government officers had administered Aboriginal affairs. He gave a description of the effects of settlement upon the Pintubi, and of the frustrated efforts of local bodies working in the field.

> The problem is not just drunks. It's a society problem of community breakdown and we've contributed to it, all of us. So let's sit down together and see what ways we can strengthen and re-enforce laws necessary. And then see, Sir, why there are so many bottlenecks in the public service system.

Cavanaugh responded.

> I know the frustrations caused by the public service. I plead guilty; but, I can faithfully report that we are speeding up. We never had a Department of Aboriginal Affairs before 1973 and we've been working under pressure and have been understaffed. You made a most inspiring speech.

The meeting was a context within which local people could publicly pressure Cavanaugh and hold him accountable. In this respect, it was an important device whereby locals circumvented intermediaries in the bureaucratic hierarchy and tried to force the minister to accept responsibility for particular issues. A key aspect of Cavanaugh's response to the ASTPB chairman was that he refused to accept responsibility for, or even the legitimacy of, any overt action upon the problems caused by drunkenness, except as it hurt the drunks themselves. Drunkenness was not a public question but an illness that had to be treated. This position left several types of local people in an uncertain situation. Indeed, it seemed to some people that Cavanaugh was leaving private citizens with the responsibility of coping with a problem the Commonwealth had itself created. Taxi drivers and publicans felt themselves in a vulnerable situation. As the objects of the most sustained accusations of racism and exploitation, they were ridden right out of any participation in the discussion at all. They argued, however, that they were often the people who suffered most from Aboriginal drunkenness. It was the petition from a local group of publicans that first heralded the coming racial crisis.

After the IAD social worker sat down, a publican rose and defended his colleagues. He noted that eight months earlier he had closed his pub because the situation was "unreal; well, it was worse than it is now". After having closed his pub, however, he received a warning that unless he served "those particular persons", he would face court charges. When he asked why, he was told he was a racist. Cavanaugh said, "You have laws. To refuse to serve someone because of his colour is an offence. But, for a pub to refuse him because he's drunk, is the law." The publican answered, "That's right, sir, but you hear over the telephone and other ways that you are racist whether you're fair dinkum or not." Cavanaugh observed, "I take it there is unanimity of opinion that there should be proper enforcement of the law." Soon afterwards he closed the meeting.

Cavanaugh's comments ignore the possibility that, from the publicans perspective, the law was unclear and that the conditions for its "enforcement" with respect to Aboriginal drunks in particular, were inadequate. Most especially, the publican was put in a situation where he alone had to judge when his customers were drunk. Given the contemporary legal and political climate, his judgments were subject to scrutiny and great negotiation. "Enforcing the law", therefore, was not as unproblematic or straightforward as Cavanaugh seemed to insist. What the publican demanded was a change in the conditions under which he worked so that his judgments might be more isolated from the wider setting and his decisions less negotiable. The reintroduction of drunkenness as an offence was crucial, in this respect, because it would have made his decisions unimpeachable, enlisted the aid of the police in their enforcement and isolated him from outside attack.

The publican's demands were politically unpalatable for Cavanaugh, so he effectively denied the relevance of the publican's problems and his own ministerial responsibility for them. Indeed, he largely dismissed him from participation in the discussion at all.

The Consequences of the Racial Tension Crisis

The most important consequence of the racial crisis was that it legitimated upgrading the power of the local office of the Department of Aboriginal Affairs. Prior to the racial crisis the Alice Springs office was subordinate to the head office in Darwin. Although it was still nominally under Darwin's control, Cavanaugh appointed a new, personally influential man as regional director and announced that the local office would eventually become an autonomous regional centre. The new regional director (who had not been associated with the Welfare Branch) was to supervise that process. Although this move meant that the DAA, the self-determination policy and the white brokers who supported it officially became more powerful in the region, it gave all local whites greater access to decision making in the administration of Aboriginal affairs. The biracial committee was one official (though short-lived) forum for this access. The point is, however, that, because the DAA had to legitimate its long-term presence in Central Australia, it had to take account of all white interests. The biracial human relations committee was but a public representation of a necessary condition of bureaucratic functioning in the local area. The point is that because they declare that the system has broken down, racial tension crises ultimately legitimate the need for bureaucratic intervention in Aboriginal affairs and thereby lead to ever-greater increases in the power of whites over Aborigines. In this respect, "racial tension" (whether interpreted as a decline in public safety, as the detribalization of Aborigines or as a manifestation of a system of racial discrimination) is part of a long tradition in the Northern Territory whereby whites use Aborigines and their alleged "problems" as political resources in their own struggles for local power.

Nevertheless, the phenomena which so many people have interpreted as symptoms of detribalization do occur and are worthy of analysis. Aborigines do live in fringe-camps. There have been major changes in domestic, marital and kin relationships among them. They do drink alcoholic beverages and often engage in violent physical interaction. Many of these phenomena threaten the basis of the social order that whites want to take for granted. The problem cannot simply be ignored by renaming it or dismissing unfruitful labels such as detribalization. In the remainder of this book these phenomena will be explained and systematically related to the way Aborigines have become incorporated into white society. Receiving emphasis will be the role of the Commonwealth government and its various Aboriginal administrations in the transformation of Aboriginal society and the generation of the conditions of contemporary Aboriginal life. In this way it will be seen how, even as they decried "detribalization", white administrators have produced and reproduced the conditions that give rise to what they consider to be its symptoms.

Australians have long bemoaned the tendency for Aborigines to gather in squatter settlements, or fringe-camps, on the outskirts of urban areas and small country towns. Because the fringe-camps are understood as the product of cultural decay and social breakdown, much bureaucratic activity has been dedicated to disguising them or preventing their emergence. Anthropologists have also tended to dismiss them as transitional phenomena irrelevant to the social reality and analysis of contemporary Aboriginal life (Reay 1945, 296–323; Reay and Sitlington 1948, 177–207; Rowley 1973, 224–40; for an exception, see Beckett 1964).

In contrast to these approaches, I want to argue that the analysis of fringe-camps is crucial for understanding the political and economic processes that have transformed how all Aborigines live in Central Australia. The significance of the Aboriginal fringe-camps around Alice Springs may be understood in the context of the emergent structure of social relationships between Aborigines and whites in the region, particularly those between Aborigines and agencies of the Commonwealth government's administration of Aboriginal affairs. Indeed, the fringe-camps properly so-called have emerged since, and as the direct result of, the increased scope of the Commonwealth government's structural involvement in Central Australian Aboriginal life since the end of the Second World War.

Notes

1. The term "racial tension" is the label most Alice Springs people used to describe these periods. I use it as an actor's label, not as an analytical term.
2. See chapter 6 for a full analysis of drinking in the fringe-camps in Alice Springs.

3

Living in the Fringe-Camps

The fringe-campers maintain a distinctive social identity in contemporary Central Australian Aboriginal society. Yet, their identity and social location lay bare the general structural predicament of Aborigines. What distinguishes fringe-campers from other Aborigines is the range and comprehensiveness of their relationships with the dominant white powers of Central Australia. Being a fringe-dweller is sociologically synonymous with maintaining a set of relatively simplex relationships with several diverse types of outside white agents.[1]

Fringe-dwellers contrast with other Aborigines who heavily commit themselves to one white agent and derive all their needs from it. All Aborigines, fringe- and non-fringe-dwellers alike, must interact with whites on unequal terms in order to survive at all. Insofar as the fringe-dwellers represent one complex strategy among others for handling the problems generated by these conditions, they both distinguish themselves and document their relevance for the understanding of other Aborigines. This approach emphasizes the transactions that fringe-dwellers make among themselves and with outsiders, rather than their moral state. It thereby makes it possible to analyse the interrelationships among individual careers, daily fringe-camp life and conditions in the wider context; for example, it suggests that being a fringe-camper is not necessarily a perpetual condition of an individual's normative orientation or cultural development. Individuals might move into and out of fringe-camps according to the development of their careers. Among other things, the fringe-camps are labour pools and reservoirs of credit for those working in the cattle industry. Consequently people who are committed to cattlework find the camps useful at certain points in the seasonal cycle of the pastoral industry. Those who find permanent urban employment, however, may not require the information or resources available in the camps and often move out of them.

Access to particular resources, however, is not the only advantage of fringe-camps. Living in the camps also frees individuals of certain obligations; in particular, fringe-dwellers are not indebted to the welfare agencies that control the rural settlements or the urban housing projects. On the contrary, the camps are places in which Aborigines can establish domestic groups and live in the urban area outside welfare housing. Stressing Aborigines' transactions with others also focuses attention on changes in the wider context which might alter the utility of fringe-camps or the capacity of people to live in them; for example, as white bureaucracies change the conditions that control access to urban housing, the fringe population might rise or be cosmetically eliminated.

The general point is that the fringe-camps are significant contexts within which Aborigines actively negotiate with and attempt to control the social forces acting upon them. They are by no means simply collecting grounds for so-called "detribalized" people. Nor are fringe-camps miniature settlements or underdeveloped suburbs. They have a singular identity relating to the specific way their residents manipulate the resources available in the camps. An adequate analysis of the fringe-camps, therefore, must focus on the conditions under which Aborigines live, their strategies for handling those conditions and the consequences which follow from the interaction of these processes. In other words, the analysis must begin with a serious look at the structure of social relationships in which Aborigines participate and which they help construct.

The Development of Aboriginal Administration in Central Australia

The fringe-camps emerged as part of the process by which whites increased their involvement with and control over Aborigines in Central Australia. How the Commonwealth government impinged upon and attempted to manipulate the development of everyday Aboriginal social life was particularly important in this process. Rowley has made an extensive analysis of Commonwealth policies and operational strategies with respect to Northern Territory Aborigines. He documents in great detail the political controversies which raged over Aboriginal policy as well as the compromises which eventually emerged as official policy (Rowley 1974, 222–340, 1972, 29–54). He pays little attention, however, to the growth and development of the actual content and pattern of the relationships among Aborigines and whites that emerged as a result of the administrative implementation of these policies; yet these relationships were the vehicle for the pragmatic materialization of the policies and constituted the social contexts within which Aborigines encountered the policies. No account of Aboriginal responses to them can ignore the social relationships which the policies helped define.

From this perspective, there was a major transformation in the administration of Aboriginal affairs after the Second World War. Indeed, although policies have changed quite significantly in the last twenty-five years, it may well be true that the organizational transformation that occurred as a result of the establishment of the Welfare Branch will have longer lasting consequences for Aboriginal–white relationships than the particular policies that various governments articulate from time to time. Although quite fundamental in its consequences, this transformation may be described quite simply. Prior to 1953 the Commonwealth government administered Aboriginal affairs either through agents not under its direct control (for example, missions and cattle stations) or through agents of its own whose primary functions lay in other fields (for example, the police and the Department of Public Health). After 1953, however, the Commonwealth government established an administrative apparatus completely under its control, the primary responsibility of which was Aborigines and which had almost exclusive control over Aborigines. In other words, with the establishment of the Welfare branch a specialized Aboriginal administration as such emerged.[2]

This transformation in the administrative apparatus of Aboriginal affairs also marked a radical increase in the power of the administration over Aborigines. Although the laws were in many respects similar, the machinery for the implementation of the laws became more efficient and highly developed. The administration began to enforce many of the laws that it had previously depended upon others to implement. These changes were fundamental: they meant that whatever policy changes occurred in 1953 and have occurred since, the organizational context within which they are administered is fundamentally different from the era prior to 1953. In comparison with the organizational discontinuity between the pre- and post-1953 periods, recent policy changes are variations on a theme. By the same token, the Commonwealth's refinement and development of the Aboriginal administration since 1953 marks a basic organizational continuity between the Welfare Branch and its descendants which might otherwise be obscured by the apparently quite radical changes in overt policy. Although Australian law no longer permits the administration to control the movement of Aborigines, for example, the administration's monopoly of most resources Aborigines need to survive maintains its basic power over them. The organizational basis for these processes was established in 1953 and has been developing ever since.[3]

The changes have had quite radical consequences for the structure of relationships between many Aborigines and the administrative apparatus. At the simplest level, the administration was able to establish its control over a greater number and range of Aboriginal people than before 1953. Prior to that time, the administration controlled little outside the urban areas and was mostly concerned with the administration of urban institutions for part-Aboriginal people. In the bush it yielded its responsibility and power to the missions, the police, and the pastoralists. Otherwise it left the Aborigines "uncontacted". It simply did not have the administrative resources to incorporate them into any systematic apparatus.[4] In contrast to its predecessors the Welfare Branch had quite extensive resources which it used actively to encapsulate whole new Aboriginal populations and to reorganize many of the Aborigines who had previously been living in contact with other white agencies. It further redistributed most of the Aboriginal population in space. The administration accomplished these tasks by developing new residential communities both in the bush and the urban areas and moving Aborigines into them. These processes expressed, and were major instruments in, the administration's increased power over and structural involvement in the everyday affairs of Aborigines.

The Welfare Branch recognized three types of Aboriginal communities: the missions or settlements, the cattle stations, and the urban housing projects. It directly controlled and/or established thirteen settlements and two urban housing projects. It also subsidized thirteen missions throughout the Northern Territory (Long 1970b, 199–200). Although the Welfare Branch left many cattle-station residents where they were and substantially yielded its authority over them to the cattle bosses, it systematically encouraged or compelled large numbers of Aborigines from the cattle regions and elsewhere to move on to the settlements. It also settled a select number of substantially part-Aborigines in the urban areas – most notably for this discussion – in Alice Springs (Long 1970b, 199–201; Rowley 1972, 35–54; Rowley 1974, 239). Between 1950 and 1965, the total population on missions and settlements in the Northern Territory increased from almost 6000 Aboriginal people to over 11,000. In Central Australia the numbers increased from under 1000 in 1950 to over 6200 in 1971. By 1971, 1850 Aboriginal people lived in Alice Springs. Most lived in houses built by the Welfare Branch or the Housing Commission. A substantial minority lived in fringe-camps. Another 1920 Aboriginal people lived in cattle stations in Central Australia in 1971 (Australian Bureau of Statistics 1971). Although there was considerable movement back and forth between these communities during my fieldwork, these population centres emerged as a result of the administration's reorganization of the Aboriginal population during the late 1940s and 1950s.

Although I have so far described these processes in terms of the redistribution of the Aboriginal population in space, it is important to realize that they involved as well significant processes of ethnic, administrative and industrial reorganization. The Welfare Branch legitimated its activities in terms of the assimilation policy. The fundamental principle of that policy was that Aborigines did not understand the norms of white middle-class Australian culture. In its own eyes the Welfare Branch's major responsibility was to teach Aborigines those norms and enable them to participate effectively in the wider society. According to the policy clients varied in the diversity of their cultural background from the most primitive to the nearly assimilated. Consequently, the policy was supposedly geared to the needs of the individual clients and administered according to their capacities. Clients were to move into the wider society as their individual progress permitted them (Tatz 1964, 13–20). There was, in other words, a graded hierarchy. The distinction

between the urban and the settlement communities was related
to what the Welfare Branch considered to be the broad distinctions within the Aboriginal community on the assimilation scale.
The settlements were for those people who were least
assimilated and understood almost nothing about white
Australian culture. The Welfare Branch offered the urban
houses to the people it considered were becoming assimilated.[5]
These broadly cultural criteria were linked to implicit racial
distinctions. Rowley notes that although the planners of the
assimilation policy explicitly disavowed racial criteria in the
public presentation and justification of their schemes, the actual
administration of the policy developed as if racial criteria were
important. This was primarily the result of the way the category
of "ward" was interpreted in administrative and legal practice. A
ward was someone judged by the administration to be unable for
special social reasons to care for himself or herself. A ward was
subject to the complete authority of the Director of Welfare. The
director controlled the movement, property, choice of residence,
and marriage rights of all "wards" and in general was responsible
for their "protection" and well-being. Although the Welfare
Ordinance of 1953 did not use racial terms to define wards, it excluded all persons with the right to vote from ward status.
Consequently, it excluded most part-Aborigines and all whites.
Only "full-blood" Aborigines were eligible for ward status.
Apparently most were so registered. Because wards were
restricted to residence on missions, settlements and cattle
stations, most rural Aborigines were "full-bloods" and most
urban Aborigines were part-Aborigines (Long 1967, 195; Rowley
1974, 239–41).

There were major administrative differences between the
three residential communities. The Welfare Branch had the
power and legal authority to interfere in the everyday domestic
life of urban and settlement Aborigines. In contrast, it substantially yielded its authority over cattle station residents to the
pastoralists. It paid the pastoralists subsidies to support their
resident Aboriginal populations and relied upon them to enforce
its regulations. In this sector, the Welfare Branch operated much
as its predecessors had been forced to operate. The significance
of this surrender might be gauged by the Welfare Branch's difficulty in sustaining its prosecution of any pastoralists for misuse of
its subsidy money. As a result of this the Aborigines living on the
cattle stations were effectively administered by their employers.

Their cattle bosses both isolated and insulated them from the Welfare Branch. They differed in this respect from their counterparts on the settlements and in Alice Springs. The Welfare Branch intervened in the most intimate and everyday domestic affairs of both urban and settlement people. It operated a communal ration system on most settlements and thereby almost completely controlled local access to food. In the urban areas it controlled most housing facilities. It legitimated its attempts to aid and manipulate urban Aboriginal families in their housekeeping efforts by pegging access to houses on displays of proper domestic husbandry. By controlling these basic domestic resources, the Welfare Branch wielded considerable power over most aspects of Aboriginal life on the settlements and in Alice Springs.

These ethnic, residential and administrative conditions also structured Aboriginal access to job opportunities. With the principal exception of part-Aborigines, Aboriginal people had primary access to jobs in the area in which they resided. Although the settlements were partially justified as "training centres", there was in fact very little work available. With the exception of the cattle projects at Haasts Bluff and Hooker Creek, Tatz (1964, 20, 71) and Long (1967, 201) report that by 1965 most settlements were still little more than ration depots. There was almost no demand for Aboriginal labour from the settlements or cattle stations. After 1965, the Commonwealth government intervened and created jobs for Aboriginal people. However, these jobs did not reflect any industrial development or the growth of a self-sustaining employment sector independent of government expenditure. On the contrary, as was documented during the cutbacks in 1976, these jobs remained vulnerable to budget cuts and Commonwealth good graces. The point was, however, that these jobs were primarily available to the Aboriginal people who lived on the settlements.

The urban work-force was similarly structured, with a very close relationship between urban residence and urban work. There was very little work for Aboriginal men in Alice Springs prior to 1960. Most job opportunities were available to Aboriginal women to work as domestics in private homes, laundries and public facilities such as the hospital. The expansion of Commonwealth agencies in Alice Springs during the 1960s created new job opportunities for men and women. Aboriginal men were frequently hired by the Commonwealth Railways, the

Department of Works, the Department of Lands and Survey and the Department of the Interior (later Northern Territory). The expansion of government spending stimulated the growth of light industrial and commercial venture in Alice Springs which also opened new job opportunities for some men. These opportunities fell open primarily to Aboriginal people who were already based in the urban setting, that is, Aborigines who were involved in the Welfare Branch's schemes to settle and assimilate them in Alice Springs. Urban employers favoured those people the government was trying to incorporate into the urban setting (Rowley 1972, 40).

As in the urban and settlement settings, there was a close link between the right to work and the right to live on a cattle station. A substantial proportion of the Aboriginal labour needed on the cattle stations out bush was recruited directly from station residents. Yet, it was frequently the case that the right to live on a station was a function of having a job on the station or a relative with a job on the station. The key variable was the state of personal relationships between cattle bosses and their workers. Although it was not necessarily so, it was often true that these links had their origins in regionally based kinship links both among Aboriginal people and between Aborigines and station owners.

There was one important exception to the rule of local recruitment in the cattle industry: the role of part-Aboriginal, often urban-based labourers. Many pastoralists preferred to hire part-Aboriginal men especially as head stockmen, fencers, well-sinkers and drovers. They also hired part-Aboriginal women as domestics. Although some pastoralists hired part-Aborigines from their own camps, this hiring practice often cut across the urban–rural distinction in employment patterns and gave part-Aborigines greater job opportunities than other Aborigines normally enjoyed. Especially this was true during the period of increased Commonwealth spending and the expansion of job opportunities in Alice Springs.

This raises a more general point. As workers and candidates for assimilation, part-Aborigines were more valuable as clients to white authorities than other Aborigines. Indeed, their ethnic identity was both an expression of their greater social value and a basic resource in establishing their value. As a result of their greater job and administrative opportunities and their greater legal freedom, part-Aborigines enjoyed altogether greater social, economic and administrative flexibility in their transactions with whites than most other Aborigines. Consequently, they maintained a distinct advantage in most areas in the competition for the scarce goods that whites monopolized.

The Structure of Aboriginal—White Relations in Central Australia

The discussion of flexibility in an otherwise highly structured and determined environment leads back to the analysis of the fringe-camps. By living in fringe-camps some Aboriginal people minimize the control outside agencies have over them and maximize their flexibility in taking advantage of what opportunities do become available. The brief analysis of the overall structure of Central Australia provides the basis for a closer look at that proposition.

The relationship between residential, administrative and industrial organization might best be summarized by saying that each of the three contexts (town, cattle station and settlement) was relatively closed and self-contained. As the case of the part-Aborigines documents, they were never absolutely closed. Moreover, the categories of people who had access to urban work and houses, for example, were never as rigid as official or commonsense models suggested they should have been (see Rowley 1972, 39). The point is, however, that by participating in a particular context, Aborigines became heavily indebted to the whites who controlled it. Because whites monopolized all the resources Aborigines needed to survive, part-Aborigines and other Aborigines alike were affected. Yet, and this is the key point, the content and pattern of transactions between particular Aborigines and particular white agents varied according to the extent and significance of Aboriginal indebtedness. These emergent characteristics conditioned the relative capacity of particular Aborigines to negotiate what under the prevailing regime was considered a "fair exchange" (Handelman 1976, 230).[6]

I have already mentioned that in general whites considered part-Aborigines more valuable as workers and clients than other Aborigines. Consequently, part-Aborigines had access to a greater range of opportunities on better terms than most "full-blood" Aborigines. Yet, a part-Aboriginal ethnic identity was neither a necessary nor sufficient resource for Aborigines to negotiate a conventional "fair exchange" from a white agency. On the contrary, some "full-blood" Aborigines negotiated deals with their employers that were conventionally considered more appropriate for part-Aboriginal or, in some cases, white workers. It is important to note that the process of recruitment into the cattle industry, for example, included techniques that served to establish or suspend the relevance of a man's ethnic identity for his relationship with his employers. The fact that some "full-blood" Aborigines negotiated a better than average deal with their cattle bosses was both evidence for, and the result of, basic interactional processes whereby pastoralists and their workers determined and often changed the significance of broader contextual conditions for their own social relationships. However, their activities were only part of a more general process. Precisely because Central Australia is such a highly stratified and heavily determined society, individual Aborigines and whites actively negotiate about the meaning of the broader conditions for their interaction. These processes of negotiation establish emergent conditions that structure the development of personal relationships and differentiate people according to the extent to which they are subject to the wider context. Four conditions are especially important: the range of peoples' relationships, the multiplexity or structural involvement of the relationships they construct, the resources people realize in their relationships, and the control people enjoy over their spatial mobility.

By range is meant the diversity of types of contexts to which an Aborigine has access or is linked. For example, an Aborgine who lives and works in only one place and who maintains no links with any other context has a narrow range; in contrast, an Aborigine who has access to several diverse types of contexts has a broad range. The range of an individual's contacts is an index of the opportunities to which the person has access. All other things being equal, the broader the range of contacts, the greater the number of opportunities there are likely to be; the narrower the range, the fewer the opportunities. This is also a measure of a person's necessary commitment to any particular context. The broader the range, the less the person must be committed to any particular context through time. Those who have access to few contexts must necessarily value and commit themselves to what is available.

The multiplexity or the structural involvement of an individual's relationship with a context refers to the content or interactional components of the relationship (Kapferer 1972, 172; Handelman 1976, 233). Handelman suggests two conditions that define the scope of structural involvement: locus and area. By locus Handelman means the individual who transacts (in his case) with the welfare department in Israel. An area is a component of household living; Handelman cites as examples employment, child care, education and housing. The scope of these two conditions may vary independently of one another; for example, one locus might transact with the welfare department over one or more areas of his household and, on the other hand, several loci in the same household might transact over one or more areas. The greater the number of loci and areas involved in the transactions between a given household and the welfare department, the greater its structural involvement, or the more multiplex its relationship with the department (Handelman 1976, 232–33). Handelman examines the resources clients can bring into transactions so as to influence the welfare department's commitment to them. For Handelman, increased structural involvement makes it more difficult for the welfare department to terminate its obligations to a client. The more the welfare department has invested in a client, the harder it is for them to withdraw from the relationship. It also follows, however, that the greater the structural involvement, the more all-encompassing is the client's indebtedness. Indeed, Handelman notes that a condition of "structural dependency" results when a client must rely on the department for help in all areas of his life. In such circumstances, his structural involvement with the department and his indebtedness is complete. Consequently, the client is "relatively powerless" to influence the flow of transactions in such relationships (Handelman 1976, 231). There are two further conditions which affect the scope of indebtedness: what an Aborigine can offer in return for access to white resources and the Aborigine's mobility. Aborigines vary quite considerably in what they can offer in exchange for white goods and services: some people offer their labour whereas others offer only their compliance with white directives. Most relationships involve elements of both. The intermixture varies and is quite significant in determining the precise nature of any given relationship. Although the value of particular resources is, of course, subject to change and situational redefinition, Aborigines who offer material or otherwise instrumental resources such as labour are in a better position that others (Kapferer 1972, 162–66).

An individual's mobility (spatial and otherwise) is in some respects a composite consequence of the other three conditions. High mobility tends to reflect a greater range of alternatives, a lower structural involvement with any particular context and a greater range and/or quality of resources to offer in exchange. Yet it is also true that the power to move spatially is itself a resource that may enable a person to minimize or even escape indebtedness to another. More generally, the capacity for people to determine their location in space is an important way of controlling the social forces acting upon them. This was especially true in Central Australia when the Welfare Branch legally restricted the rights of wards to move at their own will.

Although the possible combinations of these four conditions are numerous and quite complex, one may generally characterize the town, cattle-station and settlement contexts and compare them with the fringe-camps. Of the four contexts, the fringe-camps offer the greatest range of alternative opportunities and the least structural involvement with any white agency. As labour pools, they also provide a context within which Aborigines can realize the instrumental resources they produce. The camps also enable people to control their own mobility: they offer people opportunities that allow them to move back and forth between different social contexts and, because they are outside the spatial boundaries controlled by any particular white agency, they permit the fringe-dwellers to minimize substantially their subordination to the authorities. Although each of the other three contexts offers advantages that might be greater than those available in the camps, the camps alone combine access to advantages with a minimum of involvement in the contexts that produce them; that is to say, by surrending the particular advantages of any specific context, the fringe-dwellers maintain a structural flexibility with respect to the available advantages generally.

The settlement people were the most structurally dependent of any of the four categories. Other than a return to the bush, the settlement people had few if any opportunities for survival outside what the Welfare Branch made available. The significance of this fact was not lost upon the residents themselves. Meggitt says that the Walbiri only came into intensive contact with whites as a result of the great drought of 1924–29. They told him that, had there been no drought, they would have remained forever in the Western Desert relatively removed from white control (Meggitt 1962, 24). As it was they came into three of the largest settlements ever established by the government and became the dominant population therein. As indicated earlier, there was little work for them on the cattle stations. Those who worked on the stations tended to live there and only visit the settlements occasionally. What work they did find was government subsidized and part of the settlement apparatus. The settlement residents were totally involved with the settlement authorities. Everyone in the settlements depended entirely on the Welfare Branch for food, housing, health care, education and practically every other conceivable area of household life. Furthermore, they had little if anything to offer the authorities in exchange for access to these resources other than their compliance. The absence of work and the charitable nature of what work was available gave the settlement Aborigines little room to manoeuvre in their transactions with the white authorities. In addition to the fact that settlement Aborigines had few reasons to leave in search of work, they were not legally able to move according to their own wishes. If the authorities so wished they could either confine wards to the reserves or move them about from one reserve to another. There are indeed cases in which the Welfare Branch used this power to punish Aborigines who refused to obey its wishes.

In most respects the urban part-Aborigines contrasted sharply with the settlement wards. They were not limited to what the Welfare Branch dispensed. Although being urban-based and having urban links with welfare officers helped part-Aborigines get jobs, their work was independent of the formal welfare apparatus. Moreover, there were job opportunities in both the rural and urban areas to which they had privileged access. The capacity to offer and withdraw their labour (even if at exploitative rates of exchange) furthermore gave part-Aborigines considerably more leverage with their employers than wards had with the settlement authorities. This could be quite important especially for the most skilled men who maintained working relationships with a number of potential employers. In general, this diversity of opportunity and the absence of legal shackles on their right to move guaranteed most part-Aborigines much greater mobility than settlement wards.

However, the Welfare Branch did exert power over part-

Aborigines through its control of urban housing and domestic resources. Indeed, the branch largely monopolized these resources in the urban setting. If an Aborigine moved into a Welfare house, he committed himself to a quite extensive relationship with the Welfare Branch. Accepting a house also involved long-term transactions with welfare officers over areas of food, child care, housekeeping, marital relationships and overall social comportment. Hence, although the multiplexity of the relationships between the Welfare Branch and particular domestic groups varied, living in a Welfare house necessarily indebted part-Aborigines and subjected them to Welfare Branch control. Nevertheless, it is also true that the branch had a long-term interest in ensuring that its female clients, in particular, were "successful", meaning, in short, that they adopted a lifestyle that could be interpreted as consistent with the goal of assimilation. Because the Welfare Branch could and did use people who in its judgment "coped" well with their new conditions as evidence for the success of its overall programme, Aboriginal compliance in this regard was an instrumental and important resource. It has already been noted that the high value of part-Aborigines as workers and clients gave them considerably more room to manoeuvre with white agents than their settlement counterparts.

The situation of cattle-station residents was quite complex, and included elements of both the urban and the settlement settings. On the one hand, the cattle-station Aborigines were highly dependent upon, and structurally involved with, the pastoralists. Besides work on the stations there were few if any opportunities to earn a living. Although they hunted and gathered to supplement the food supply, they owed their jobs, much of their food and, in the final analysis, their right to live on the properties to the pastoralists. They were indeed restricted to what the pastoralists chose to dispense. The pastoralists' power was strengthened by the fact that the Welfare Branch effectively transferred to them its authority over station people. It was also true, however, that the pastoralists needed the labour the Aboriginal people offered in order to operate their properties. They also needed to obtain it at an exploitative rate of exchange. The pastoralists did not and still do not refrain from using physical violence against their Aboriginal workers.[7] The absence of alternative possibilities also tied Aborigines to the pastoralists who hired them. Yet, unlike the settlement Aborigines, they did have room to manoeuvre: they could use their labour and their close knowledge of the pastoralists, particularly of their intimate affairs, to bargain. This did not mean that they could strike for better wages or conditions; on the contrary, for many years they were not paid cash wages and they still work for less than an equivalent value for the labour they exchange. However, many were better off than the settlement Aborigines. There was a solid base for the station residents' widely held view that in comparison with their own lives, the settlement Aborigines were lean and hungry (Stevens 1974, 167). Indeed, it was quite true that many Aborigines regarded work in the cattle industry as a major way of escaping the control of the Welfare Branch.

The rest of this chapter is a detailed presentation of the position of the fringe-camps in this analysis. For the moment there are four preliminary and general observations to be made that will be tested as hypotheses with the detailed data:

Fringe-campers maintain relationships with a great range of contexts outside their own domestic groups. Consequently, the fringe-camps offer a range of opportunities to their residents, particularly in the field of employment.

The relationships between the fringe-campers and outside contexts are relatively simplex. Fringe-campers are less structurally involved with any one white agent than most other Aborigines.

The fringe-camps enable Aborigines to realize resources they can offer in exchange for access to white-controlled contexts.

Fringe-dwellers have a greater capacity to control their own mobility than many other Aborigines.

These four features engender an overall structural flexibility that is uniquely characteristic of fringe-camp life and constitutes its chief utility. However, it is important to note that a necessary condition, as well as long-term consequence, of living in the fringe-camps and of taking advantage of their flexibility is that fringe-dwellers restrict their material demands to what is necessary to meet their fundamental subsistence needs. Given the impoverished environment within which they live, Aborigines must establish quite multiplex relationships and incur substantial debts to whites if they are to acquire anything much beyond their basic food requirements. It is obvious that many Aborigines do so, but the point is, that in so doing they increase their indebtedness and commitment. They also cease (or even fail) to be fringe-dwellers. People become fringe-dwellers by limiting such transactions and keeping their debt low.

The Emergence of Fringe-Camps in Central Australia

In the Introduction it was suggested that fringe-camps properly so-called only emerged during the expansion of the Commonwealth government's involvement in Aboriginal social life under the Welfare Branch. Doubtless, Aborigines have lived on the outskirts of Alice Springs since the earliest days of white settlement. However, the point might well be made that the earliest white settlements constituted little more than fringe-camps on the outskirts of Aboriginal society. This is noted in order to stress the dynamics of the political and economic relationships between blacks and whites in the region. The question of the relative identities of the "settlement" and the "fringe" can only be resolved with reference to the distribution of power between them. Hence, Aboriginal fringe-camps can only be said to have emerged as the whites began firmly to establish their political and economic control over Central Australia and Aborigines. The transformation in the administrative apparatus of Aboriginal affairs under the Welfare Branch radically increased the power and control of the Commonwealth government over Aborigines, and it was that same transformation that established the conditions for the change in significance of the fringe-camps. Indeed, it is precisely the case that the fringe-camps as they now exist only truly emerged during, and as a response to, the increased power of the Welfare Branch.

At the beginning of the century there was an Aboriginal camp immediately adjacent to the original telegraph station at the Alice Spring, a deep section of the Todd River which eventually gave the town its name. The telegraph workers distributed rations and hired mainly domestic labour from the Aboriginal camp. Although a ration point, this camp appears not to have been administered in any direct way. When the railroad arrived in Alice Springs in 1929, the telegraph station was moved to a site in the town near the railhead. The Aboriginal people, however, were moved to Hermansburg, the Lutheran mission west of Alice Springs. This followed J.W. Bleakley's report and appears to have been justified by fears that the railway workers posed a moral and physical threat especially to Aboriginal women.

Bleakley wanted to avoid what he called "trouble . . . owing to the approaching Railway Construction Works" (Bleakley 1928, 18–19; Rowley 1974, 270). The Bungalow, the original institution in Alice Springs for part-Aboriginal children taken from camps in the bush, was shifted west to Jay Creek for the same reason.

After the railway workers left and the threat apparently dissipated, the Bungalow was installed in the old telegraph facilities and a new Aboriginal camp began to grow in Alice Springs on the site of what is now the Anzac Oval. White people hired Aborigines from this camp as domestics, goatherds and fowlkeepers. Between 1929 and the outbreak of the Second World War the camp shifted to a stretch of land between the western boundary of the Bungalow Reserve and the Charles River (see figure 1). According to my informants this camp was

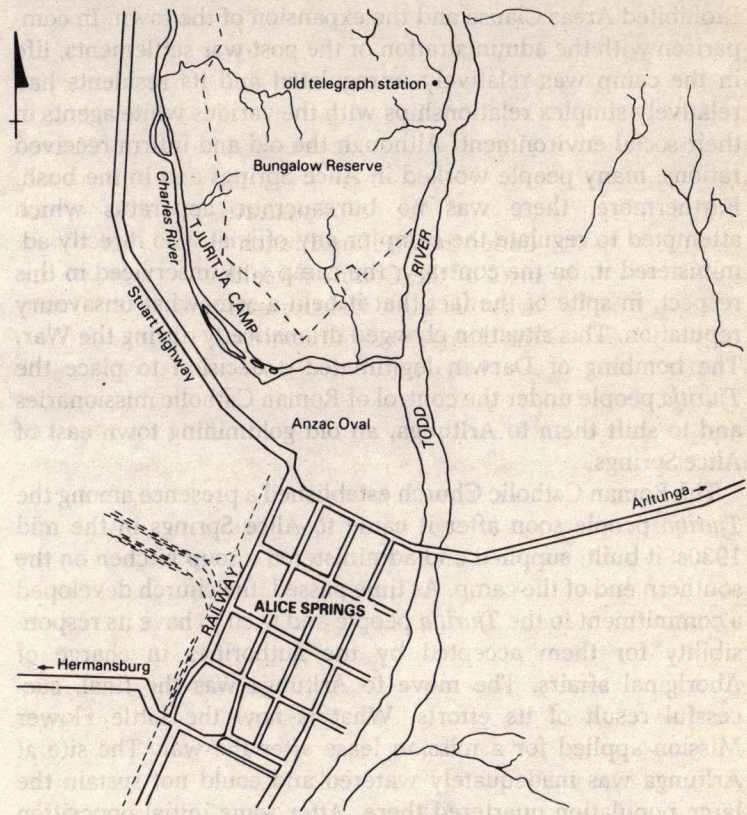

Figure 1   Map showing location of *Tjuritja* camp in the 1930s

called *Tjuritja*, the name which also identified the eastern Arunta people. Although a substantial proportion of its residents were apparently Aboriginal people from the immediate area and regions further east, the camp was also a gathering place for Aborigines from the north of the town. Indeed, it was a kind of boundary between northern and southern groups. The Aboriginal attendants of the camel trains that moved north and south, for example, used to change in the *Tjuritja* camp. If the trains were coming from the south, southern Aborigines handed over the camels to northern Aborigines in the camp; the same procedure worked in reverse.

The interesting thing about this camp was its apparent independence. The presence of Aborigines in the urban areas was regulated by law. And it seems probable that the shifts in the *Tjuritja* camp's location reflected the restrictions of the Prohibited Areas Clause and the expansion of the town. In comparison with the administration of the post-war settlements, life in the camp was relatively unregulated and its residents had relatively simplex relationships with the various white agents in their social environment. Although the old and infirm received rations, many people worked in Alice Springs and in the bush. Furthermore, there was no bureaucratic apparatus which attempted to regulate the camp or any official who directly administered it; on the contrary, the camp was unserviced in this respect, in spite of the fact that it held a somewhat unsavoury reputation. This situation changed dramatically during the War. The bombing of Darwin legitimated a decision to place the *Tjuritja* people under the control of Roman Catholic missionaries and to shift them to Arltunga, an old goldmining town east of Alice Springs.

The Roman Catholic Church established a presence among the *Tjuritja* people soon after it came to Alice Springs in the mid 1930s: it built, supplied and administered a soup kitchen on the southern end of the camp. As time passed, the church developed a commitment to the *Tjuritja* people and tried to have its responsibility for them accepted by the authorities in charge of Aboriginal affairs. The move to Arltunga was the final, successful result of its efforts. What is now the Little Flower Mission applied for a mission lease after the war. The site at Arltunga was inadequately watered and could not sustain the large population quartered there. After some initial opposition the mission was granted a lease and moved to its current site at

Santa Teresa, 300 kilometres southeast of Alice Springs. It was in this manner that the Aborigines who first lived on the "fringes" of Alice Springs were removed and subjected to the direct control of the mission authorities.

New fringe-camps began to emerge after the war and the Welfare Branch was established. In the light of the Welfare Branch's total activities, it is significant that the majority of people who eventually became fringe-dwellers came from two sources: the Welfare houses in Alice Springs and the two government settlements (the Bungalow and Amoonguna) in the town's immediate vicinity.

Some of the earliest fringe-dwellers were escapees from the Bungalow. During the Second World War the part-Aborigines at the Bungalow were evacuated to Balaklava in South Australia and the army transformed the institution into one of five Aboriginal labour camps that stretched along the Stuart Highway from Alice Springs to Darwin (Long 1967, 193; Rowley 1974, 332–33). After the war the Commonwealth reassumed civilian control of the Bungalow and made it into a settlement for "full-blood" Aborigines, initially administered by the Native Affairs Branch. Between 1953 and 1961, however, administration passed to the Welfare Branch. The Bungalow embraced an expanse of hills running north along either side of the Todd River. The actual buildings were the original structures used by the telegraph station and later by the children's institution. They were located next to the Alice Spring and the Aborigines were camped in the surrounding hills.

Some Aborigines, however, refused to live on the Bungalow settlement and ran deep into the hills outside its boundaries, where they supported themselves by hunting and gathering. As all of the Bungalow's residents were wards under the provision of the Welfare Ordinance of 1953, it was not legal for them to live outside the settlement without the administration's permission. Systematic searches were made for the escapees and those found were returned to the Bungalow. In spite of the administration's efforts, people continued to run away and live on its "fringes" hidden in the hills.

In 1961 the Welfare Branch closed the Bungalow and shifted its people to Amoonguna, a new settlement ten kilometres southeast of Alice Springs (see figure 2). This provoked further proliferation of the fringe-camps both in number and spatial distribution. Some Bungalow residents refused to make the

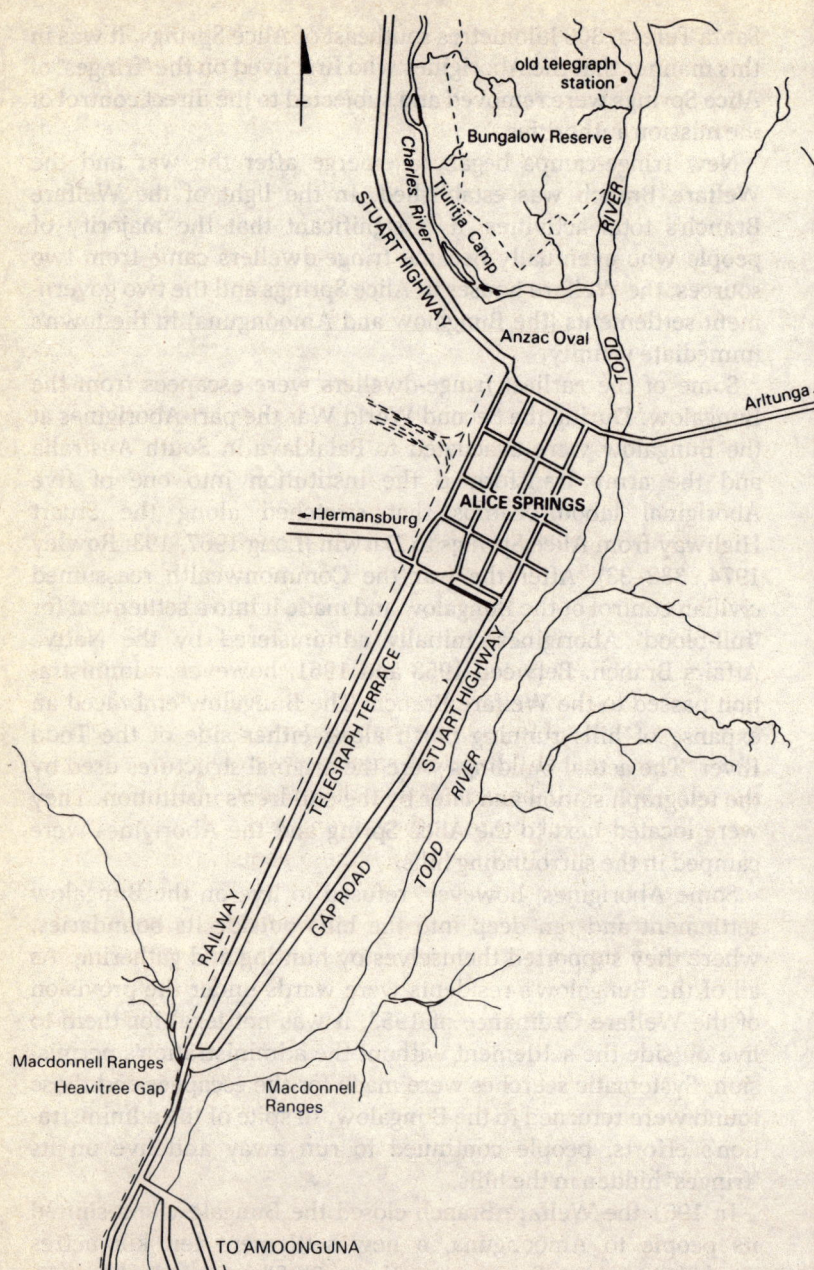

Figure 2 Map showing direction of Aboriginal settlement of Amoonguna, set up after the Bungalow settlement was closed in 1961

move to Amoonguna and a few people continued to hide in the hills north of Alice Springs; others established new camps along the base of the ridges south of the town in the vicinity of Amoonguna itself. According to Sister Leslie Grey, a welfare officer who was working in Alice Springs at the time, these fringe-camps tremendously embarrassed the Director of Welfare who again gave orders for the people to be returned to the settlement. Sister Grey said that the camps cast the Welfare Branch in a bad light and opened it to criticism from southern journalists and tourists. Although the welfare officers proceeded cautiously (according to Sister Grey), their efforts were unsuccessful and the fringe-camps continued to appear. This process apparently continued until the Welfare Ordinance was revoked and the Welfare Branch lost its power to control the movements of wards in space. Many fringe-dwellers settled down and remained in their camps.

The Welfare Branch also contributed to the rise of the fringe-camps in a more direct manner. It evicted from the houses those part-Aborigines who in its eyes failed to maintain a lifestyle consistent with the assimilation policy. Although the Welfare Branch justified such action in a variety of ways, it was especially quick to act against people who in its opinion drank too much liquor, failed to pay rent, or otherwise abused the houses. The Welfare Branch "demoted" some people and put them into less well-equipped houses "lower" down the assimilation hierarchy. However, it barred others from access to any type of welfare house at all. Consequently, these people had to establish camps on vacant land on the outskirts of town.

Some fringe-camps emerged in another way which combined elements of the two processes just described. Some Aborigines refused ever to move into houses the Welfare Branch offered them. Although they had the right to live in the urban area and had houses available to them, they turned them down. The welfare officers tended to explain such anomalous behaviour in terms of ingrained, culturally determined preferences for living outside in the open air. The fringe-dwellers, however, saw the situation in a different light. By living in the camps and staying out of the welfare houses, they undermined any basis the Welfare Branch might have had to control them. They maintained control over their own movements and thereby their flexibility with respect to the social environment as a whole. Indeed, I suggest this is the key to the whole development of the

fringe-camps in the post-war era. By minimizing their transactions with the Welfare Branch, the fringe-dwellers limited its
power over them.

Given the situation I have just outlined, it is evident that the
emergence of the contemporary fringe-camps cannot be understood apart from the development of the Welfare Branch.
Although Aborigines have been living on the outskirts of Alice
Springs for over eighty years, there is a fundamental difference
between the pre-war and the post-war camps. Whether it was as
the result of their own efforts to escape the Welfare Branch's
power or of the Welfare Branch's use of its power against them,
the Aborigines who became fringe-dwellers after 1953 did so as a
result of the conditions created by the increased power and
structural involvement of the welfare apparatus in their everyday lives. The Welfare Branch established the context within
which the camps emerged and to which the fringe-dwellers
reacted. None the less, it is also true that the specific points
made about the relationships between the fringe-dwellers and
the Welfare Branch hold generally for the campers' links with
the outside, white-dominated world. Fringe-dwellers can no
more escape the implications of their general dependence upon
whites than they could finally escape from the Welfare Branch.
What is significant about the camps is that they create conditions
that enable some Aborigines to manipulate the content and
pattern of their relationships with whites and, thereby, partially
control the effects of their dependence upon them. I want to examine this process further now in the context of the contemporary situation.

Fringe-Camps in the Contemporary Situation

There were at least fifteen fringe-camps distributed around Alice
Springs during my fieldwork. With the notable exception of the
camps located on the banks of the Todd River, all were located
on the immediate outskirts of town. The total fringe population
varied between approximately two hundred and five hundred
people. The smallest camps numbered as few as one domestic
group. The largest camps, such as Mt Kelly, housed ten or more
domestic groups and populations as large as sixty people. In
addition to these fifteen camps, there were others that tended to
appear and disappear. Although fringe-dwellers tended to shift

their camps frequently and although many of the camps I knew had only recently been established, most of the people had first started living in camps during the reign of the Welfare Branch and as a result of the processes outlined above. The Welfare Branch had been dismembered for almost two years when I entered the field, yet many of the political and economic conditions that had originally generated the camps still prevailed. Welfare agencies still controlled the kind of housing most Aborigines could afford and the job market was even tighter than normal during my fieldwork. As a point of structural flexibility in an otherwise highly structured and determined context, the camps continued to be highly significant to the contemporary context.

It was suggested earlier that fringe-dwellers maintain relationships with agents in a wide range of contexts outside their own domestic groups and that, consequently, there are a relatively wide range of opportunities open to them. Although I do not have detailed data on all the camps, it was certainly true that they all maintained links into both the urban and the rural contexts. I interpret their location as a basic index of their links into the urban context. Although they did not live in conventional houses, they did live inside the city limits of Alice Springs. As I will describe below, this fact was meaningful to the campers themselves and was crucial to their social identity as they interpreted it. Their close proximity to urban resources was also significiant in the more material aspects of their lives. Jobs for unskilled Aborigines were extremely scarce during my fieldwork and unemployment in the fringe-camps was highly visible. Nevertheless, fringe-campers had access to urban employment. Practically every adult in Mt Kelly, for example, had worked in Alice Springs. Some people (especially women working as domestics) had in fact done most of their work in Alice Springs. Fringe-campers also had privileged access to certain special urban work projects funded by the Commonwealth government.

Living in the urban context also gave fringe-dwellers privileged access to social security pensions. The core of practically every camp in Alice Springs was a group of pensioners who included the aged, supporting mothers and invalids. Although there were no geographical restrictions on who was eligible for pensions, the administrative machinery outside the urban areas was inadequate to ensure that people who were entitled to pensions in the rural areas actually applied for and received them. That depended primarily upon the diligence of local mission, settlement and pastoral authorities, some of whom did make pensions available to the Aborigines with whom they associated. None the less, large numbers of people did not have proper access to these benefits. CAALAS discovered this fact when it began making extensive bush trips in 1974. Consequently, it took application forms on the trips and encouraged people to register. It further met stern resistance from the Department of Social Security when it suggested that special social security field officers be appointed to travel the bush to enrol people. In contrast to the rural situation, however, the urban welfare officers actively tried to ensure that those people, particularly women, who were eligible for pensions, received them. Urban residence was therefore a distinct advantage in the competition for social security benefits.

What was especially interesting about pensions was that once obtained a pensioner was not required to engage more actively with the urban welfare officers; for example, the pensioner was not required to live in an urban house. Quite to the contrary, a pension enabled a person to move at will. It was a relatively untrammelled form of income which did not require recipients to go into debt to a white agency. All a pensioner had to do was to appear fortnightly at the post office to receive the cheque. Moreover, pensions were continuous forms of income; as they did not vary according to the demands of the labour market, they were highly suitable as the basis for the construction of the domestic economy of fringe-camp life. Indeed, pensions were the economic centre of the fringe-camps and pensioners occupied crucial positions as income centres and sources of credit for those who were out of work.

Of the thirteen major fringe-camps at least ten regularly supplied labourers to particular cattle stations on a regular basis. Mt Kelly provided labour to six different cattle stations during my fieldwork. Although some new links were formed during my stay, most of the jobs came from pastoralists who had known Mt Kelly men for many years and preferred to hire them before anyone else. The pastoralists usually drove into the camp looking for the men they knew. If those they wanted were unavailable for some reason, they usually hired someone else from the camp. Although Mt Kelly may have been exemplary in this situation, the fringe-camps as a whole were labour pools for the cattle industry.

The fringe-campers' links into the rural context, however,

were not limited to cattlework. On the contrary, most had links into the settlement and mission as well. Many of the people were born in the rural context and had migrated into Alice Springs as adults; for example, most of the Mt Kelly people originated on cattle stations north of Alice Springs and still had kinsmen living there; a few had kinsmen living at Warrabiri Settlement who regularly visited Mt Kelly and camped there whenever they came to town. Although it is common to assume that "urban Aborigines" are cut off from their rural origins, this was not so for most fringe-campers. On the contrary, they kept up their kin links in a variety of ways. Perhaps a more important point is that the fringe-campers were usually committed to the white agency which dominated the rural contexts into which they were linked. I have discussed briefly the Mt Kelly peoples' commitment to the cattle industry. Other campers reflected an equivalent commitment to the missions, for example, from which they had come. Indeed, one of the most important ways that rural agencies such as the mission affected the urban setting was through their links into the fringe-camps.

Table 1 Rural links of fringe-camp dwellers in Alice Springs, 1976, showing number of places by category with which each camp was linked

Camp	Cattle station	Mission	Settlement
A	8		
B	6		2
C	1		
D	2	1	1
E	2	1	
F	2	1	
G		1	
H	2	1	
I		1	
J	1		
K			1
L	3	1	
M	1	1	

The contemporary fringe-campers maintain links into a broad range of contexts in the Central Australian setting. Unlike the people who live in the houses in the town, on the cattle stations, or on the settlements, they are not committed to any single context. Rather, they have diversified their commitment. This diversification opens up a wider range of opportunities for many of them than would be available if they were to commit themselves to any single other context. Although many of the fringe-campers are "full-blood" Aborigines, they shared in the general advantages of the urban part-Aborigines in the competition for jobs and other income possibilities.

It is important to note, however, that the fringe-campers share in the urban employment and income opportunities without having to invest heavily in the urban setting. In particular, they are outside the immediate administrative control of the welfare authorities because they do not live in urban houses. By the same token they have access to the cattle industry without having to live on the cattle stations. Hence, although fringe-campers have a wide range of links, the links they maintain tend to be relatively simplex. They use different links to satisfy their needs in different areas and tend not to depend upon any single white agent to satisfy them all. Moreover, different people in the camps tend to have links into different contexts. For example, the Mt Kelly men work in the cattle industry. Although most Mt Kelly women have worked in the industry in the past, none did during my fieldwork. On the other hand, women tended to monopolize pensions and access to urban-based welfare resources. This means that while the camp as a whole is heavily linked into the wider context, few individuals have access to all contexts. Although Mt Kelly as a whole is heavily dependent upon the outside world to subsist, no single individual within it is structurally dependent upon any single context. No one is heavily indebted to any single white agent. Consequently, in comparison to other Aborigines, they are relatively independent of the power of all white agents in the region.

Because pastoralists recruit workers from the fringe-camps Aborigines can realize their labour as a major resource in the camps. Yet, given the camps' visibility and access to welfare resources, fringe-dwellers can also realize those features of their social identities that are relevant to the welfare administration. For example, single mothers are eligible for supporting mothers' pensions. Indeed, the local welfare workers encourage women with children who associate with men considered irresponsible by the welfare authorities to apply for pensions. In this way, "single" mothers can transform their control of children into a basic resource to legitimate their domestic income.

It is important also to note, however, that the fringe-camps are contexts within which their residents can pool resources for each other. Although the Mt Kelly people remained comparatively independent of outside white agencies, it is precisely for that reason that they risked failing to meet their basic subsistence needs. Men were especially vulnerable to irregularities and discontinuities in their source of income. But because the Mt Kelly people were collectively linked into a wide range of contexts, they were able to bridge the structural gaps between them and the discontinuities in each others' incomes by sharing and developing patterns of assistance and credit. The Mt Kelly people were able to realize resources for each other as well as supply them to outsiders.

The fringe-campers' high rate of spatial mobility was a condition, a consequence and a basic resource of fringe-camp life. Because the men in particular had to move in order to work, they had to be willing to leave in order to take advantage of the opportunities the camp made available to them. Indeed, the greater the range of opportunities available to any individual, the more mobile that person must be. This forces individuals to minimize their commitment to any particular context, including the fringe-camp itself. By being heavily committed to any context a person becomes embroiled in multiplex relationships with agents in it. Such relationships make it more difficult for the person to depart in the event that another, perhaps ultimately more favourable opportunity emerges (Kapferer 1972, 102–4). In such cases these with a relatively wide range of resources to exchange would inhibit their own chances for long-term survival. In summary, the fringe-campers' high rate of spatial mobility emerges from their access to a range of alternative outside contexts, a low structural involvement in any particular context and a great range and quality of resources to offer in exchange for access to those contexts.

The power to move spatially is itself a resource that people use to minimize or even escape their involvement in any particular contexts. Fringe-dwellers tend to leave particular contexts when it is no longer absolutely necessary for them to participate in them. For example, many of the Mt Kelly men have the right to live permanently on the cattle stations where they work, yet when the work is finished, they usually leave the station and return to town. Moreover, despite the availability of work, they sometimes simply leave for what they call a "holiday". They gloss these visits by saying they get lonely in the bush or want to have a drink or two in town. Such "holidays" are a display of the individual worker's productivity and close ties to the boss, as will be argued in chapter 6. It is important to note that such moves minimize the extent to which the men are indebted to pastoralists and communicates the men's independence to them. By leaving during periods of no work, they fail to accumulate debts for which they are not offering work in exchange. By leaving when there is work, they document the extent to which the pastoralist depends upon them and values the work they do perform.

The very location of the fringe-camps is itself significant and marks the unwillingness of the fringe-campers to commit themselves to any context in particular. As is well known, the camps are on the "fringes" of the town, but it is more accurate to observe that the camps are really quite outside the effective administrative boundaries of any context in the region. The fringe-camps are located outside either the settlements or the cattle regions. They are almost all located on vacant crown land inside the Alice Springs town boundary. Although nominally under the control of the Lands and Survey Branch, Department of the Northern Territory, no one actively administers vacant crown land. The Lands and Survey Branch was more effective in preventing Aborigines from acquiring leases to vacant crown land during my fieldwork than it was in denying them its use. No other local or Commonwealth agencies are willing or politically able to control the fringe-camps. Indeed, the Alice Springs Town Council has tried a number of times in recent years to "have something done" about the fringe-camps, but they have had limited success.

In understanding the structural processes through which the fringe-camps have come to be located where they are, it is important to realize also that the fringe-campers themselves consider their place in space a vital component of their self-identity. They are not unaware of the political significance of their location. On the contrary, they interpret living outside the boundaries of any white-dominated context as a basic mark of their independence of the power of white authorities and white society as a whole. By the same token, because living in the camps gives them privileged access to the resources whites control, they distinguish themselves from other Aborigines who are not so favourably placed. So it is that the essential sociological characteristics of the fringe-camps — that is, their access to, but independence of, other white-dominated contexts in Central

Australia — are basic components in the fringe-campers' view of themselves as identities operating in the total regional field.

Conclusion

Ethnic heterogeneity has been a characteristic of fringe-camps for many years. Given the long history of official attempts to segregate the three ethnic categories in Central Australia, one of the most striking things about the fringe-camps is the mixture of black, "coloured", and white people living in them. The presence of "full-blood" Aborigines and part-Aborigines in the camps has already been mentioned. Of special interest (as well as special worry to welfare officials since the very beginning of white colonization) is the presence of white men in the camps (there were no white women in the camps during the period of my field-work). Indeed, white men are especially significant given the long history of attempts to keep them out of Aboriginal camps (Rowley 1974, 236). Moreover, although the restrictive laws were legitimated as necessary to protect Aboriginal women from sexual abuse and exploitation, there has always been and still is what many officials consider a disturbing tendency for Aboriginal people to encourage and protect certain types of white men in the fringe-camps. This has been such a basic part of fringe-camp life that some white men in Alice Springs have lived in the camps for over twenty-five years and raised families. Although some whites as well as some blacks do visit the camps for various reasons, some white men are vital parts of the fringe communities within which they live.

Given what I have said about the opportunities available in the fringe-camps, it should not be too surprising to find white men living in them. Although no white person ever experienced the kinds of legal disabilities to which Aborigines were long subject, most of the white men who live in the camps were engaged in the same kinds of work as Aborigines. In particular they worked in the cattle industry and held unskilled jobs in the towns. Consequently, the camps offered these kinds of white men the same opportunities they offered Aborigines, that is, information and social connnections through which they could get jobs and credit during periods of unemployment.

It is equally important to note that white men offered reciprocal benefits to Aborigines. Because many employers preferred to hire white men, white workers were often a key point around which Aboriginal fringe-dwellers organized their own employment strategies and maintained access to jobs. Moreover, white men have always received cash wages and have never been legally restricted in what their money could buy. Consequently, they could provide Aborigines with the cash and valuable items – not least of which was liquor – that Aborigines could not obtain for themselves. In fact, Aborigines often made such exchanges necessary conditions for whites living in the camps. In general, therefore, white men made good spouses and offered Aborigines opportunities they might not otherwise have had. In other words, the crucial point which explains the real significance of white men to Aborigines and relates them to the broader issues of fringe-camp life is that their presence in the camps suspends the relevance of the Aborigines' ethnic identity for major domains of their lives. Aborigines who could incorporate white men into their everyday kinship and social relationships were thereby able to overcome some of the disabilities they experienced as Aborigines. Not only could they obtain such items as liquor, they gained access to cash, better job opportunities, and in general established better control over their life chances.

This relates directly to the significance of the fringe-camps as a whole. Fringe-camps are points of structural flexibility in the otherwise highly determined social environment of Central Australia. I have set them in the context of the largely successful attempts of the Commonwealth government to make the basic spatial, political, industrial and ethnic divisions in the region coincide and be mutually supporting. From this perspective, the fact that Aborigines attract and involve certain kinds of white men into everyday fringe-camp life is an essential element of their overall strategies to minimize the effect and undermine the whole edifice which white authorities have been trying to erect in Central Australia. The very presence of white men in the camps flouts the authorities and makes the overall fringe-camp life that much more viable. White men in the camps do not, therefore, simply exploit black women or take advantage of Aboriginal ideas of reciprocity. Rather, they are crucial to the techniques Aborigines have tried to adopt to survive in the region.

Notes

1. The terms "simplex" and "multiplex" are the subject of some debate in the transactional literature. In this book I use these terms in an effort to characterize briefly different degrees of what Handelman (1976, 282–83) calls "structural involvement". He avoids the use of "simplex" or "multiplex" and refers instead to "multiple links". I have adopted Handelman's indices of structural involvement, yet I require a set of terms that distinguishes between different degrees of structural involvement, which Handelman does not provide. In line with a suggestion of Max Gluckman, Garbett distinguishes between manifold and multiplex relationships. By manifold relationships, he means relations which involve multiple transactional elements. In contrast, multiplex relationships involve multiple normative elements (Garbett n.d.). Again, Garbett's terminology does not allow me to compare the relative complexity of relationships that are not single-stranded but that none the less are constituted by different degrees of structural involvement. Kapferer distinguishes between relationships which contain either instrumental or societal components. Kapferer calls relationships that develop on the basis of either one or the other "simplex", and those which contain both "multiplex" (Kapferer 1972, 172). In my use of the terms "simplex" and "multiplex" I am trying to indicate different degrees of structural involvement, that is, I use the terms comparatively. I use Handelman's notion of "area" to compare the transactional elements which constitute the emergent relationships between Aborigines and whites. Although most such relationships contain multiple links, some contain fewer transactional elements than others. I use the terms "relatively simplex" and "multiplex" to distinguish between relationships with fewer or more transactional elements.

2. The Native Affairs Branch began working earlier than this. It was especially active in establishing the rudiments of what later developed into the complete system of settlements for Aboriginal "wards". However, I stress the role of the Welfare Branch because it had the money, the power, the administrative apparatus and a fully developed welfare ideology to implement the changes outlined and which the Native Affairs Branch only initiated. Although the Native Affairs Branch was a specialized organization, it was not until the Commonwealth established the Welfare Branch in 1953 that an organizational context emerged which could effectively create the conditions for the full development of the new approach. The significance of the Native Affairs Branch is that it marked the gradually emerging new direction in the Commonwealth's activities.

3. The dismembering of the Welfare Branch has had important effects on the structure of relationships between Aborigines and the Commonwealth government. However, the Welfare Branch fully encapsulated Aborigines within the wider Commonwealth administrative apparatus, so that, although Aborigines look to the Department of Social Security to provide them with pensions, they now work within a context almost totally dominated by one agency or another of the Commonwealth government. This was not true prior to 1953 and is the direct result of the Welfare Branch's work. This process of encapsulation will be stressed in this chapter.

4. The Commonwealth did make some early efforts in these directions prior to the Second World War. It appointed T.G.H. Strehlow as a patrol officer to work among many of the western desert groups which inhabited the southwestern border areas of the Northern Territory; it also established a few ration depots. However, the resettlement process was only developed

completely under the aegis of the assimilation policy and the administration of the Welfare Branch of the Northern Territory Administration after 1953.

5. The urban houses were, of course, also ranked (see Rowley 1972, 40–41).

6. I use the term "fair exchange" to refer to the actor's assessment, not as an absolute or outsider's judgment.

7. I collected reports of physical violence between most Mt Kelly men and their cattle bosses – the problem is considered in detail in chapter 5. For independent evidence of this fact, refer to Stevens (1974). I suggest that physical violence establishes the relevance of a worker's ethnic identity as an Aborigine. Insofar as he tolerates violence from his boss, he documents that he is not subject to the "lazy" and "cheeky" impulses pastoralists often ascribe to Aborigines. Men who work in the Central Australian cattle industry must show that they are reliable in this manner; otherwise they will develop poor reputations and find little work.

4

Urban Aboriginal Women and Welfare

Because Aborigines in Alice Springs use control of their domestic groups to legitimate access to the resources to sustain them, the domestic group has become the key context within which they negotiate for the basic necessities of life. This situation is the result of the attempts of the Commonwealth government to support and control urban Aborigines in Central Australia. Because women have privileged access to welfare resources, they have more secure domestic livelihoods than men, and men often depend upon them for their basic requirements. The conditions under which women acquire welfare benefits, however, encourage them to minimize their relationships with men. These conditions have encouraged major changes in relationships between spouses and between parents and children. New types of marriage, new kin-naming patterns, and new types of domestic organization have emerged as people compete for access to the means to support themselves. Because the extent to which Aborigines must transact with whites depends upon their access to domestic resources, the analysis of domestic politics is essential for a full explanation of the social significance of fringe-camps and of the broader issues of black-white relationships.

The Primacy of the Domestic Group

Relationships between blacks and whites in Central Australia have changed extensively since the earliest days of white settlement. When whites first moved into the area, many Aboriginal domestic groups retained their political and economic autonomy. As Elkin has noted, particular domestic groups were able to react to white incursions in different ways (Elkin 1951, 164–86). Such a range of responses was possible precisely because Aborigines were essentially organized in terms of individual, relatively autonomous domestic groups. The actions of one domestic group did not necessarily imply anything about the reactions of others. In the context of a more highly organized state, such a diversity would probably not have been possible. As many whites first entered new regions in small domestic groups, it is possible to characterize the early history of white settlement as a confrontation of two domestic economies – one based on hunting and gathering and the other based on pastoralism. The early white settlers raised cattle and occasionally sold them on the market. They could not always sell their cattle, however, and, during bad times, had to become subsistence cattleherders. They were able to relate to the conditions of the cattle market in this way primarily because they could operate a domestic economy which sought in the first instance to provision itself (Sahlins 1974).

Under these circumstances it was possible for each domestic economy to retain its fundamental autonomy and, at the same time, establish relationships with the other. In the early days, Aboriginal domestic groups moved back and forth between the two domestic economies, depending upon particular circumstances. White domestic groups entertained relationships with Aborigines without necessarily becoming subservient to Aboriginal society. Insofar as these conditions held, there was a period marked by the articulation of two (essentially domestic) modes of production. The difference was that one (the white pastoral economy) was also linked into a wider market economy that sporadically purchased its products.

The full incorporation of the Central Australian pastoral industry into the world market and the encapsulation of Aborigines in a well-organized, powerful state bureaucracy fundamentally changed these conditions (see appendix 1). Aborigines lost direct access to the means of their material production and reproduction. The state bureaucracy penetrated Aboriginal society at the level of individual domestic groups through its ration and family stabilization plans. Aborigines thereby also lost control of the processes of their own cultural reproduction. These processes subordinated what had previously been their autonomous, domestic mode of production to the urban-dominated mode of production that was extending its control throughout Central Australia. As these processes developed, the controlling moment of Aboriginal society passed from its individual domestic groups to agents of white society. Central Australia emerged as a culturally heterogeneous region organized by one mode of production.

The key feature of Aboriginal society that has continued from immediate pre-colonial times to the present is the primary significance of the domestic group and its economy. Many Aborigines still operate an economy of "concrete and limited objectives" (Sahlins 1974), but it is crucial to observe that Aborigines do not control their means of social production. On the contrary, contemporary Aborigines have constituted a domestic economy in an effort to minimize the penetration of outside forces into their lives and limit the effects of having to transact with white authorities on totally unfavourable terms. The contemporary significance of the Aborigines' domestic economy emerges from their current political and economic subordination to whites, not from the survival of their pre-colonial domestic mode of production (Beckett 1977; Hartwig 1977; Larbalastier 1977).

Aboriginal fringe-dwellers minimize their transactions with whites in two important ways: they underuse the material resources white agents control and make available to them and they work less than otherwise they might. A major consequence of these tactics, however, is that most fringe-dwelling domestic groups can reasonably expect occasionally to fail to support themselves (Sahlins 1974, 42–74). As well as limiting their demand for material goods to what is necessary to sustain their domestic groups, fringe-dwellers deliberately exploit fewer opportunities for material gain than white authorities make available to them. Moreover, because they restrict their material demands, they occasionally have a relative surplus income.

The Mt Kelly people describe their escapes from welfare authorities with tremendous enthusiasm and they boast of houses they have rejected or destroyed. They deny they are poor and take great pride in the amount of money that flows through the camp. They are conscious and inveterate spendthrifts. Many Mt Kelly people spend large amounts of money on items most white officials consider wasteful, particularly liquor. Because these habits have caused many of them to lose welfare houses and develop bad reputations with the welfare officials, their boasts and the actions which enact them are not idle or unconsciously irresponsible. On the contrary, they reflect a general unwillingness to curb their own patterns of behaviour according to the rules of the welfare authorites. The fringe-dwellers are willing or able to accept what the welfare officials offer only on their own terms.

The ideas the Mt Kelly people have about the money available to them are not ill-founded. Occasionally, there is an actual surplus in the camp. In particular, the money which the young men earn working on the cattle stations is not necessary for any domestic group − or even for the young men themselves − to survive. As long as they work out bush, the young men survive on the food supplied by their boss. The basic subsistence needs of most domestic groups, on the other hand, are met by social security payments of various kinds. The fact that surplus cattle money flows into and out of Mt Kelly sustains its residents' self-image as an affluent people. It is primarily the surplus cattle money which finances the very large drinking sprees that occasionally punctuate Mt Kelly life. By limiting their domestic requirements to correspond with the size of their pension incomes, the Mt Kelly people, and fringe-dwellers generally, are able to spend irregular windfalls on items of conspicuous display. They also use some surplus to extend credit to productive workers who are temporarily short of basic resources.

Fringe-dwellers also work less than they might. The situation is of course quite complex, given that over 50 per cent of the Aboriginal labour force is unemployed in Central Australia. There was also a slump in the cattle market during my fieldwork which further restricted the labour demand for the Mt Kelly men particularly. None the less, fringe-dwellers withhold their labour from the market for reasons of their own. Because single mothers have access to pensions, they do not have to work. Although most Mt Kelly women worked for some time during their lives, their work periods supplemented their pension incomes and were often interrupted. Even the Mt Kelly men take advantage of fewer opportunities for work than are sometimes available to them. Not all able-bodied men work the same amount. Some men have reputations as hard workers: whenever their bosses drive up, they get up and work for several months at a stretch. Others are willing to work only for a week or two. As they pack their swags, other Mt Kelly people smile and crack jokes about their chances of working for longer than it takes to sober up. Although some men work sporadically because they leave jobs early, even the "hard workers" take extended breaks or bypass chances to work. Often, men come in from the bush quite unexpectedly. They say that they were lonely or wanted to do some good drinking. In the same way, men delay their bosses for a week or more while they engage in one last round of heavy drinking. To delay one's boss is a mark of pride and displays the fact that a man's boss prefers him to all others (this is analysed extensively below). Suffice it to note that it also limits the extent to which men transact even with their major source of income.

Neither men nor women always have jobs when they want them. Although fringe-dwellers may have better access to jobs than other Aborigines, it is hard to deny that Aborigines face a grim employment situation. However, fringe-dwellers keep their own schedule and withdraw from work when it suits them. Because of the low pay and even because it exchanges labour for wages, work compromises Aborigines in their relationships with whites. Access to work constitutes a debt to an employer that is basically inextinguishable. Its effects can only be controlled by leaving work. The "walkabout" makes sense in these terms as the correlate of an economy of limited ends and strategy to minimize indebtedness.[1]

Some domestic groups fail to make their own living in the fringe-camps. In Mt Kelly there were three families whose only income during my fieldwork was child endowment. More generally, most domestic groups can reasonably expect to fail to feed themselves at one time or another. It is common experience that individuals who have more money than they know what to do with at one time will, at other times, be broke and unable to work.

These three aspects of the domestic economy establish the significance of pensions and condition relationships between men and women in the fringe-camps. Pensions meet peoples' basic domestic requirements. Moreover, once an individual qualifies for a pension, he never has to work or necessarily interact with white authorities again. Although most families occasionally cannot feed themselves, pensions never fail. They are a continuous source of income and, therefore, the basis of the domestic economy. The key point for the rest of this analysis, however, is that women have privileged access to continuous pension incomes and, therefore, substantially control the domestic economy. Because men work, they must regularly interact with whites and necessarily fail to provision themselves occasionally. Their sources of income are highly compromising and discontinuous.

Insofar as women establish control of their own domestic groups (in particular, of their children), they legitimate access to the means to support them, and withdraw into their boundaries. If men are to survive, they must legitimate access to what women control. This relationship between continuous and discontinuous incomes establishes the basic significance of the domestic group to fringe-dwellers and constitutes the conditions under which men and women negotiate about access to the basic resources they all need to survive.

The Domestic Group and the Administration of Urban Aboriginal Affairs

An important theme in Hartwig's and Beckett's discussions is the role of the state in regulating the relationships between the capitalist and pre-capitalist modes of production (Hartwig 1977, 131–39; Beckett 1977, 79). It is primarily the significance of the state in this matter that justifies the term "internal colonialism". It is the action of the state in trying to maintain the pre-capitalist mode of production in order to reproduce cheaply the physical and basic social bodies of the labour force that is crucial in establishing the conditions for "articulation" instead of "dissolution" (Wolpe 1975, 248–49). My point is that precisely the opposite happened in Central Australia. The more effectively the state penetrated Aboriginal society, the more the domestic mode of production dissolved.

By 1971, 1850 Aboriginal people lived in Alice Springs (Australian Bureau of Statistics 1971). Most lived in houses built and rented by the Northern Territory Administration, Welfare Branch or the Housing Commission. A large minority lived in the fringe-camps. Most Aborigines moved in Alice Springs as part of the process by which the Welfare Branch attempted to resettle and assimilate primarily part-Aborigines in the town. Although there was work there for part-Aborigines, the urban Aboriginal community was not based upon patterns of industrial labour. It emerged as the result of the transactions between the welfare administration and the Aborigines in the course of the implementation of the assimilation policy.

The Welfare Branch used the assimilation policy to interpret and justify its own activities and those of its clients. The fundamental principle of the policy was that Aboriginal people did not understand the norms and values of white, middle-class Australian culture. The Welfare Branch's major responsibility was to teach Aborigines those norms and thereby enable them to participate effectively in the wider society. According to the policy Aborigines varied in the diversity of their cultural background from the most primitive to the nearly assimilated. Consequently, the policy was to be administered according to the individual needs of the clients. Aborigines were to move into the wider society as soon as their particular, individual progress permitted (Tatz 1964).

Tatz observes that the two major aims of the assimilation policy were to teach Aboriginal people the value of steady work and to inculcate in them a sense of financial responsibility (Tatz 1964). My own information substantiates this view. In their conversations with me, Sister Leslie Grey and Mrs Helen Thatcher, the two welfare officers who worked with the Alice Springs population throughout the Welfare Branch's regime, presented these two values as the key components of white, middle-class life. They also expressed the opinion that Aboriginal people had a circular sense of time which prevented them from planning ahead and acting responsibly to ensure their long-term prosperity. Consequently, they thought Aboriginal people devalued money and work. They lived only for the moment and satisfied immediate needs. When they accumulated resources they spread them among their kinsmen and saved nothing. The welfare officers explained these traits as survivals of the traditional hunting and gathering economy and of the communal kinship structure. In order to become assimilated, Aboriginal people had to adopt a linear sense of time and begin to plan for the future. Such planning, however, required Aboriginal people to work steadily, manage their finances responsibly and deny their kinsmen.

The Welfare Branch used raciocultural models of social organization to justify the construction of the urban and settlement communities and the recruiting principles by which it populated them. It is essential to observe, however, that a model of conventional, middle-class family life was implicit in and a vital component of the assimilation policy. The object of the Alice Springs housing programme, in fact, was to create the conditions necessary for Aboriginal people to establish stable, happy families in the urban setting. Welfare officers considered a "normal" family life necessary for Aboriginal children to advance successfully toward assimilation and for the white community to accept them. Sister Grey wrote of the importance of adequate living conditions (unpublished manuscript 1955, 3–4).

> Most whites regard a black or coloured skin as a sign of inferiority. It should be realized that the crossing of the Aboriginal race with ours does not produce a physically decadent human specimen as many suppose. On the contrary, it has been proved that under normal living conditions the offspring display a hybrid vigour which is surprising and interesting. Backwardness is often a symptom of some home conditions; a diet of excessive carbohydrates, lack of parental guidance, excitement of life in a crowded area, quarrelsome neighbours, too many late nights, drunken parents, irregular meals and bedtimes, lack of books and other recreational facilities. When these conditions are remedied, the results are apparent as has been proved by those who have experienced the changeover.

Although Sister Grey was describing a general picture of what she considered domestic disorder, she based it upon her image of life in what was called Rainbow Town. Rainbow Town was an area south of Alice Springs in which a number of austere cottages were built for the resident part-Aboriginal population just after the Second World War. The name was derived from the multiplicity of types and shades of people who lived there. According to Sister Grey, "low class whites", "half-castes", and "full-bloods" all lived there under what she considered "camp conditions". The old cottages had very few facilities. One aim of the new housing programme was to remove people from Rainbow Town and place them in new houses with more modern conveniences. The Welfare Branch moved people into the new houses when it judged they wanted to adopt the new lifestyle and were able to cope with its greater responsibilities (Rowley 1974, 40–41). The important point, however, is the interdependence of proper housing and a healthy domestic environment. A good house was both a consequence of progress toward assimilation and a necessary condition for further progress. Sister Grey and Mrs Thatcher were responsible for assisting Aboriginal families in this dual process of domestic development.

The model of conventional, middle-class domestic life had different implications for men and women. It included models of male and female activities based on what the Welfare Branch considered to be male and female roles in the wider society. Men were supposed to work in the competitive world and women were supposed to be good mothers and careful housekeepers. Settling families into urban houses meant training men and women in their respective roles. The Welfare Branch's image of domestic life, however, did not fit with the conditions to which they tried to apply it. In particular, most Aboriginal men had to leave Alice Springs and engage in cattlework for long periods in the bush away from their families. Consequently, by administering its policy on the basis of models of conventional male and female roles, the Welfare Branch produced contradications in the very organization of the domestic group. Of special interest is the fact that Aboriginal parents were often forced to choose between committing themselves to their relationships with each other or to their relationships with their children. Because the Welfare Branch offered special support to mothers who devoted themselves to the care of their children, this dilemma was particularly acute for women. It is also important to note that, with the exception of the relatively few men who could find work in Alice Springs, this policy also compelled Aboriginal men to choose between being good workers and resident fathers. It was often impossible for them to be both. The consequence of these dilemmas emerged as definitive elements in the development of everyday domestic life.

Tatz observes that the Welfare Branch's policy on jobs for men was confused. There was little demand for Aboriginal labour outside the settlements. Furthermore, the welfare officials could not decide whether or not to invest heavily in creating jobs on the settlements. Tatz suggests this reflects their indecision about whether the settlements were "transitional camps" or "permanent rural communities" (Tatz 1964, 60–71). The Welfare Branch initiated the Haasts Bluff cattle project but Haasts Bluff required only a limited number of select men. Little was done to provide the job training the assimilation policy required. As a result, the outlying settlements became large-scale ration depots and food was provided free of charge.

In Alice Springs, however, the Welfare Branch pursued its employment policy for men more vigorously. It did little to create new jobs or to train men but it pressured men to work. If men did not work, the Welfare Branch considered them irresponsible and failed to support them. It extended this attitude to men living on the Bungalow, the settlement for "full-blood" Aborigines. Pastoralists and drovers regularly recruited workers from this settlement and, in this respect, it was unlike other settlements further out in the bush. The Welfare Branch seems, therefore, to have defined its residents in a manner similar to the town's part-Aboriginal people. They refused to ration men there and on some occasions they forced unemployed men to leave the settlement and banished them from the urban environment.

The Case of the Banished "Bludgers"

In March 1953, the Bungalow was faced with a food shortage for its Aboriginal residents. In a letter dated 26 May 1953, the acting district superintendent asked for an increased ration and explained the situation at the settlement.

> At present the method of rationing adopted at the Bungalow is as follows:
> 1. School children numbering approximately 45, are fed directly from the kitchen five days per week.
> 2. Fresh meat is supplied daily to workers and their families.[2]
> 3. Aged and infirm then receive a ration of meat until stocks are exhausted.
> During the past week, 116 adults and 94 children were rationed, for whom, according to the correct ration scale a total of 1,141 lbs. of meat should have been available, whereas in fact only 558 lbs. were distributed as follows:
>
> | | |
> |---|---|
> | 65 lbs per day from the butcher | 455 lbs |
> | 137 x 12 oz tins of corned beef | 103 lbs |
> | | 558 lbs |

He observed that the Aborigines at the Bungalow received a "grossly inadequate diet" and recommended it be upgraded. He suggested specifically that the supply of fresh meat from the local butcher be increased to 110 pounds of boneless beef per day and that an extra half bullock per week be brought from Jay Creek Settlement (Department of the Northern Territory, Welfare Branch 1953).

The acting director of Native Affairs approved the request for more food. Part of the problem was that the Bungalow lacked a communal dining room. The Aboriginal people collected their rations from a central distribution point and returned to their camps to eat. Consequently, the welfare officers could not control who ate what. They thought that this meant "ineligible people" shared the rations. Ineligible people were primarily men who were unemployed, rationed at work, or "holidaying" on the settlement, none of whom were included in the number rationed.

The settlement superintendent wanted to ration them. He

suggested that unemployed men be offered rations in exchange for work around the settlement. Although it is not clear, there is evidence that he implemented this plan. The director of Welfare did not respond to his suggestions, however, and only ordered him not to ration men who were fed at work. He further observed that funds were short and turned down the request for money to build a dining room.

By January 1953, the Bungalow population had grown and there was again a food shortage. A daily average of 197.5 people received rations on the settlement. Although the approved ration scale required 492 kilograms (1083 pounds) of meat per week to feed that number of people, only 350 kilograms were provided. In this instance, the acting district superintendent noted that "no alteration is recommended to the existing set-up" (Department of the Northern Territory, Welfare Branch 1953). Instead, the welfare officials began to move against men they thought should not be sharing the food.

The reports suggest that, by February 1954, all women with children were considered eligible for rations and that "nursing and lactating females", the wives and children of employed men, and children in general, received rations. A report dated 2 February 1954 also lists that 3.2 unemployed men on an average daily basis received rations. However, on 17 February 1954, the acting district superintendent noted that unemployed men were no longer getting rations unless waiting return to their homes. There was still no communal dining room, however, and so it was difficult to police the decision. Unemployed men continued to cause problems.

On 11 August 1954, a patrol officer reported to the acting district superintendent that he and the settlement superintendent had conducted a survey of the unemployed men at the Bungalow. They found fourteen such men and questioned them about their employment plans. Six hoped to get jobs soon and the others had "no employment in mind". He reports, further, that "All the above boys [sic] except [two] were told that they would be returned to their country unless they could find employment within a week". He also suggested a follow-up inspection be carried out the next Monday, and "action taken to remove able-bodied natives who have no employment or suitable excuse for their idleness" (Department of the Northern Territory, Welfare Branch 1954). No further reports on this matter appeared in the files I examined.

In 1957, however, the welfare officials responded in a similar
fashion to problems caused by wards who drank alcoholic
beverages (it was illegal for them to do so). On 8 July 1957, the
Bungalow's superintendent sent a list of "Wards: Drinkers and
Disturbers of the Peace" to the acting district welfare officer in
Alice Springs. The list contained the names of twenty-six men. In
response, talks were held with the local publicans who agreed to
stop furnishing wards with liquor. In addition, a meeting was
called at the Bungalow during which the welfare officers warned
wards to stop drinking. They said that if any ward was convicted
twice in twelve months for drinking liquor, he would be
removed from the town area for one year. It was also decided
that persistent offenders should be sent immediately to isolated
settlements, especially Hooker Creek.

In his report of 24 January 1958, the district welfare officer of
Alice Springs stated:

> It will be noted that the number of wards residing at the Bungalow
> has been considerably reduced since ... the period ending 15
> November 1957. This has been mainly due to the efficient manner in
> which Manager F. has applied himself to the problem of dispersing
> those people who are unable to justify their presence in the town
> area. Movements were taking place to settlements and to station
> properties where they belong.

With respect to employment, the district welfare officer
reported:

> several wards have flatly refused to accept employment.
> To date fifty-some drinkers and what may be called part-time
> loafers have been removed from the town area.
> Of those who have refused work a recommendation has been for-
> warded to you requesting a committal order in respect to B– T–.
> The remainder have been warned to either leave the town area of
> their own volition or by transport provided, failing which committal
> orders would be applied for their removal to remote areas.

The reason the welfare officers gave to justify their action
against the men are important. They described the men as
loafers and disturbers of the peace. In the first case, the men ate
food intended for the aged, the sick, mothers and children. In the
second case, they allegedly broke the law, caused fights, and
generally disrupted the peace. From the welfare officers' point of
view, these men had clearly failed to learn the value of work as a
worthwhile occupation. Consequently, the solution was to send
them to work and banish them from the town.

The Welfare Branch could not banish part-Aboriginal men because they were not wards. Yet, welfare officers adopted the same attitude towards them: able-bodied men who did not work were irresponsible and did not deserve the privileges of urban life. There was, however, a general shortage of work. Furthermore, there was a particular shortage of urban work, and urban work was a necessary condition for men to assume all the roles projected for them by the Welfare Branch.

Most men worked in the cattle industry where work patterns were necessarily irregular. Pastoral workers alternated long periods out bush with periods of unemployment and no income. Consequently, it was difficult for men to work and run urban-based families in the manner specified by the welfare policy. Moreover, pastoral workers often engaged in hedonistic types of behaviour which welfare officers understood as manifestly deviant and not conducive to stable family life. Aboriginal men, therefore, were caught in an insoluble dilemma.

The Welfare Branch understood the role of women in a different way. It clearly expected women to be mothers and housekeepers. It supported them in that role in a way it did not support men. Women and children received rations, for instance, but they were not expected to work for them: it was sufficient that they be mothers and care for their children. The Welfare Branch greatly elaborated this view of women in its work in Alice Springs.

In 1953, the branch appointed two women, Sister Leslie Grey and Mrs Helen Thatcher, as welfare officers to work with the Alice Springs population. Their main project was settling part-Aboriginal families in the new houses the Northern Territory Administration was building. Although they had male clients, they were appointed principally to work with women and children. They visited their clients at home regularly, encouraged women to attend prenatal clinics, to send their children to school regularly, and "to maintain a reasonable standard of living in the home" (Report of Female Welfare Officers . . . 1958). Furthermore, they assisted their clients with rations, accommodation and general counselling in times of need.

The Welfare Branch also justified action toward particular women in terms of its image of the female role. It gave families better houses on the basis of how well they kept the house. This was primarily the woman's responsibility. It also took legal action against women it suspected were neglecting their children. Sister Grey told me that the welfare officers each had diaries in which they recorded salient notes on their clients' domestic habits. If a woman began to leave her children unattended, drink heavily, neglect the washing or otherwise fail in her duties, the welfare officers warned her. After several warnings, the Welfare Branch would ask the police to summons the derelict family to the court. If the magistrate decided the children had been neglected, he committed them to the care of the state and removed them from their parents.

The Welfare Branch also intervened in the affairs of some part-Aboriginal families in a more direct manner. The assimilation policy included an assumption that part-Aborigines would not advance rapidly if they associated extensively with other Aborigines. Consequently, part-Aboriginal children who lived in remote areas or homes that were considered unsuitable were forced to live in institutions in Alice Springs. In one sense the assimilation policy only echoed an idea that had been hallowed in theory and practice for many years in the Northern Territory (Rowley 1974, 231). In the context of the resettling of part-Aboriginal families in Alice Springs, it took on special significance. The removal of part-Aboriginal children who were neglected or lived in remote areas far from educational opportunities directly affected the internal organization of urban Aboriginal households. The point was that most urban-based men had to travel to remote places in order to work. If their wives accompanied them, they had to surrender their children to the care of the Welfare Branch and put them into institutions. Women faced a dilemma in which they effectively had to choose between being wives and being mothers. They could not travel with their husbands and care for their children in the way the Welfare Branch demanded. If women tried to do both, the Welfare Branch took legal action against them and formally committed their children to institutions.

The conditions of life, however, favoured the residential stabilization of women in Alice Springs. There was a substantial demand for Aboriginal women to work as domestics in private homes and laundries. Unlike most men, therefore, women could work and live in the town. After 1961, single women with children became eligible for child endowment and supporting mothers' pensions. They could support themselves without having to work or take a husband. The Welfare Branch, moreover, supported working and single mothers. It found women jobs and arranged babysitters. Women in town received their pensions in cash (Tatz 1963, 90–91). The Welfare Branch and Housing Commission offered rebates to pensioners. Hence, single mothers could live in town even though their incomes were low. The branch extended special assistance to single mothers. As Sister Grey informed me, the welfare officers often encouraged women to apply for pensions, live without men, and independently support their families; the advice depended on the men with whom the women associated.

The Welfare Branch justified its activities in Alice Springs in terms of fostering stable urban family units. Given this emphasis and the actual conditions of everyday life in Central Australia, the evidence suggests that women emerged as the focus of the Welfare Branch's special attention and as the key to the long-term success of the assimilation process. The point is that women could take on an ideal welfare identity more easily than men and, thereby, justify continued support (Handelman 1976). By the very nature of their work, men could not be everything the Welfare Branch expected. That and the exuberant types of behaviour pastoral workers often exhibited made most men the very antithesis of the ideal welfare client. Women, on the other hand, had firm job opportunities in Alice Springs. The Welfare Branch elaborated upon that fact and solidified their position in the town. It encouraged women to become the heads of their domestic groups and thereby transformed the structure and social signficance of Aboriginal domestic groups in the urban context.

The Significance of the Domestic Group

As a result of these processes, matricentric or matrifocal families emerged in Alice Springs. Similar developments have also been reported for Aboriginal families in Adelaide, Melbourne and rural towns in New South Wales (Barwick 1974; Gale 1970; Rowley 1974). Matrifocal families have also been the subject of considerable study in other parts of the world, especially in the Caribbean and the black ghettos of the United States (Hannerz 1969; Smith 1956; Solien de Gonzalez 1961, 1965, 1969). Matrifocal families are quite common in situations similar to those I have described for Alice Springs; that is, contexts in which women control a basic resource that permits them to care for their children and remain residentially stable while men must move around. Matrifocal families have emerged most commonly in situations where men must migrate seasonally to work but cannot or do not take their families with them. Hannerz cautions, however, that "structural constraint" explanations of family form are incomplete without consideration of "what people think, feel and say about the relationship between male and female, as it is and as it ought to be" (Hannerz 1969, 77). He devoted considerable attention to the ways that mainstream middle-class and ghetto-specific ideas about marriage, sexual morality and male and female roles affect family life in the Washington ghetto he studied. His description is graphic in its portrayal of the social reality of ghetto marriage. In general, Hannerz presents the most complete discussion of matrifocal families available. However, Hannerz and the other writers have ignored the relationship between family form and the significance of the domestic group as a social unit. In spite of his sensitive attention to the details of Soulside residents' views of marriage and the family, Hannerz does not describe the ways in which the people use particular family ideologies to legitimate attempts to control their domestic groups. He takes the domestic group for granted and thereby fails to make clear why family forms are important. Hence, although Hannerz's description is ethnographically detailed, it tends to freeze the situation and ignores the fact that domestic politics are fluid, constantly negotiable and subject to great change.

In the light of these criticisms there follows a discussion of the relationship between the significance of the domestic group and the emergence of new types of marriage and kin-naming patterns among contemporary Aboriginal people in Alice Springs. In particular the focus is upon the link between marital relationships and the control of children. A major consequence of the analysis thus far is that the control of children is the key to the control of the resources necessary to maintain one type of domestic group: by maintaining control of their children, women are able to gain access to pensions and other welfare support; and such a strategy often requires them to commit themselves to their children at the expense of their relationship to their spouses. The more general point, however, is that the choice between husbands and children is, in fact, a choice between two types of domestic organization. The new types of marriage and kin-naming patterns are related to the emergence of these new possibilities. People use them to describe and legitimate particular domestic arrangements and the control of resources they command. From this perspective, therefore, the new marital and kin ideologies are both expressions of and basic resources in the negotiations that shape everyday domestic life in Alice Springs.

In a highly stimulating analysis, Sahlins attempts to relate particular types of kinship systems to the ability of particular societies to command surplus production from their constituent domestic groups (Sahlins 1974). Specifically, he suggests that kinship systems that encourage an extensive identification of collateral kin with lineal relatives command greater surpluses and generate more intensive economic systems than systems emphasizing lineal descent. The key factor is the relative isolation of the immediate family or domestic group from the rest of the community. The more isolated the domestic group, the lower the total societal production and the smaller the economic surplus beyond basic domestic needs. Sahlins's point is that lineal descent systems tend to isolate the basic domestic group more than systems that extend domestic ties along collateral lines (Sahlins 1974, 123).

Although Sahlins does not say so, his analysis suggests that a domestic group that wanted to legitimate isolating itself from the wider community might adopt a kin ideology which stressed lineal filiation or descent. It is therefore significant that Aboriginal families in Alice Springs have begun to change their ways of reckoning filiation and their ideas about marriage. In particular, some families have begun to trace filial linkages through the matriline and to deny the social significance of marriage. Indeed, some families have adopted a kin-naming system in which male and female children carry their mother's surname and socially repress the significance of fathers in the family system altogether. It is not surprising that such families tend to be matricentric. These changes have accompanied and legitimate the emergence of isolated, female-dominated domestic groups as a major social unit of contemporary Aboriginal social life in Alice springs.

During my fieldwork, Aboriginal people in Alice Springs recognized three types of marriage: "firestick", "kangaroo" and "proper". A firestick marriage is one contracted and celebrated according to Aboriginal customary practice; a proper marriage is contracted during a civil or religious ceremony recognized by white Australian law; and kangaroo marriages are simply *de facto* relationships. In Mt Kelly, for example, thirteen couples lived in some kind of marriage relationship. Of these, twelve were kangaroo relationships and one was a proper marriage. There were also six people in the camp who had earlier maintained marital relationships with other people but who were then living alone. Two of these had lived together in a kangaroo relationship for over thirty years; although never celebrated, it was normatively correct according to Aboriginal customary law.

It is important to grasp that the Mt Kelly people deny that kangaroo relationships are marriages at all. People living in this relationship, when asked, insist that they are "just living together". It is not always easy to distinguish between casual, short-term liaisons and a kangaroo relationship. The Mt Kelly people have no hard and fast rules; rather, they generally recognize that couples who have children and keep a separate camp form some kind of domestic unit. The key point seems to be a recognized willingness to share domestic resources, of which children and the establishment of a separate camp are conventional markers. The Mt Kelly people assert vigorously the qualified nature of the mutual commitment between two people involved in a kangaroo relationship. Women are particularly keen to distinguish between what they owe a man in a marriage and their obligations in a kangaroo relationship. In the midst of domestic quarrels, for example, women point out to their spouses that they are not married to them only living with them. Sometimes women wave the child endowment money they receive in their spouses' faces and deny they need them. Indeed, women generally seem to prefer kangaroo relationships to proper marriages.

One important dimension of this process is the way women use surnames. It is very uncommon for a woman to adopt her spouse's surname upon establishing a kangaroo relationship with him. Rather, they most commonly keep their maiden (usually their mother's) surname. Those women who do adopt their spouse's surname tend to reassume their maiden names during arguments and periods of domestic trouble. There was even one case in Mt Kelly in which the man adopted his spouse's surname. Women frequently pass on their own surname to their children. In some Alice Springs families this matronymic pattern has now extended to the fourth generation below the original ancestor. There were three families in Mt Kelly in which some members

traced their surnames through the matriline back three genera-
tions. In these cases the original ancestor was a white man.
Sometimes women take their spouse's name and pass it on to
their children. In this way they mark their commitment to their
spouse and usually surrender access to welfare support.

There is one large family in Alice Springs that illustrates the
full range of possibilities in this kin-naming system. Mrs
Percival, the family's elderly mother, had *de facto* marital
relationships with four white men during her life. She told me
that although her first three husbands had sometimes been
harsh, they had all been good men and taken good care of her.
Her fourth husband, however, was an evil and irresponsible
man who neglected her and her children. Mrs Percival had
children by all four men. She gave the children of her first three
husbands their father's surname. After her fourth husband left
her, however, she reassumed her father's surname of Percival,
and passed it on to the children of the last man. She claims that
her father was an excellent man. She refuses to mention her
fourth husband's name and recalls him with evident disgust. Her
children as a group carry four surnames. Her sons have each
made proper marriages and passed their own surnames on to
their children. Her one daughter (who was the last man's child)
has established only kangaroo relationships and named all her
children Percival.

Terry and Isabel Sharp, a Mt Kelly couple, had a proper
marriage. Isabel adopted Terry's surname and passed it on to all
her children, including George, her son by another man. Terry
was a highly regarded stockman and worked out bush for almost
his entire life. Isabel lived with him throughout his career. They
had six children. Because Isabel travelled with Terry, they had
to send each child to an institution in Alice Springs when they
came of school age. Mrs Thatcher, the welfare officer in charge
of the Sharps, told me that Terry and Isabel agreed to surrender
their children only after the Welfare Branch threatened to take
legal action against them. It warned them they had to place the
children in institutions so they could attend school or face
committal proceedings in the Alice Springs Children's Court. The
Sharps decided to give up their children "voluntarily".

The point is that Aboriginal people manipulate ideologies of
marriage and filiation to describe and legitimate particular
domestic situations. In particular, women make statements
about their marital relationships by manipulating how they trace

their own filial links and those of their children. In those situations in which women withold a firm commitment to their marital relationship, they present their domestic groups in terms of an ideology of matrifiliation. In those situations in which they commit themselves to their marital ties, they downplay their matrifilial links and present their domestic identity in terms of their husband's family.

These manipulations and different patterns of domestic commitment have profound implications for the emergent composition and career of particular domestic groups. They mark different ways of provisioning domestic groups and two types of domestic organization. The point is that the Welfare Branch adopted different tactics toward particular domestic groups depending upon how it assessed the fate of the children involved. It supported women who committed themselves to their children and maintained a stable home; in other words, women who did not commit themselves firmly to any marital relationship with a man. This was especially so if the men with whom mothers associated were "low-class" or had jobs that were not conducive to establishing conventional family life. It pressured women to withdraw themselves from such men and maintain their own households. This established a field in which Aboriginal women could manipulate their marital identities with men so as to establish control of their children and thereby legitimate access to welfare's support. Through this process, a matricentric form of domestic organization emerged. In contrast, women who invested in their relationships with their husbands committed themselves to their husbands' sources of income and to a different domestic organization. In most cases, the Welfare Branch not only refused to support such women, but took away their children. The domestic group was then split into two sections: the parents travelling from job to job and the children living in institutions in Alice Springs.

Conclusion

This analysis has highlighted the significance of the domestic group to contemporary Aboriginal people in Alice Springs and has shown the interrelationship between the ways different people relate to the outside, white-dominated society and their emergent domestic organization. On the one hand, the nature and complexity of different people's links to whites has an important effect on the composition and organization of their domestic groups. There are basically two types of domestic organization in Alice Springs: the matricentric type and one in which parents live together separately from their children. These types emerge as women, in particular, commit themselves to two different ways of provisioning their domestic groups. In the matricentric type women establish control of their children, minimize their relationships with men and support themselves on welfare benefits. In the other type of domestic organization, women commit themselves to their husband's income, surrender control of their children to local welfare agencies, and forgo welfare benefits. These different types of domestic organization also establish secondary conditions that affect the way Aboriginal people must interact with agents of the outside society. Of particular importance is the possibility that women who support themselves on pensions can limit their outside links and engage in few relatively simplex relationships with whites. Women's strength lies in withdrawing into the confines of their domestic group and exploiting it as a basic resource in their attempt to survive. Women are structurally placed to construct a more perfect fringe-dwelling identity and existence than men.

This analysis makes sense only if it is understood that Aboriginal men and women in Central Australia operate in a field dominated by whites. The contemporary significance of the domestic group, the ways people manipulate marriage and kin ideologies and attitudes toward pensions and urban houses can be explained only in the context of Aboriginal attempts to survive in the face of the white monopoly of all necessary resources. There is no longer any alternative mode of production in which Central Australian Aborigines can escape white power. They must engage in external relationships to use and manipulate white-controlled resources.

Notes

1. Australians use the term "walkabout" to refer to the alleged tendency of Aborigines to quit a place before completing whatever task may be engaging them. Whites explain this tendency by invoking the Aborigines' "customary" need to conduct religious ceremonies or their inherent need to wander as nomads.
2. On the basis of other remarks in the records I think these men were settlement employees. Men who worked outside the settlement were supposed to have been rationed by their employers.

5

Finding Work in the Central Australian Cattle Industry

This chapter is the first of a two-part argument about the position of Aboriginal men in the fringe-camps around Alice Springs. This chapter analyses how men find work and construct careers in the Central Australian cattle industry. The next chapter shows how having a good cattle boss and sharing what is received from the boss (particularly in the form of liquor) guarantees a man's credit. The argument is that men require access both to work and to sources of domestic credit if they are to survive. Unlike women, they cannot easily commit themselves to or exploit one type of income-earning. Indeed, men must usually work if they are to receive credit and receive credit if they are to work. For most Mt Kelly men, for example, the cattle industry is the most promising as well as the preferred source of work. Because cattlework is subject to systematic discontinuities, the men must often rely on pensioners for credit during key phases in their career if they are to continue to work or survive. If men are to become fringe-campers and take advantage of the opportunities fringe-camps offer, they must enlist the support of fringe-dwelling creditors, most particularly, of fringe-dwelling women.

An important consequence of this argument is that men must interact with white authorities more comprehensively than women. Even if they intend to live in fringe-camps and minimize their involvement with whites as much as possible, men must extensively transact with, and commit themselves to, whites in a more radical way than women. Consequently, their perspective on the wider society and on their own identities is different from that of women. In general men have had to make the demands of white society part of their own consciousness in a way many

Aboriginal women have been able to avoid. Nothing highlights this more than the fact that women often force men to transact with and present themselves in terms of white agents in order to establish their collateral for the credit women control. Women use men to establish indirect access to white resources without having to surrender their domestic isolation.

Mt Kelly and the Cattle Industry

Fringe-camps give their residents access to employment opportunities in the rural and urban areas. Nonetheless, many fringe-dwellers, particularly the Mt Kelly men, expect to find work primarily in the cattle industry. It would be impossible to understand Mt Kelly without reference to the growth and development of the cattle industry.

Most Mt Kelly people were born on Bullion and Gumtree, two adjacent cattle stations approximately 250 kilometres north of Alice Springs. Those who did not come from these two stations worked primarily on the group of stations northeast of Alice Springs. Although most Mt Kelly people maintain an identity as part-Aborigines, they are of Anmatjira, Kaiditja and Arunta origins, the groups of Aboriginal people whose pre-colonial territories lay in the northeast sector of Central Australia. The Mt Kelly people born on Gumtree and Bullion stations have known each other since childhood and consider each other kinsmen. They all maintain social relationships with the Aboriginal people who still live on the two stations and visit them frequently. The station people also tend to camp in Mt Kelly whenever they come to Alice Springs. In other words, the Mt Kelly people originally came from and still maintain their links into the cattle communities to the north (see appendix 2).

Most Mt Kelly adults worked in the cattle industry at some point in their lives, including the twelve pensioners and twenty-one people who were in the work-force during my fieldwork. Of the people in the work-force, fifteen (two women and thirteen men) worked in the cattle industry for at least one week during my fieldwork. Eight of the many men who worked during this time considered the cattle industry the most promising long-range source of jobs and worked to develop their careers in it.

The facts shown in appendix 2 indicate the extent to which the cattle industry affects the rhythms and development of everyday

Mt Kelly life. At the most mundane level, the camp's population varies radically according to the demand for labour in the cattle industry. When there is work, the camp population drops and few people other than the pensioners may be found there. On the other hand, the camp is largest and its population most heterogeneous during slack or holiday times. The camp is largest during the summer seasons around Christmas when there is no work for at least two months and the men all come home for an extended visit. Individuals return to Mt Kelly for short visits due to illness, because they have lost their jobs, or simply for drinking bouts of various lengths. The ebb and flow of the population marks as well the rise and fall of the flow of money into the camp. There is a core of pensioners who usually live in the camp and receive continuous incomes. It is the custom in Central Australia for the men working on the cattle stations to be paid only when they leave work. When the men arrive home from the bush, they usually have large sums of money in their pockets. The camp's income is greatest at that moment. The amount of money drops as the men spend their earnings and return to work. While they are away, only the pensions continue to fund the camp and its overall income reaches a minimum.

The arrival of men and money also coincides with a radical change in the tone of Mt Kelly life. Although pensioners throw drinking parties during the weekend after their cheques arrive, the truly great drinking sprees occur only when the "working men" return home from the bush. When the men drive up in the back of their bosses' cars, the people who have stayed at home sing a great cheer. Often they shout the name of the man who is head stockman, sing his praises, and call him by the name of the station where he works. The men give their immediate kinsmen and close friends meat or other gifts from their bosses, go to town and cash their cheques and return again with several cartons of beer and many flagons. They throw open parties for anyone who wants to come, including people from other places in Alice Springs. The parties often go on until the early hours of the morning and the men return to the hotels several times for more liquor. Although people insist that others should "sit down the good way" and drink quietly, fights are not uncommon during these great sprees. As the money runs out, the scale and exuberance of the spree declines, the men limit their drinking to weekend bouts or evening sessions in the pubs, and Mt Kelly life tones down. The departure of the men once again marks a return to pension life and the small parties that punctuate it.

There is a sense too in which these variations in the rhythms of Mt Kelly life mark the relative prominence of the male and female domains of life. Although there are certainly men who receive pensions, women dominate access to welfare benefits. Although some women work in the cattle industry as domestics or camp cooks, pastoral work is associated with men. The rise in income, in the camp population and in the exuberance of camp life tend, therefore, to be associated with the relative prominence of men and their social identities. By the same token, the decline in camp population, money and general toning down to camplife marks the fading of the male world and the emerging prominence of women. These trends more generally are associated with the rise and fall of the relative prominence of domestically generated resources and resources derived from the world of work. Mt Kelly is interesting and significant because it is a social field within which its residents bring together and interrelate these broader worlds.

Recruitment and Opportunities for Pastoral Work

Employment opportunities for Aboriginal people in Central Australia are extremely limited. Although in recent years the Commonwealth government has increased the number of jobs available for Aborigines in Central Australia, over 50 per cent of the Aboriginal people in the work-force are unemployed (1971 census). Hence, the value of any job is quite high. The Mt Kelly men are quite privileged in this respect relative to other Aborigines: they have access to jobs in Alice Springs. During my fieldwork, for example, one man found work in a local Aboriginal organization as a field officer; three others obtained jobs on special works projects established to hire unemployed fringe-dwellers; and several had worked for the Commonwealth Railways, the local abattoir and other agencies that hire unskilled labourers in Alice Springs. The Mt Kelly men were particularly fortunate because the camp was also a labour pool for the cattle industry. For over twenty years, several pastoralists recruited their workers from Mt Kelly, so the Mt Kelly men were well placed to get what few jobs were available to unskilled Aboriginal workers.

The cattle market was extremely depressed during my field-work. The United States had imposed restrictions on importing Australian cattle and, consequently, pastoralists did not need many men to muster, brand or drive their herds. Some pastoralists were even forced to let their equipment deteriorate because they did not have the cash necessary to maintain it. There were whole regions of Central Australia in which only one or two stations were hiring workers. Consequently, although the Mt Kelly men worked, they worked considerably less than they might have otherwise expected. In spite of this contingency the overall employment pattern I witnessed was characteristic of cattlework generally.

Cattlework is subject to systematic discontinuities and breaks in employment opportunities. There is little work available during the summer hot season. In Central Australia, herds are normally left to wander over the paddocks during the summer. There is usually some work available for head stockmen mending fences, windmills and other equipment but most men suffer at least a two-month break. Few skilled stockmen expect to work for one pastoralist throughout their careers. Pastoralists die, sell their properties or simply discharge their workers. Stockmen also think it wise that men work early in their careers for several pastoralists in order to sharpen their skills and become widely known. Moreover, stockmen do not consider all pastoralists good employers. On the contrary, they consider some men "bad bosses" and prefer to work for "good bosses" who "look after them properly". The overall demand for Aboriginal stockmen has also declined in the last twenty years. The end of droving and the construction of fences seriously eroded opportunities, particularly for the least skilled workers. The increased indebtedness and small profit margin of most pastoralists make it difficult for them to support extra workers.

These structural and historical features of the Central Australian pastoral industry mean that, although the Mt Kelly men might well occupy a relatively privileged position in the industry, they expect and must anticipate periods of unemployment. Their hedge against the vagaries of pastoral employment is their capacity to find new jobs and to obtain credit during slack periods. Critical to these procedures, however, is the range and nature of their relationships with pastoralists and fellow Aborigines. Men who maintain good relationships with several pastoralists have a greater chance of finding jobs. By the same token, if men are well thought of by their Aboriginal peers, they are more likely to receive credit when they cannot find work and have no money. (The question of credit is considered in the next chapter.)

There are a number of ways pastoralists recruit men for a season's work. The local office of the Commonwealth Employment Service lists cattle jobs and stock and station agents advertise in the local press and select workers. By far the most common procedure, however, is direct personal recruitment. When pastoralists need workers, they often contact men they have known and found satisfactory in the past. Some recruit their workers directly from the station camp. Others travel into Alice Springs and find men, particularly in the fringe-camps. Alternatively, they rely upon workers or other trusted individuals to recommend men they consider suitable. In other words, recruiting depends upon interpersonal relationships. The most reliable way for an Aboriginal man to get a job, therefore, is to establish close, personal relationships with pastoralists or with other Aboriginal workers who already maintain such links.

The recruiting process in the cattle industry works in the context of Central Australia and often opposes the general structural conditions of the region. In particular, the recruiting process either exploits or suspends the relevance of the location of Aboriginal workers and their ethnic identities. Many pastoralists recruit their workers from the Aboriginal camps on their own stations. Pastoralists and other commentators sometimes suggest that local recruiting is part of an agreement whereby Aborigines work and give their boss the use of the land in exchange for access to their sacred religious sites. According to this explanation, the basis of the Aborigines' link to the station is their primeval religious relationship to the land. If that were the case, the Mt Kelly men would never work. They live no less than 150 kilometres from any pastoralist who hires them. Although there are no Aborigines living on the stations where they work, pastoralists drive to Mt Kelly to recruit men, bypassing more conveniently located Aboriginal populations on neighbouring stations, missions and settlements. Pastoralists avoid keeping Aborigines on their properties (and on one occasion during my fieldwork even ejected a group) by hiring the Mt Kelly men. They do not hire Aborigines merely because they live close at hand. The right to live on a property as well as the opportunity to get jobs while living away from a property depends entirely upon the relationship between pastoralists and workers.

The Mt Kelly men's advantage might also be explained by their part-Aboriginal ethnic identity. Central Australia has a reputation as a region highly stratified by very rigid ethnic boundaries. Aborigines and whites talk in terms of three distinct ethnic categories: white, "half-caste" or "coloured" part-Aborigines and "full-blood" Aborigines. Alternatively people refer to whitefellows, yellowfellows and blackfellows (Meggitt 1962; Rowley 1974; Stevens 1974). Although these terms have been used throughout Australia, they have developed rather specialized meanings in the context of the Central Australian cattle industry. In addition to the differences in material possessions, political and economic power, and prestige conventionally assigned to these categories, the terms also name the components of a basic model of the local hierarchy of skills, division of labour and responsibility, and relationships between the work roles in the cattle industry. In general, "whites" are the owners, managers and highly-skilled role-players. They are the "bosses". "Blackfellows" are "the boys" who, by virtue of their special skills in tracking and animal work, make good cattleworkers. It is conventionally thought that part-Aborigines have the physical capabilities of the blacks and some of the white man's intellectual ability. Consequently, they often play roles midway between the other two categories (in particular head stockmen, well-sinkers, drovers) and perform tasks that require mental and physical dexterity but little planning. In general, pastoralists consider part-Aborigines more intelligent than "full-blood" Aborigines and prefer to hire them.

Many local people (including the Mt Kelly men themselves) would therefore argue that pastoralists hire them because they are part-Aborigines. However, the explanation in terms of the ethnic preferences of the pastoralists is incomplete if not altogether inaccurate. William Samuelson, the man who enjoys the greatest prestige in Mt Kelly and who is the role model for the camp's young stockmen, is a "full-blood" Aborigine. He worked for the same pastoralist for over twenty-five years and, although now retired from active stockwork because of a back injury, still receives money and presents from his old employer. He also enjoys a standing right to live in his boss's station at any time. His boss still publicly considers Samuelson his head stockman and hires Mt Kelly men under Samuelson's control.

This is all true in spite of the fact that Samuelson is a "full-blood" Aborigine. Moreover, Samuelson is not a unique example.

In the light of this kind of evidence, it would perhaps be easiest to disregard ethnic categories and assert that they are nothing but the components of a folk model which has little relevance to the sociological analysis of Central Australia (Peters 1967). This would ignore the fact that whites and Aborigines take account of the implications of the ethnic model in interaction and negotiate the situational significance of that model for their relationships with each other. They cannot merely disregard it. As particular blacks and whites fill in the details of their relationships, they actively legitimate or suspend the model's relevance for any particular transaction or relationship. The same is true for relationships based on spatial contiguity. Away from particular relationships (for example, in the context of legislative debate or interviews with anthropologists) these models may be invoked and on such occasions they unproblematically maintain their validity as typifying relationships. In everyday life their significance must be established by the actors themselves. The problem for analysis is to determine under what conditions and how they are made relevant or irrelevant in particular situations.

The conditions that establish the relevance of the ethnic model in the cattle industry emerge as pastoralists recruit their workers and construct the relationships that legitimate recruitment procedures. Specifically, the relevance of a man's ethnic identity is established as he constructs what the Mt Kelly men call his "reputation" that is, his identity as a good or bad worker. Indeed, a man must construct a good reputation precisely because of the otherwise constraining limitations of the ethnic model. Given the prevailing views on the capabilities of the average Aborigine, an Aboriginal man who establishes a good reputation thereby largely suspends the relevance of his ethnic identity for his transactions with pastoralists. This is particularly true for "full-blood" Aborigines, and it is also true for part-Aborigines. It is conventionally assumed that part-Aborigines can develop along one of two ways. The behaviour of a part-Aborigine who fails to perform as expected is explained in terms of "the blackfellow coming on in him". On the other hand, if he performs adequately, he has successfully repressed the "blackfellow" and developed his white blood. In other words, a man's reputation does not necessarily correspond to the general ethnic models. Rather, the significance of a man's reputation is the way in which it distinguishes him from or makes him an exemplar of general categories. In this way it establishes the relevance or irrelevance of those categories for him.

In its narrowest sense a man's reputation documents how skilled in cattlework other people consider him. It is a description and product of the relative success of his training process. There have never been any major training programmes for stockmen in Central Australia. Consequently, men have to learn cattlework on the job. A man's first employer is particularly crucial in teaching him and establishing his initial reputation. Aboriginal men do not all have equal access to their first jobs. On the contrary, several factors structure the entrance of new workers into the industry.

As mentioned above, many pastoralists think that part-Aborigines have greater potential as employees than most "full-blood" Aborigines. The Commonwealth government officially supported the pastoralists' view for many years and systematically tried to prepare part-Aborigines for work on the cattle stations. Although it did not establish schools that offered instruction in the techniques of cattlework, it did finance institutions designed to teach part-Aboriginal children the rudiments of European culture and thereby prepare them for later vocational training on the job (Rowley 1974). The police were responsible for finding part-Aboriginal children in the bush and were empowered to remove them from their mothers. Prior to the Second World War there were two institutions in Central Australia that received the children: Hermansburg Mission and the Bungalow. After the war and the official inauguration of the assimilation policy, other similar institutions were established. The two most prominent in Alice Springs were administered by the Anglican Church: St Margaret's and St Anthony's. The children lived in the institutions and attended school in the town. These institutions functioned as recruiting grounds for young stockmen and domestic labourers. Pastoralists who wanted young part-Aboriginal men or women could recruit directly from them. Through these institutions the Commonwealth acted as an agent between pastoralists and prospective employees and established the initial contacts upon which some pastoralists and their workers built closer, long-term relationships.

Relatively few Aborigines had the opportunity, involuntary or otherwise, to attend school and acquire special access to potential employers. Most had to rely upon indirect links through kinsmen who already worked for a pastoralist. It is in providing ready access to men who already had jobs that spatial proximity has its most important effect upon recruiting in the cattle industry. A man who needs a job can invoke a kin tie to legitimate moving into a station camp where he thinks jobs might be available. Aboriginal women played an important part in this process particularly prior to 1940. In many respects, Aboriginal women were the points of articulation between the pastoral economy and the domestic economy of the pre-war Aborigines. The shortage of white women in the outback prior to 1939 is well documented (Bleakley 1928, 10). Although it was illegal some white men cohabited with Aboriginal women. It was not uncommon for the Aboriginal woman's kinsmen to join her as the pastoralist's main workers. Moreover, the children who were born from such relationships often had priority over other people both as workers and even as heirs to the estate. Although all such children were categorized as part-Aborigines and, therefore, subject to removal, pastoralists (as well as Aboriginal women) sometimes hid them on the station. The police also overlooked the children of those pastoralists they favoured or otherwise had to respect. The situational negotiability of ethnic identities in Central Australia might be gauged by the fact that those part-Aboriginal children who eventually did inherit their father's or grandfather's station now are considered "white".

Station camps were a context in which well-established workers could give aspiring workers the chance to learn the business and get to know the pastoralist. The fact that even Mt Kelly functions as a recruiting ground in this way documents the significance of the social relationships between pastoralists, workers and potential workers in this process at the expense of merely spatial conditions. There were five men in Mt Kelly who had direct personal relationships with one or more pastoralists. These pastoralists recruited almost all their workers from Mt Kelly. Whenever they needed men, they drove into the camp, contacted their main employees and indicated if they needed extra workers. The Mt Kelly regulars filled their bosses' needs from young men in the camp or other friends around Alice Springs. Young men who had earlier lived in Mt Kelly often came back to the camp looking for work. I observed several such men get jobs through their relationships with the Mt Kelly men who had regular employers. On one occasion I witnessed a young Mt

Kelly man begin his career in the cattle industry with a job on Jefferson Downs, a station whose head stockman lived in Mt Kelly and was then cohabiting with the young man's sister.

To be a stockman a young man has to become skilled in the techniques of cattlework. His training also includes learning what kind of man pastoralists hire; in other words, they must learn the cognitive and affective aspects of the social identity of a good, reputable worker (Berger and Luckman 1972, 94). In the context of the Central Australian pastoral industry a man must pay special attention to ensuring that he is perceived as having what might be called a proper motivational structure; by this is not meant the actual psychological impulses that prompt a person to act, but, following Mills and Schutz, those particular personality traits that other people publicly assert prompt a person to act. In this sense a man's motivational structure is a composite label others ascribe to him, not necessarily a feature of his own personality (Schutz 1976; Mills 1940). The significance of a man's publicly documented motivational structure is related to the overall significance of the motivational structures conventionally ascribed to the three ethnic categories in Central Australia. Ethnicity is made relevant in everyday life in the cattle industry precisely through these notions.

In contrast to whites, Aborigines are typically understood to be cheeky, unable to manage their own work and unreliable. They tend to "go walkabout" and manifest the rather casual attitudes said to have been characteristic of hunters and gatherers. Although such notions are quite common, F. Stevens provides data documenting these points for the pastoralists in his sample. He collected this data in an attempt to determine the reasons why pastoralists opposed paying Aborigines the award wage. He ends up explaining the results of his opinion poll in terms of "genuine problems of communication in the everyday running of cattle stations" (Stevens 1974, 66–67). Few pastoralists have ever bothered to learn an Aboriginal language, he notes, and suggests that better working conditions and increased acculturation for both groups might undermine these attitudes.

Stevens's analysis misses the point. What provides a clue to the significance of his data, however, is his observation that pastoralists and managers tend to individualize their assessment of certain workers' abilities. Stevens says, "Indeed, there was a surprising departure from the tendency to depersonalize Aboriginal workers in other circumstances. Such comments as

'Johnson would be supreme' or that 'no white man could match X' were fairly common" (Stevens 1974, 66). Although he provides no explanation for this fact, it is as important as the results of his survey data. The survey data is nothing other than a profile of the motivation structure ascribed to the typical Aboriginal worker. It is a model against which the performance of particular men is measured and their own reputations built. The exceptional "Johnsons" of the industry are significant precisely because they have constructed reputations that suspend the relevance of the model in their particular cases. Their reputations, in turn, legitimate the exceptional nature of their relationships with their employers. Indeed, the pastoralists Stevens interviewed agreed that these exceptional men were worth the award wage.

These responses to Stevens's inquiries neither marked the liberal attitudes of some pastoralists nor were special pleading displayed for Stevens's benefit. Rather, the process of creating exceptions to the conventional typifications of Aboriginal motivation is precisely the way the recruiting process works in Central Australia. Those men who work are all exceptions in one way or another. If a man is not an exception to the type of the "lazy blackfellow", he does not get a job. A crucial part of a man's education in the cattle business, therefore, is learning how to display exceptional motivations.

I was once told a story about a famous white pioneering pastoralist and his part-Aboriginal son. The white father had the habit of tying his son to white-oak yard posts and horsewhipping him. According to my informant, the father whipped his son in order "to beat the blackfellow out of him". The son was not alone in his experiences. The Mt Kelly men all told me stories of how their bosses physically and verbally abused them. They described how even "good bosses" assaulted them with stockwhips and subjected them to other kinds of physical punishment. Moreover, the Mt Kelly men agreed that a limited amount of such treatment was legitimate and an essential part of their "education".

Cameron Sharp, a nineteen-year-old Mt Kelly part-Aborigine, told me about the time his first boss whipped him. It was early in the morning and the men were preparing their horses for work. The season was fresh and, as is common in Central Australia, the horses had not been ridden for several months. Consequently, they were "a little bit wild". In addition, Cameron had chosen to

ride a young colt that was only newly broken and quite unused
to riders. When he mounted, the colt bolted and began to buck.
The boss ordered Cameron to pull the colt up tight, but Cameron,
too, was inexperienced and let the animal run. The boss grabbed
a stockwhip and flailed into horse and rider. Cameron said that
the boss tried to teach them both how to work properly in this
way. Cameron said further that he thought he had learned from
the experience.

Another older Mt Kelly part-Aborigine, Don Corcoran, told me
about his youth on Nijambah station. He was born on the property and worked there for over forty years. As a young boy he was
responsible for the boss's vegetable garden — watering it and
scaring away the crows. Occasionally he stole some
watermelons. When the boss discovered his misdeeds he whipped him. Don ran away several times as a result. If the boss
caught him running off, he shot at the boy with his rifle. If he
refused to stop, the boss rode after him on his horse and returned
him to the station, where he was whipped again. Don outlived
his boss and remained on the property for several years. Eventually he had a major argument with the new owner and left.
When I went around to the Alice Springs home of the new
owner, the boss refused to speak with me. I told him I wanted to
discuss Don. He simply said, "Oh, that cheeky bastard" and
refused to spare any more time. Don, on the other hand, once
spotted the boss walking down the main street of Alice Springs.
He cursed his old boss and said, "I gave that man the best years
of my life and now look at me. What have I got for it? Nothing."

Alfred Samuelson was an old white drover and small-time
pastoralist who employed William Samuelson for over twenty-
five years. He once told me a story about William that occurred
before they began working together. William was working for
another white pastoralist on a station northeast of Alice Springs.
One day the boss began to stockwhip him. Apparently, when
William thought the punishment had gone too far, he turned and
beat his boss badly. According to Alfred, the only thing that
prevented William from killing the boss was a knife at his belly.
The interesting thing was that Alfred did not disapprove of
William's response. On the contrary, he used the story to
disparage the other pastoralist. Alfred praised William and said
that he was the only "blackfellow" who had ever got up in the
morning before Alfred himself. He said that William had never
been a "cheeky" worker. Alfred observed that he had never had

to stockwhip William and wondered about the other boss's good sense. He did not doubt the general utility of the whip and only questioned its use in the case of this worker, a man who worked hard and was not cheeky. In his opinion William did not require what was otherwise a regular feature of boss–worker relationships.

Without quantitative evidence of the number of times pastoralists use or threaten to use violence against their workers, it is difficult to know whether Stevens is correct in saying there is less violence now than in 1946 when the Berndts studied the Northern Territory cattle industry (Stevens 1974). Aboriginal men working in the industry still expect violence, understand it as a key element in their relationship with pastoralists and generally consider it legitimate. Violence is significant because it determines the relevance of an Aboriginal man's ethnic identity to his identity as a worker. When a pastoralist whips an Aborigine, he puts the man in an insoluble dilemma. If the worker refuses to be whipped, he documents that the "blackfellow" is still "in" him. He shows himself to be "cheeky" and unreliable. Consequently, he undermines his relationship with his boss, loses his job and jeopardizes his wider reputation. If he intends to keep his job, establish good relations with the boss and construct a reputation as a "good boy", he must submit to the stockwhip. Only by submitting to the violence can a worker document that he has a motivational structure appropriate to the job as stockman and the identity as a boss's boy.

The account of the white father who beat his part-Aboriginal son described earlier provides evidence for the argument that pastoralists are operating on what they consider to be the typical motivational structure of Aboriginal men even if they have some of their own "blood". Indeed, the case is particularly enlightening given that the boy was part-Aboriginal and supposedly had the potential to develop in either direction. The boy inherited from his mother the potential to manifest "blackfellow" traits. He had likewise inherited from his father the potential to repress those traits and cultivate his white characteristics. When the father whipped the boy, the boy could show he had repressed his black instincts only by responding appropriately to the whipping and otherwise working well.

Don Corcoran's case is equally instructive as an example of a part-Aboriginal man who eventually, in spite of repeated whippings and many years, could not repress his "blackness". He was a "cheeky" man, according to his ex-boss. After a major crisis they severed the relationship and Don had to leave the station. Don considered his boss a "bad boss", a man who gave him nothing in spite of what he considered to be the labour of his entire life. The notion of "good" and "bad" bosses will be discussed below. For the moment it is enough to note that Don and his boss together linked "cheekiness" and prevailing notions of a fair exchange between pastoralists and their worker: Don was cheeky and his boss was bad. This was the typical way of describing a relationship that had broken down. It was the exact opposite of the way men with stable relationships with their bosses talked. The result of Don's transactions with his boss was that he lost his job and assumed an identity more appropriate to a "blackfellow". He had no job and no stable relationship with a boss.

William Samuelson was an example of a "blackfellow" who by virtue of his relationships with Alfred Samuelson assumed a position and social identity more typical of a part-Aborigine. Indeed, given the way Alfred talked about him, he seems almost to have established the identity of a white man. According to Alfred, William got working in the mornings even before Alfred himself, a unique characteristic for a "blackfellow". William was such a fine worker, in fact, that Alfred denied he ever needed to be whipped. White men (at least those men pastoralists considered to be really white) were never whipped as far as I know: they did not need to have the "blackfellow" beaten out of them. By saying that William did not need the whip, Alfred suspended the relevance of his obvious "black" origins and said that he was something altogether special. This legitimated the transactions and relationship between the two men, which were themselves considered something special and highly prestigious in Mt Kelly.

The Mt Kelly men accept the legitimacy of the violence and consider it part of their education because they are aware of its significance for their relationships with pastoralists and their long-term career prospects. It is a forced choice in which either course of action is disagreeable but one side less so than the others (Walters 1972). Through violence they learn to be "good boys", that is, to adopt the proper attitude toward pastoralists. On one occasion I witnessed the case of a Mt Kelly man who risked having his reputation redefined as a result of gossip which questioned his demeanour. Barry Corcoran, Don's son, had worked for one pastoralist for over nine years. As a result of a major argument they had in the bush during a muster, however, the boss dismounted Barry approximately sixteen kilometres from the station house and forced him to walk in. Barry left the boss's employ. This happened before I moved in to Mt Kelly but while I was there Barry informed me that he was worried about what his previous boss thought of him. Barry's fellow workers at the station had informed the boss that they had heard Barry "rubbishing" him in a local Alice Springs pub. Barry was concerned lest the boss get angry and spread the word that Barry was a "cheeky" worker. At the time Barry was having difficulties with his new boss and did not want to jeopardize his career further. The gossip of his ex-workmates risked doing just that.

In his study of the Sicilian Mafiosi Blok argues that violence emerges as a means of social control in encapsulated regional political orders when "the State fail[s] to monopolize the use of physical force and [has] to yield its sovereignty to local power holders" (Blok 1974, 176). Blok's thesis describes more accurately and establishes the conditions for what Rowley and others have labelled the perpetuation of "frontier conditions" in Central Australia (Rowley 1974). Given Blok's perspective one might observe that the "frontier" does not vanish with the development of a state apparatus which nominally or even through the agents of local police appears actually to have established administrative control of a region. Rather, one must stress the extent to which the state in practice relies upon "local power holders" to carry out its responsibilities. It has been described in earlier chapters to what extent the Commonwealth government both officially and tacitly relegated its power and responsibility for Aborigines to pastoralists. Blok's analysis properly suggests that such a relegation is a necessary condition for the kind of violence described here as part of the relationships between pastoralists and Aboriginal workers.

It is important to realize that pastoralists are not, strictly speaking, brokers, as Blok and Adams use the term (Adams 1970, 320–21; Blok 1974, 7). Unlike the Mafiosi, pastoralists own the means of production and do not depend upon their control of Aborigines to maintain the state's support for their power in the region. They do not use violence to control a vital resource (Aborigines) at the local level which is necessary for them to keep the support of the power holders in the larger domain in which they are encapsulated. On the contrary, although the Commonwealth government can effectively do little to stop violence between pastoralists and their workers, news of such violence is not well received at the national political level and tends to undermine the pastoralists' overall legitimacy. A more important point, however, is that violence is not a simple means of social control, but a recruiting technique that identifies men and forces them to choose between having a boss and not having one. Men who cannot tolerate violence do not get bosses.

I suggest that all the "exceptions" to the general personalized rule that Stevens found were men who had proved themselves able and willing to tolerate violence. The point is that violence controls pastoralist–worker interaction and conditions the development of their relationships through its relevance for the complex negotiations that construct and legitimate the social identities of particular pastoralists and their workers. The significance of men's social identities, on the other hand, itself emerges from the political and economic dependence of Aboriginal workers on their pastoral bosses. As a mechanism by which the fate of particular men is determined in an overall highly structured field, the importance of violence lies not in its general properties as a means of social control but in its specific properties as a means of differentiating men; and in this context, precisely because it differentiates them, it controls them. Violence is as important as the wages and side benefits a boss pays his workers. The capacity to offer violence and wages marks the power and identity of the boss. The willingness to accept violence and wages marks the dependence and identity of the worker. Violence not only expresses the boss's power, it constructs and legitimates it.

Debt and Avoidance Patterns between Pastoralists and Workers

Relationships between pastoralists and workers in Central Australia are of the type Radcliffe-Brown analyses in his classic essay "On Joking Relationships"; that is, they involve "both attachment and separation, both social conjunction and social disjunction" (Radcliffe-Brown 1952, 91). On the one hand, pastoralists need their workers' labour and the workers need an income. On the other hand, their relationship is based on a structural conflict over the proceeds of the total operation, in particular over the results of the workers' labour. Radcliffe-Brown notes that "social disjunction implies divergence of interests and therefore the possibility of conflict and hostility, while conjunction requires the avoidance of strife". Given this set of conditions, he asks, "How can a relationship which combines the two be given a stable, ordered form?" (Radcliffe-Brown 1952, 92). His answer is that such relationships can be maintained either through joking or through avoidance.

Insofar as violence is a crucial component in the processes whereby pastoralists and workers develop their relationships, conflict and hostility are not necessarily repressed. It is important to note, however, that violence is limited primarily to the early, formative stages of a developing relationship. Mature relationships between pastoralists and their workers are marked by patterns of avoidance. The shift from violent interaction to avoidance is crucial and marks a major change in a worker's emergent relationship with his boss. It indicates that the relationship has become established and henceforth must be marked by a mutual concern for maintaining face in ordinary, everyday social interaction.

Radcliffe-Brown argues that the content of transactions between the parties to a relationship varies according to the degree of respect that must be shown among them (Radcliffe-Brown 1952). He suggests that joking, for example, occurs between equals and marks a symmetrical relationship. Avoidance occurs between unequals and characterizes asymmetrical links. The relationships between pastoralists and their workers (both experienced and inexperienced) are certainly unequal. The shift from violence to avoidance marks, however, a change in the character of the unequal relationship: there is a change from a relationship between people who owe each other little and remain relatively uncommitted to a relationship between committed, indebted people. As the commitment and mutual obligations between pastoralists and their workers grow, violence fades and avoidance becomes a more prominent aspect of their interaction. These ideas suggest a way to specify the problem of asymmetry more precisely than does Radcliffe-Brown. Avoidance occurs when the conflict of interests between the parties to a relationship is great (perhaps even irreconcilable) and, when the debt or dependence of one party upon the other is perpetual or understood to be irredeemable. From this perspective avoidance in a general sense socially represses expressions of social disjunction. Its logic, in other words, is the reverse of joking.

In the Central Australian cattle industry, respect is maintained and face saved when everyone recognizes the dependence of the workers upon their bosses but, at the same time, avoids overtly introducing the fact into everyday interaction. The power of the boss remains unstated and expressions of it are socially relegated to the anomalous moments of untrained awkwardness and "out-of-line" behaviour characteristic of the useless and the untrained. Evidence for this proposition comes from the way the Mt Kelly men conceptualize what they call good bosses and bad bosses. There are two basic components of a "good boss": he "looks after" his workers and he leaves them alone to do their work unsupervised. A "bad boss" is a man who only pays his workers the minimum wage and who directly supervises the entire day's work. The Mt Kelly men recognize, of course, that the boss has the right to pay men nothing other than the legal minimum and to attend to every detail of the station's operation. They prefer to leave bad bosses, however, and find jobs with good bosses. Indeed, they treasure good bosses and endeavour to keep them. Men who manage to acquire good bosses indicate by that fact alone that they are "good boys", that is, highly skilled workers. On the other hand, bad bosses can usually only attract "bad boys" and bad boys must settle for bad bosses.

Both components of the identity of good bosses imply interaction patterns of avoidance. In the first place, a good boss does not require his workers to articulate their dependence upon him for their livelihoods. Good bosses pay all their workers more than the basic wage. They also legitimately pay their prized workers even higher wages. A good boss gives his men special things he anticipates they might need; for example, at the beginning of the mustering season, he might give his head stockman a new pair of boots or a new hat. He also permits his best men to live on the station even during slack periods. Alternatively, he finds them summer work or picks them up at their own homes away from the station when the season starts. A good boss also grants his men beef and extra money to give to their kinsmen. If his men are stranded in town without money, a good boss lends them cash or arranges credit for them at a local stock and station agent. In addition to these more or less regular concessions, a good boss helps his workers in emergencies. On one occasion, for example, I witnessed a boss bring his head stockman's wife into town in order to give birth in the Alice Springs Hospital. I saw another boss pay a $300 traffic fine of one of his workers.

A boss does not grant all of these concessions to each of his workers, and nor do they expect him to do so. On the contrary, only the best, most prestigious workers can reasonably expect to have access to all these kinds of resources. A discussion of the significance of this fact for relationships among workers and their peers occurs in the next chapter. The point to notice now is that ideally a good boss grants these items to his workers without having to be asked or without any dispute. Men act as if what is in fact a privilege is a worker's right by virtue of his close relationship with the boss. Insofar as the boss recognizes his responsibility as boss and meets his workers' needs as they arise, he upholds this fiction. At the same time, he gives his men what only he has the power to provide them with, without making the basis for their exchange overt, public and discrediting. In other words, a good boss avoids making his identity as boss relevant to everyday interaction between himself and his workers. A bad boss, on the other hand, awkwardly minimizes his responsibilities and makes his workers publicly recognize their dependence upon him. He expresses his power and insists his workers do likewise.

Good boys also have responsibilities of this type toward their bosses. Most significantly, a good boy never inquires or negotiates with his boss about his pay. Rather, he takes his job, has faith in his boss's goodwill and accepts his pay at the end of the job. If the boss consistently disappoints a good man's expectations the worker simply leaves and reidentifies his previous employer as a bad boss. A skilled, well-respected worker need not tolerate a bad boss. He can leave and find another job with confidence. A worker who leaves a bad boss and finds other work gains added prestige in the eyes of his peers. By the same token, a man who consistently submits to a bad boss and cannot find another loses his peers' respect.

It often happens that the goods a pastoralist presents to his workers are loans. A pastoralist who buys his head stockman a new pair of boots, for example, does not necessarily make his worker a gift. More often, he takes the cost of the boots out of his workers' final pay cheque. The mark of a very generous boss is that he puts his best workers heavily into debt for long periods of time. There is, therefore, a close association between indebtedness, respect and avoidance in the relationships between pastoralists and their workers in Central Australia. I have argued up to this point that the prevailing avoidance patterns socially repress expressions of the boss's power over his men, but I have said little about the components of the boss's power. The link between indebtedness and avoidance, however, suggests something about the conditions that maintain the boss's power and long-term relationships between pastoralists and workers. For the boss to take the cost of items such as new boots out of his worker's cheque suggests, of course, that there is a direct exchange of a worker's labour for the item he receives. From this limited perspective, boots are simply a form of payment in kind. This is only partially true. The debt a worker incurs includes more than just the cost of the boots. When a pastoralist presents his worker with a pair of boots or grants a cash loan, he thereby guarantees and indicates that he will give his man the work necessary to repay the loan. Insofar as workers stay indebted to their employers, they retain access to work. Work is so scarce for most Aborigines in Central Australia that men compete to go into debt to a boss. The primary debt men owe their bosses for access to a job (as distinct from the secondary debts they owe for particular items), is, therefore, substantially irredeemable. It is the long-term basis for the pastoralist's power over his workers. The avoidance patterns are principally associated with the social repression of the primary debt; that is, by being a good boss a pastoralist socially denies both that he has the power to grant primary debts and that his men vitally depend upon him to do so in order to live.

This suggestion raises the question of the second component of the identity of the "good boss" and the avoidance patterns associated with it. In addition to meeting his workers' needs, a good boss avoids his men during the workday. In the morning a good boss informs his head stockman what he wants done. He then goes away to do his own work and leaves the men to implement his instructions without his supervision. If a boss avoids his men during the workday, he thereby communicates his trust in their skill and sense of responsibility. This is important because the only resource a worker can offer his boss in exchange for what I have called the primary debt is his skill as a worker. As I stated previously, a man's skill determines the extent to which he depends upon any particular pastoralist (be he a good or bad boss) for his livelihood. If a man is highly skilled, the force of the primary debt he owes his employer is considerably less. Some men are so skilled and reliable that pastoralists compete to acquire them. These points relate also to my comments about secondary debts. Only a man who is highly skilled commands many gifts and secondary loans from his employers. From this perspective a pastoralist who properly "looks after" his men and leaves them alone during the workday communicates a message about the extent to which their positions in the social order have been reversed: he communicates the fact that he depends upon their particular labour more than they depend upon the resources he controls. Insofar as a pastoralist avoids his men, he represses the fact that he is the boss.

How does the problem of horsewhipping relate to these points? In terms of the argument I have just presented, horsewhipping stops when a pastoralist recognizes his worker's skill, that is, when he must begin to avoid his worker. For the workers themselves, therefore, the full significance of horsewhipping emerges in terms of its function as a prelude to avoidance. A man is not proud simply that he has been horsewhipped; rather, the mark of pride is that he has been horsewhipped but is now avoided. Men do not consider bosses who whip their young workers necessarily bad bosses. A good boss instructs new young men well, including teaching them how to present themselves. Young men experience violence when they transgress the conditions of avoidance. Bosses must teach those conditions and young men must learn them. When that occurs, a man's training is over, the violence stops and avoidance emerges.

Conclusion

In conclusion there is a problem of major importance in boss–worker relationships in Central Australia that deserves consideration – the use of kinship terms. Aboriginal workers regularly extend kinship terms to their bosses. For example, they often call their bosses uncle, father or brother-in-law. They often cast requests to their bosses in the idiom of kinship and talk as if their bosses were part of the customary Aboriginal kinship order. More radically, workers who maintain particularly close relationships with a pastoralist adopt his surname as their own. William Samuelson adopted the name "Samuelson" after he had become Alfred Samuelson's head stockman and chief worker. William also claims to have adopted earlier the surnames of two other white employers, both of whom had died. Consequently, as was customary among Aboriginal kinsmen, he refused to mention their names.

It would be incorrect to dismiss these practices as either a survival of customary Aboriginal social norms or a mere mystification. They must be set in the context of the contemporary situation, in particular the context of boss–worker relationships. I suggest that these naming practices are radical extensions of the sociological significance of the avoidance practices just analysed. The kinship idiom makes certain responsibilities appear to be non-negotiable. If a worker asks his boss for a favour using the term "brother-in-law", he invokes obligations outside the context of their boss–worker relationship that are mandatory. In other words, the kinship idiom nullifies the social significance of the worker's debt to his employer. It makes it appear that the boss has permanent debts and obligations to his worker and, by extension, to his worker's kinsmen. By the same token, the use of the kinship idiom in interaction is not merely a rhetorical mystification but an interactional device whereby Aborigines transform needs they experience in the short term into long-term commitments. In this idiom, Aborigines do not recognize that the goods they obtain from their employers derive from a dependent relationship born of basic economic necessity. The kinship idiom casts such goods in the context of long-term relationships that recognize few debts and legitimate all demands as simply part of what is expected between "relations". The kinship idiom legitimates a kind of endless credit with no interest. In this sense it finishes the job that avoidance began; in other words, it negates the meaning of primary debts.

Kinship is a total idiom: it suggests an interdependency rooted in the very nature of things which is indissoluble. For this reason, it seems a particularly appropriate idiom for the kind of dependency relationships that exist between pastoralists and their workers. Of particular significance is the dual emphasis on violence and "looking after" so characteristic of these relationships. It appears that the kinship idiom encodes the total power of the pastoralist to violate and to sustain his workers. The kinship idiom is a mystification, but one which vividly marks the components of the relationship as it stands.

6

The Gift of the Spirit: A Theory of Drinking

The consumption and sharing of liquor in the Aboriginal camps around Alice Springs is related to the patterns of dependence and interdependence among the people described in the preceding chapters. Aboriginal people try to develop funds of credit to counter the long-term uncertainties in their sources of livelihood by spending current surplus income on liquor for the general communities they live in. Specifically, men use money they earn from pastoral and unskilled urban work to share liquor and thereby legitimate long-term access to domestic resources (namely, pensions) that women substantially control. For their part, women manipulate their control of domestic resources to legitimate claims upon the resources men control. Among Alice Springs Aborigines liquor also marks an individual's personal productivity and affluence. Indeed, liquor's capacity to make subtle distinctions on the theme of personal independence and thereby present social collateral accounts for its wide use in exchange. It is for these reasons that drinking is fundamentally related to the ways in which Aborigines assess their own social situations, rationally adapt to current circumstances and thereby participate in (if not determine) the construction of their social lives.

A "social problems" approach has previously dominated the analysis of drinking among contemporary Australian Aboriginal people. Most analysts view the use and alleged abuse of liquor as a symptom of the "breakdown of traditional society". According to this view, Aboriginal drinkers selfishly gratify themselves at the expense of meeting their obligations to their families and the wider community. As a result the physical health of individuals

deteriorates and the community as a whole becomes disorganiz-
ed. The gradual decline in the practice of and respect for the
customary religious beliefs is often said to be a particularly
significant consequence of drinking. This approach presents
drinking liquor as part of a general syndrome of problems that
hinders the adaptation of Aboriginal people to white society and
interprets excessive drinking as a phenomenon of transition, as
part of what happens to Aboriginal people as they change their
normative orientation from customary tribal values to white
Australian values. Different writers describe this process in different terms (for example, psychiatric, biological, or structural-
functional). They all agree, however, on the disruptive and
maladaptive function of liquor for Aborigines (Albrecht 1969;
Bain 1969; Cawte 1972; House of Representatives Standing Committee on Aboriginal Affairs 1977; Millar and Leung 1974;
Rowley 1973; Sackett 1977; Stanner [1958] quoted in Becker
1964, 337). A similar approach has also largely determined the
analysis of drinking among North American Indians (Graves
1967, 306; Honigman 1973, 253; Levy and Kunitz 1973, 219;
Robbins 1973, 115).

At one extreme this view of drinking is altogether un-
sociological and based on crude psychoanalytic concepts which
depict contemporary Aboriginal society as "sick" and composed
of neurotics (Cawte 1972, 50–52). From this perspective drinking
liquor is culturally meaningless and socially pathological. More
sociologically sensitive observers, however, have tried to explain
patterns of Aboriginal drinking in terms of their social context
and to discover their social significance (Beckett 1964; Sackett
1977). Few analysts have recognized that the consumption and
sharing of liquor are in fact processes of social organization with
which Aborigines meaningfully construct their social world
(Robbins 1973). Rather, most analysts consider drinking liquor a
deviant activity, especially in what appears to be excessive
amounts. For these reasons even sociologically informed interpretations have to date failed to explain Aboriginal drinking
activities.

It is undoubtedly true that drinking has untoward effects on
some people. The understanding of drinking among contemporary Aborigines will not advance, however, until moral
judgments about its effects on traditional society and about the
irresponsibility of people who drink are suspended. Drinking
should be related through a sociological analysis to the processes

by which Aborigines make and remake their everyday social world. The analysis of drinking might begin with the recognition that Aborigines construct their relationships with each other through the sharing of liquor. Indeed, sharing liquor is a fundamental way in which some Aborigines order their contemporary communities.

Credit and the Sharing of Liquor

A number of analysts have noted that liquor is a valued item in the exchange patterns of some Aboriginal communities (Albrecht 1969; Beckett 1964; Sackett 1977; Waddell 1973), yet none has made this observation the starting point of a more general analysis. For example, Beckett states that people approved the sharing of liquor "since it involves merrymaking and excitement" (Beckett 1964, 42). Sackett follows a number of other analysts in observing that men who treated their peers generously to liquor could reasonably expect food and more drink in return because "the traditional system of reciprocity still operates" (Sackett 1977, 92). For them the relationship of liquor to transactions in other kinds of goods is unproblematic, but there was more to what they observed than mere excitement or traditional norms of reciprocity. It is crucial to relate the sharing of liquor to the sharing of other goods, particularly food. Moreover, a thorough analysis must link transactions in food and liquor, for example, to the conditions that determine their availability to various categories of people.

The data Beckett and Sackett present are quite interesting in this respect because the communities they studied share many characteristics with Mt Kelly. In particular, the men of all three communities work primarily in the cattle industry and maintain links with other people whose main forms of income are social security pensions of various types. The preceding chapter analysed how men establish themselves in the cattle industry, and it was noted that even highly skilled men must anticipate breaks in their work periods. The summer stand-down, the death of pastoral bosses, the sale of stations and other reasons make cattlework irregular and subject to systematic (as well as contingent) discontinuities. Men with access to several employers can usually find new jobs when necessary but they must occasionally rely on credit from other people to survive and stay available for future work. Pensioners are key sources of credit to the Mt Kelly workers. Unlike discontinuous cattle income, pensions are continuous. Pensioners usually have surplus income they can lend to people who are less fortunate and they are sometimes eager to lend money to people who under normal circumstances have access to other resources, such as cattle wages. By granting credit, a pensioner lays claim to the debtor's productivity.

In the context of domestic credit, a man's boss acquires a critical significance. A man's boss guarantees his credit and substantiates his identity as a productive worker. A man with many bosses has access to extensive credit. If a man has no bosses, few people will grant them anything but the most modest subsistence. Such men receive charity, not credit. Given the breaks in cattlework, few men could work in the industry without access to occasional sources of domestic credit. The general point is that few men could survive without access both to work and to credit. Most men require access to both in order to have access to either. Without work and credit, men neither work nor acquire credit.

The concept of credit is not immediately transparent. There are different types of credit and different types of social entities that grant it. The two types of credit are realized and potential. Realized credit is the sum total of goods and services an individual has actually received on credit. Potential credit is that volume of goods and services an individual could legitimately acquire on credit if necessary. The exact relationship between an individual's realized and potential credit is variable and subject to negotiation. Characteristically the amount of an individual's potential credit is not explicitly stated. Rather, there are crucial moments when an individual's credit rating is made public. For example, when a man first receives credit, his creditor might make general statements about his worth and the relative size of his potential credit. In the context of a longstanding relationship, there are occasions on which (often mutual) declarations of good-will and credit worthiness must be made if potential credit is to be maintained. Such statements tend to be vague. When a man's credit is exhausted or nearly exhausted, his creditor might require special documentation of his position and explicitly state the limits of more credit.

Two types of social entities grant credit: specific people and generalized collectivities. Individuals grant both realized and potential credit. However, it may also be true that a man enjoys a reputation for credit worthiness within a greater or lesser range of people. Although an individual's specific creditors belong to the range of people who recognize his credit worthiness, the important point is that the greater range may also include people who have not yet but might actually become specific creditors. These potential creditors are important especially in an uncertain context in which the fate of an individual's specific creditors and of his relationship with them fluctuates.

A complex field of uncertainty surrounds potential creditors. A man cannot generally know who (if any) among his potential creditors will be able to grant him credit when necessary. More fundamental problems emerge from the fact that the potential credit granted by general collectivities is often quite tacit, that is, no one may ever state the amount of credit an individual might potentially enjoy. Furthermore, no one may explicitly agree to act as a creditor in the future. Indeed, individuals might deny obligations to extend credit when asked. In order to establish a fund of potential credit among a generalized collectivity, therefore, an individual must develop means to articulate what his potential creditors may wish to keep tacit. This is especially true in situations in which credit resources are scarce and the demand is high.

These ideas about credit provide the basis of a theory about the use of liquor and the relationship of liquor to other items of exchange among contemporary Aboriginal people in Alice Springs – the full scheme is developed below. Note for now, however, that the "binge drinking" or "sprees" for which white bushmen were earlier so famous and which are now the focus of so much attention in some Aboriginal communities are particularly appropriate ways of establishing potential credit among a generalized collectivity. They are public affairs in which varying numbers of people accept a highly valued good from an individual who often makes his "generosity" explicit. Such sprees are rational adaptations to situations in which individuals may experience quite radical changes of personal fortune in the course of their careers. In such situations, individuals must develop credit, deny short-term benefits for long-term opportunities and commit themselves to the well-being of the community in order to secure their own well-being. Aborigines in Alice Springs live in such a situation.

The intersection of the defined characteristics of credit produces a four-cell property space: realized credit from a specific person; realized credit from a generalized collectivity; potential credit from a specific person; and potential credit from a generalized collectivity. Particular forms and items of exchange fall into each of the four spaces in Mt Kelly.

Realized credit from a specific person. People in Mt Kelly grant others credit in the form of domestic resources, that is, as food, small amounts of money and occasionally liquor from the creditor's personal supply. Such credit is usually repaid in lump sums of money after the debtor returns from a period of employment. Otherwise people who obtain credit may in turn support past creditors with food, money or liquor. The paradigmatic exchange of this kind is between the men who work on cattle stations and their close kinsmen, especially their parents. It is important to note that the men cannot rely exclusively upon their kinsmen for credit. Although most men initially turn to close kinsmen, the majority eventually also must recruit creditors from non-kinsmen, especially affines. The parents of a man's spouse are crucial sources of credit. Otherwise, men have to find credit among totally unrelated people both inside and outside Mt Kelly.

Realized credit from a generalized collectivity. The only credit the generalized collectivity in Mt Kelly could grant was the right to live in the camp. Since the ultimate right to live in Mt Kelly was determined by the heads of the individual camps, even this was highly circumscribed. Yet, particular people were more or less welcome in Mt Kelly as a whole. Moreover, the kind of credit an individual could ultimately expect to receive was related to how widely recognized was his right to live in the community. This was especially true for white men given that the community frequently had to protect them from the attacks of welfare officers and other agents of the wider society. In general, the right to live in Mt Kelly gave some access to the resources available there.

Potential credit from a specific person. Individuals maintained their good standing with creditors in a variety of ways. A man was basically credit-worthy if he was affluent, that is, if he possessed the capacity to generate wealth (Sahlins 1974). Men with a number of good bosses or with a good job in town are locally considered affluent in this sense; so, too, are pensioners. However, individuals have to work to keep their credit-worthiness. They have to pay their debts. They also must present their creditors with small gifts on appropriate occasions. When men return home from the bush, for example, they usually pay their creditors a lump sum of money and give them presents: bottles of wine, a case of beer, a night on the town, a side of meat from the boss or perhaps some tailor-made cigarettes. Individuals present these gifts directly to their creditors. They do not present them as parts of public dispersements (although specific creditors sometimes attend such occasions).

There is also a system of exchange widely dispersed throughout the Aboriginal population of Alice Springs that falls into this category. It so happens that pension day and payday fall on alternate weeks. Pensions arrive at the post office on every other Thursday. Workers are paid on the Friday of the week following pension week. On pension days, many pensioners give closely related workers ten dollars from their pension cheques. Occasionally, they also give them small bottles of port or other gifts. On payday, the workers return the ten dollars and also occasionally make small gifts. The exchanges are almost always exactly balanced. I observed these exchanges break down only when one party could no longer afford to reciprocate or during quarrels. I suggest, therefore, that these exchanges are markers of social relationships and potential credit among individuals.

Potential credit from a generalized collectivity. The sharing of liquor comes into its own during the great sprees of Mt Kelly life. Although there are small sprees each weekend, the greatest such occasions occur when the young men return from the bush and "shout" the entire community to large quanitities of beer and invalid port. The distinctive thing about the sprees is that there are few restrictions on who may participate and share in the liquor: everyone in Mt Kelly is welcome, and kinsmen and friends who live elsewhere often visit the camp and share the drink on such occasions. Although I never saw anyone denied liquor, it is probably true that strangers or enemies may not join the parties. The major point is that the sprees are unrestricted affairs and open to all comers within the broadest possible range of the Mt Kelly people's social universe.

Although the sprees are open, their social composition is not undifferentiated. Some people in Mt Kelly refuse to attend either particular people's sprees or sprees generally. Three adults (two women and one man) do not drink liquor in Mt Kelly. Sometimes they wander over to the site of the sprees, imitate humorously the slurred speech of the drinkers and comment wryly on the scene. Usually they remain in their own camps and officially ignore the festivities.

There are, however, people who drink liquor but rarely attend sprees. If they do arrive on the scene, they usually bring a bottle of their own. Once I was sitting in the camp of a young man who never attends sprees. His uncle came over and invited him to a drink. The uncle hardly ever works and is usually dependent upon his close kinsmen for everything. However, on this occasion he had just returned from a two-week stint out bush and was treating all comers to liquor. The nephew refused the invitation and said that he never went to anybody else's camp for a drink. On the other hand, the nephew drinks considerably and regularly supplies beer to the other young men of the community. Indeed, the uncle usually depends upon his nephew for liquor. I interpret the nephew's rejection of the invitation as a refusal to become in any way indebted to his uncle. By denying his uncle's liquor, he prevented the older man from repaying past debts and establishing credit for the future. He thereby maintained his uncle's indebtedness and his own control over what he had to grant him in the future. The point is that the nephew did not consider the uncle a potential creditor, nor had he ever depended upon him in the past. Hence, he was able to refuse his uncle's gift. Because the uncle was generally considered to be "rubbish" and the nephew was trying to establish himself as an independent, self-reliant man, it would have been unseemly for him to have accepted the liquor. By rejecting it, he marked clearly his relationship with his uncle and made a statement about what he considered to be his social identity.

This analysis holds for the other people who refuse to attend sprees or take their own liquor. They are pensioners who have secure incomes. Moreover, they have constructed what are locally considered highly successful and significant careers. They regularly support other members of the community and enjoy reputations as "good", that is, generous, people. They are the most prestigious people in Mt Kelly. They also each maintain quite aggressively independent self-presentations. It is significant that they maintain a set of dyadic, balanced-exchange relationships. By staying out of the sprees these people maintain control of the flow of goods and services between themselves and the community. They thereby mark and maintain their independence of others. They also ensure that they maintain control over the claims for credit others might lodge. They can grant and refuse credit as it suits their interests. The credit they grant is expensive because it does not emerge from a background of debt or obligation. Their reputations for generosity, indeed, depend upon the fact that they grant credit in the face of no obligation or apparent need to do so.

Who then attends the great sprees? There are always a certain number of people who "come for the grog", people who, it is known, either cannot or probably will not ever reciprocate. They are the camp's "rubbishmen" or casual visitors who happen to be around on the big day. An individual's willingness to shout such people rebounds to his own credit and documents his "generosity". It constitutes evidence of his disinterestedness in the transaction. However, the relationship between the host and the majority of his guests is more complex. In many respects the sharing of liquor has all the elements of gifts which "are voluntary, disinterested and spontaneous but which are in fact obligatory and interested" (Mauss 1969, 1). Other than the rubbishmen there are essentially two categories of people who attend sprees: a man's fellow workers and people (often women) in his social universe who control domestic resources. The point is that by shouting these people a man constructs potential access to jobs from his fellow workers and potential credit in domestic resources from the rest. It is again important to note that the sprees are not restricted gatherings. Although a man's close kinsmen often attend the sprees, they are not usually alone: non-kinsmen also attend. Furthermore the sprees are not domestic gatherings and no food is served. Indeed, for a spree to be most successful a man has to attract both non-kinsmen and people outside his own domestic group. In such a way, he creates an obligation among people who might otherwise owe him nothing. In the last analysis, it is important to note that the people who attend sprees also have an interest in the host. By coming to the spree, they make a claim on further resources the host might offer then and in the future. Debts of liquor and the credit they imply constitute resources for gaining access to the host's productivity and are a means of competing for his attention.

It is important that the sprees are held in public. Given the tacit and therefore uncertain nature of potential credit, a public demonstration of indebtedness is important in actually establishing an enforceable credit obligation. The element of display is crucial in at least two ways. It forces someone who wants liquor and perhaps other resources to come forth and accept it before an audience; and the number of people who actually come to a spree and accept liquor is a measure of the host's value to the people in his social universe. Hence, liquor debts are established in settings that visibly mark the relative value of the credit which might be offered in exchange. The broader the range of people a man might call upon for credit, the less dependent he is upon any one source, and, all other things being equal, the less valuable is each one to him. Given this observation, it is therefore all the more significant that some of the most generous people never attend sprees. By staying out of the sprees, they counter the effect of the public display and rely upon private negotiations between themselves and people who want credit.

The cost of credit is quite high and bears a direct relationship to what men spend to repay past debts. In effect, men must spend everything they make beyond what they need to meet their basic needs and repay old debts on liquor for the community as a whole. It is men who successfully appear to exhaust their surplus resources on liquor for the community who develop "generous" reputations. The rate at which men so spend their resources is also important. It indicates the confidence they have in their capacity to return to work and thereby once again displays their value. In other words, the sharing of liquor on a grand scale portrays a familiar three-party set of transactions. The sharing of liquor does not mark a direct return on past credit. On the contrary, it depends upon the existence of a third agent between a man and his creditors who grants him the means to earn the goods to repay his debts. In the case of the men who work out bush, the third agent is their cattle boss. The cattle boss mediates between a man and his creditors and between original and repaid credit. However, the cattle boss also provides men with more than they need simply to repay past debts and survive in the meantime. Indeed, by working for a cattle boss men produce a yield above and beyond their initial credit and basic needs. It is that yield which men spend on the grand liquor sprees. Quite seriously, the liquor is the *hau* or "spirit" of past credit. By throwing great sprees to all comers, men return the yield of their past credit to the ultimate source of all potential credit and thereby maintain their right to ask for more (Sahlins 1974; Mauss 1969).

So it is that liquor marks a man's affluence or productivity. The more liquor a man provides, the greater his apparent surplus.

His surplus both directly measures his past relationship with his boss and promises further production in the future. Two interesting points follow from this. The longer men are out bush and, therefore, the longer between sprees, the greater their production and credit-worthiness; the time a man spends out bush is itself an element in his display of value. It is also true that the time a man spends in town when he might otherwise be able to work out bush equally displays his productivity. By displaying his boss's willingness to wait upon him, a man documents vividly his productive capacity and the source of his worth. It is for this reason that men sometimes voluntarily break work and come into town to drink. Unto itself, this produces a characteristic work pattern in which men alternate between work out bush and drunken binges in town. A drunken binge is a display of productivity, confidence and collateral.

Liquor and the Theme of Personal Independence

Among the Mt Kelly people, an individual's productivity measures and establishes the conditions for independence from others. Because liquor marks an individual's productivity, it takes on its broadest significance as a measure of personal independence and thereby becomes somewhat autonomous from the realm of credit and interpersonal assistance. Indeed, it is precisely liquor's capacity to make subtle distinctions on the theme of personal independence that accounts for its wide use in the exchanges I have described.

The process of sharing liquor has two properties that promote its use in this way. First, as a fluid substance, liquor can be divided into greater or lesser amounts of no predetermined size. It is also true, however, that liquor comes packaged in established, well-known units. Each unit of whatever size has value.[1] Hence, a man can make very precise and subtle distinctions between people simply by varying the amount of liquor he shares with them. He can compel others to share his liquor from a communal cup which is passed around or he can make personal gifts of small bottles or flagons of port and cans or cases of beer. Units of liquor can be matched to fit the occasion and carefully mark the nature of the relationship between the donor and recipient as well as their relative prestige.[2] For example, it is as significant that a man accepts a mouthful of port from a communal cup as it is that his host offers it. Second, an individual may not convert liquor he receives in a public distribution into credit of his own with other people, that is, he must consume the liquor on the spot. Unlike the gift of a whole, uncooked pumpkin, for example, an individual may not save liquor and pass it on to someone else at a later date. This limits the range of debt and highlights the significance of the liquor transaction to the relationship between the host and his guest. Again, these properties of sharing liquor display the obligations being created in an unambiguous way.

It is also important to note that the type of liquor an individual drinks is a key component of social identity and mark of prestige. The Mt Kelly people rank the various types of liquor available in Alice Springs. Although there was some dispute, the rank order from most to least prestigious was as follows: spirits (rum was the most common spirit drunk in Mt Kelly although some people preferred more exotic drinks such as ouzo); beer; invalid port or sweet sherry; and methylated spirits. The Mt Kelly people rank individuals according to the rank of the liquor they drink. Spirit and beer drinkers often regard port as an inferior drink and look down upon port drinkers. Port drinkers tend to rebuff such pretensions, especially if they claim to drink beer only when nothing else is available. Beer and port drinkers alike disparage people who drink methylated spirits. Indeed, the Mt Kelly people categorize and rank whole groups of people according to what they think is the locally prominent drink. For example, the Mt Kelly people refer to the people who live in the Todd River as "Todd frogs". They regard the "Todd frogs" as inferior people who are "no-hopers" on their way to death. They also regard the Todd as a dangerous place. If a Mt Kelly resident moves into the Todd, the other residents express concern for his safety and encourage him to come home. According to the Mt Kelly people, the distinguishing feature about the "Todd frogs" is that they drink methylated spirits. The Mt Kelly people say that such people will "drink anything" and tell stories of "Todd frogs" who were poisoned to death after having drunk from flagons they found lying in the creekbed. The stories allege that hostile whites occasionally put strychnine in half-empty flagons to catch unsuspecting drunks.

A number of characteristics define this local categorization of liquor. People rank themselves according to the cost of their favourite drink. Those who spend more rank themselves higher than those who spend less. At one level this is a straightforward marker of an individual's affluence. However, the cost scale is also related to an individual's alleged capacity to control his drink; for example, beer drinkers consider those who drink port to be "grog mad", that is, unable in a complex sense to hold their drink. The point is that port is higher than beer in alcoholic content per dollar spent. It takes less to get drunk. Consequently, beer drinkers allege that people who drink port are only interested in getting drunk as quickly and cheaply as possible. Again, port drinkers deny these allegations. However, they and the beer drinkers consider meth drinkers "grog mad". In other words, the cost and alcoholic content of particular types of liquor is metaphorically linked with an individual's ability to control himself. The putative desire to get drunk quickly (be under the control of liquor) is related to an individual's power to be independent of other people. The capacity to spend more and control oneself while drinking marks the truly independent man.

The Mt Kelly people use these meanings of liquor to chart the ups and downs of an individual's career as well as to label people. For example, the Mt Kelly men use the type of liquor they drink to mark changes in their personal employment situations. When I first started fieldwork in Alice Springs, George Sharp had been unemployed for six months and was living on credit from his parents. They shared their liquor with him as well as their food. Because they preferred to drink port, George also drank port. However, George began to work for a local Aboriginal agency in April 1975. When I moved into Mt Kelly in May, George remarked that he no longer drank port, only beer and ouzo. According to George the change in his drinking tastes signalled a whole new phase of his life. He declared that he was altogether more responsibile for himself than he had been in the previous five years. Drinking beer instead of port marked his intention to continue in his newfound ways. The men who worked out bush frequently made similar statements to me. The cattle market was depressed during my fieldwork and work was short. The young men spent more time than usual in Mt Kelly living off their creditors. After the men were out of work for some time, they had to depend on others for liquor. They usually had to drink port. However, when they returned to Mt Kelly flush with their cattle wages they commented that they too have given up port and only drank "this stuff", pointing to the cans of beer they carried about with them.

The logic of this marking system also works in the other direction. People comment upon "downward" changes in a man's drinking tastes. If a man who usually drinks beer begins to be seen drinking port, people know he is running short of money. People know he is broke when he begins to drink port only from other people's flagons. People present their own situations in such terms as well. One night I was walking around Mt Kelly when I saw a light coming from Ronnie Elliotson's house. Ronnie was living in Mt Kelly against his wishes and on the sufferance of Terry and Isabel Sharp. He had earlier lived with his family in his own caravan on a private site adjacent to the camp. However, he had lost his job and fallen behind in his loan repayments. When the caravan was repossessed he had moved into Mt Kelly. He was a charity case and dependent upon the Sharps. When I poked my head through the door, I found him sitting disconsolately on his bed. He complained bitterly about Terry and Isabel and bemoaned their abusive ways. He noted that before he had often fed the Sharp children when Terry and Isabel had drunk all the food money in plonk. All they did now, however, was rubbish him. They would not find him so soft-hearted in the future. Ronnie remarked, "In those days I had two refrigerators: one half-full of meat, and the other full of beer".

Ronnie's link between meat and beer was significant. On several occasions I witnessed people get up from sprees and stagger off toward their own camps. Sometimes an individual would walk a certain distance and vomit into the dirt. The people remaining at the spree often would watch and comment upon the contents of the vomit, especially if only fluid appeared to come out. On such occasions people shook their heads and said that the sick person had stopped eating. He only drank plonk now. The point is that such remarks were only ever made about the most dependent people in Mt Kelly. The fact that they vomited only fluid meant that no one was feeding them. In other words, they no longer had access to a domestic group that would give them food. Rather, they could get charity solely at the all-comers' sprees at which only liquor was served. A person without a family is absolute rubbish. There is only one step lower than this in the mind of the Mt Kelly people: to move into the creek and become a "Todd frog". Although the move horrified the Mt Kelly people, a number of men were forced by circumstance to adopt this tactic.

The Mt Kelly people also associated drinking liquor with the sophistication of white urban life. The Mt Kelly people claim to be able to handle liquor, unlike the "myall blackfellows" from the bush. The different types of liquor graded degrees of sophistication. Spirit and beer drinkers consider themselves more sophisticated than port or methylated spirit drinkers. George Sharp, for example, preferred to drink ouzo. He was very widely travelled; during his tour of duty with the Australian army, he had fought in Borneo, Malaysia and Vietnam. The Mt Kelly people considered him very sophisticated. The fact that he drank ouzo (an expensive and very unusual drink) marked his uniqueness. His taste for mushrooms and Chinese food bespoke the same sophistication.

More generally, liquor creates the opportunity for displays of connoisseurship. The Mt Kelly people all have particular likes and dislikes in brands of liquor. The railroad from Adelaide was the major means of freight transport to Alice Springs from the south; on one occasion, about two weeks after floods had cut the line, the local supply of the most popular brand of invalid port ran dry. Consequently, the Mt Kelly people had to purchase what they considered off-brands of port. As they drank the different brands they commented extensively on their relative merits and demerits. Some types were too sweet, others too bitter. Everyone was overjoyed when the rail service resumed operation and the regular brand again became available. Some people display a perhaps more telling preference: they prefer to drink sweet sherry rather than port. Sweet sherry, they claim, does not destroy the appetite or leave a hangover. A man can drink sweet sherry all night and still eat or go to work the next day. Invalid port, they note, leaves a man so drunk he fails to eat and cannot possibly work. This highlights my earlier points about food, employment and liquor. Note however that connoisseurship constitutes an exercise of skilful judgment in which a concern for the taste of the liquor is asserted at the expense of its effect. Insofar as others respect a man's taste, they legitimate his judgment and his right to have a preference. They authenticate his claim to be interested in liquor for something other than its intoxicating powers. They thereby accept his implicit claims for knowledge and independence.

In general, liquor signifies power and affluence. The person who purchases the bottle and shouts others at a spree is known as "the boss". I have analysed elsewhere the significance of the term "boss" to the Mt Kelly people. In general, white men are bosses. By claiming to be the boss of the bottle, an individual associates his capacity to buy liquor and his own social identity with the power of whites. Although this interpretation may seem far-fetched, its force was made vivid to me one night in Mt Kelly. I was returning to my caravan when I heard someone singing in Don Corcoran's camp. I walked over and found Don and Larry Rainer drinking invalid port. Don was providing the liquor. Larry rarely worked and always depended upon others for his drink. When I walked up, Larry turned to me and said, "When I drink, I'm whitefellow, not a blackfellow. We (Larry and Don) are two whitefellows."

Larry's comment raises the question of how the Mt Kelly people interpret being drunk. For them getting drunk is a shedding of shame. This affected my interaction with some people. Once I was sitting in George Sharp's grandmother's camp. A number of people were gathered around drinking, including George's wife. We were discussing her home country and the question of her language arose. She was from a cattle station north of Tennant Creek and spoke a language quite alien to the Arunta and Anmatjira spoken in the camp. I asked her if she would teach me a few words. She said she would, but only after she had become drunk, she added. She was too shy otherwise, she said. I was quite friendly with one middle-aged woman in Mt Kelly who was a paraplegic. I ran most of her errands and bought all her liquor. I tried several times to discuss her life history when she was sober. However, each time she refused sheepishly. I eventually gave up my efforts and resigned myself to the snippets I had gathered from gossip and odd talk. One day she rolled up in the wheelchair apparently quite drunk. She said that it was okay now, she would give me her life story.

The Mt Kelly people did not reserve this interpretation of their drunkenness for me alone. A couple of people explicitly told me that they lost shame when they drank. They also commented that they were much more forward with whites when they were drunk. I saw this in action one night when the Country Party of Alice Springs organized a public rally to petition the Labor government to reinstate subsidies on freight charges on the railroad. The subsidies had been important in giving pastoralists more profit on the cattle they railed south. I attended this rally with George Sharp. We had been out hunting kangaroos and, as was our custom, had consumed a fair amount of beer during our expedition. We showed up at the rally feeling no pain. About midway through the rally, the Speaker of the Northern Territory Legislative Assembly got up to speak. He began to abuse the Labor Party and encourage people to send telegrams to Gough Whitlam demanding the subsidy be reinstated. George began to harangue the speaker in return. He yelled that the speaker should petition Canberra for better housing for Aborigines and he continued to heckle the rally for the rest of the evening. He was one of the few Aborigines at the rally and the only one to speak. The next morning he commented to me that he probably would have said nothing had he been sober.

I hesitate to analyse this process in terms of a loss of agression-control or the absence of norms of drunken comportment (Fink 1960; Sackett 1977). Drunken behaviour is not the only way Mt Kelly people reject white society (Beckett 1964). Such theories ignore the fact that the Mt Kelly people themselves interpret the experience of drunkenness in much the same way they interpret liquor, that is, as an experience of personal power. Insofar as the people interpret being drunk as an experience and expression of their personal power, drinking makes action possible; in other words, it helps create the conditions for people to enact their images of personal power both among themselves and with others.

Liquor, Children and Domestic Income

The discussion of food and liquor returns this discussion to the beginning of the analysis. Men and women use resources from the non-domestic and domestic domains, respectively, to justify access to, and control of, resources derived from the other. In the light of the analysis of liquor, therefore, it is significant that two related trends have emerged in recent years: women have begun to drink liquor and men have begun to assume direct control of domestic resources, especially children. It is difficult to date or measure the strength of these trends, yet it is clear that they are developing.

Beckett states that Aboriginal women did not drink liquor in his field area (Beckett 1964). Although for the last twenty-five years welfare officers have removed children from women in Alice Springs they considered hopeless drunks, the number of women who drink regularly seems to have increased considerably. Women are among the heaviest drinkers in Mt Kelly.

They take particularly active roles and often sponsor the regular, small sprees that occur each pension weekend. From my observations, there is little reason to suspect that the Mt Kelly women are unique in the town. It is also true the Mt Kelly men take an active interest in their spouses' children. I observed one man banish his wife and keep his daughter. It is more common, however, for men to proclaim publicly that they will foster the children their spouses have borne to other men. Indeed, such a proclamation seems a major sign that a man and woman intend to establish a connubial relationship. I would like to suggest that these trends mark the attempts of men and women to coopt each other's subsistence resources and tactics. By manipulating liquor, women are trying to legitimate access to male resources. For their part, men hope to gain direct access to domestic resources and control their women by caring for the family's children.

Why should these trends have developed? It is significant that opportunities for Aboriginal men and women have declined considerably in Central Australia over the last ten years. Although women still enjoy privileged access to the resources welfare agencies control, the demand for female labour in Alice Springs has dropped since the introduction of cash wages in 1967. It is now very difficult for women to supplement their pension incomes. Moreover, supporting mothers face an inevitable decline in their pension incomes as their children mature. These circumstances have introduced a degree of uncertainty in the long-term position of women which was earlier substantially limited to men. Older women have responded to the new situation by becoming grandmothers. That is, they have tried to assume control of their daughters' children and thereby extend their rights to welfare support. It is now common to find large households in Alice Springs composed of an older woman, her daughters and her grandchildren. There is one such domestic group in Mt Kelly. However, I suggest that these circumstances also explain why women have begun to drink. By shouting other people to drink when their pensions are at a peak, they develop long-term credit to meet the day when their pensions begin to decline. They also legitimate claims upon the resources their men produce in the meantime.

The opportunities for men have also declined. Although there has been a minor expansion of job opportunities for men in Alice Springs in recent years, there has been a major decline in the demand for labour in the pastoral industry. The uncertainty previously inherent in pastoral work has been augmented by the general shortage of jobs. Access to secure, alternative sources of domestic income have become even more important for men. Hence, they too have begun to use children as a resource. However, these circumstances have also encouraged men to invest even more resources in liquor. The award wage is significant in this context. Since 1967 Aboriginal pastoral workers in the Northern Territory have qualified for the award wage. Although the wage is still low compared with most forms of urban work, it is substantially higher than the sum Aboriginal men previously enjoyed. It also includes a substantially greater proportion of cash which, as mentioned above, is paid in one lump sum at the end of each employment period. It has been noted that men have to spend any surplus income they earn on liquor for the general community in order to maintain their right to credit. If this is so, it is possible to understand that the award wage has actually provided greater surpluses than were previously possible, and thereby more money to spend on liquor. Hence, precisely because men face an increasingly difficult employment situation, they must spend ever more on liquor.

These circumstances explain why there has been a general increase in the level of drinking among Aboriginal people in Alice Springs: they are trying to develop funds of credit against long-term uncertainties by spending current surpluses on liquor. There is keen competition for legitimate access to increasingly scarce sources of domestic income. The rights to control liquor and children are crucial resources in these negotiations. The attempts by men and women to gain control of liquor and children generated many conflicts and much violence in Mt Kelly.

Conclusion

Liquor and the exchange of liquor are key elements in the processes by which the Mt Kelly people construct their social lives It involves relationships between men and women, parents and children, creditors and debtors, the powerful and the weak, sophisticates and the naive, the independent and the dependent, domestic and non-domestic groups. Liquor invokes the entire social universe of Mt Kelly. Indeed, its exchange often mediated between Mt Kelly's various contrasting elements in crucial ways. Was liquor in Mt Kelly a total prestation? I think that in spite of its capacity to express the total social identities of the parties to a transaction, liquor was not a total prestation; this was because it linked individuals not groups with relatively ephemeral, impermanent relationships. However, I pose the question in order to suggest ways to analyse drinking in other Aboriginal communities which may perhaps still be organized in terms of corporate kin groups. It may well be, for example, that the massive drinking sprees that periodically occur on settlements in Arnhem Land are latterday potlatches in which various local groups shout each other to liquor. It is certainly true that liquor has become an important item of ceremonial exchange elsewhere (for example, in the Te-exchange among the Enga). Perhaps an analysis of drinking on these settlements in terms of exchange might reap dividends.

As for Mt Kelly, it is clear that liquor is a major form of what Bourdieu calls "symbolic capital" (Bourdieu 1977, 181).

> Once one realizes that symbolic capital is always credit, in the widest sense of the word, i.e. a sort of advance which the group alone can grant those who give it the best material and symbolic guarantees, it can be seen that the exhibition of symbolic capital (which is always very expensive in economic terms) is one of the mechanisms which (no doubt universally) makes capital go to capital.

Notes

1. The significance of this might be gauged by comparing the value of a mouthful of port with a mouthful of food.
2. Professor Meggitt says that, among the Enga, packaged units of liquor (especially cartons of beer) are now units of value in the Te-exchange cycle (personal communication).

7

Violence, Debt and the Negotiation of Exchange

In the preceding chapter, the sharing of liquor related to patterns of credit and domestic exchange in Mt Kelly was explained. However, the conditions under which people recognized the commensurability of particular items in exchange was not discussed; for example, that people would exchange liquor for domestic resources was taken as relatively unproblematic. It was observed that people do not always want to recognize a debt and the public nature of drinking sprees was explained in that context. This chapter will extend the implications of that observation by noting that the relative commensurability of exchange items is negotiable – subject to situational redefinition – and that it is a major problem in the everyday life of Mt Kelly. Of major importance is the point that the patterns of interpersonal violence which regularly punctuate Mt Kelly life emerge from the problem of commensurability. Violence erupts in situations in which key exchange items are rendered incommensurable. Because liquor is such an important item in the exchange relationships of the Mt Kelly people, violence often erupts during drinking sessions. However, liquor is merely one (albeit highly significant) exchange item and is related to other, broader spheres of exchange. The overall significance of violence, therefore, must not be understood as limited to liquor-dominated contexts. Rather, violence must be set in the context of all exchanges in Mt Kelly and the social relationships they help create.

Some Theories of Violence

The analysis of interpersonal violence among Australian Aborigines has developed no more than the analysis of drinking liquor. Violence is usually linked with drinking as a symptom of cultural breakdown, frustration and stress, particularly in so-called "detribalized" communities (Cawte 1972; Fink 1960; Rowley 1973). This approach uses elements of frustration-aggression theory and alienation theory (Dollard 1967; Berkowitz 1972; Fanon 1967). The argument asserts that because Aborigines (or colonized peoples in general) cannot express their outrage against the colonial order through revolution, they must discharge frustration among themselves. Rowley notes, for example, that violence among contemporary Aborigines is a manifestation of their disunity and resentment in the face of "overwhelming social forces" (Rowley 1973, 236). The main function of violence, according to this analysis, is catharsis and mystification.

Although violence among the Mt Kelly people is certainly related to the structure of their relationships with white society, the frustration-aggression theory takes no serious notice of that fact. Alienation theory emphasizes the structure of domination within which indigenous people must live, but neither approach treats violence as anything more than an expressive explosion and each limits its analytical significance to its bio-psychological effects upon aggressors. They completely ignore the interactional significance of violence, that is, how violence affects the social relationships among the aggressor, the victim and the wider audience. They deny explicitly that violence helps restructure interaction and can be an active component in the ways people define and construct their social relationships. Violence is a form of deviance that must be cured either through therapy or revolution.

Although it has not yet been applied to Australian Aborigines, there is a large body of literature that explains interpersonal violence in terms of an overarching culture or subculture of violence (Wolfgang and Ferracutti 1967, 95-164; Toch 1972, 71). The subculture of violence thesis argues that in some societies there are norms that compel men to respond violently in certain circumstances. The strength of this approach is that it notes that interpersonal violence is legitimate in some societies. Insofar as it counters the idea that interpersonal violence must necessarily be deviant, it corrects certain aspects of the frustration-aggression hypothesis. Yet, like the frustration-aggression hypothesis, it interprets violence as merely part of a syndrome or cultural complex. Violent behaviour is simply the result of a normative orientation toward violence. As Blok notes, it is therefore tautological and poses no problems for analysis; rather, it stops inquiry by reifying norms and decontextualizing violent interaction (Blok 1974, 176).

Toch's attempt to integrate the subculture of violence thesis with the typologies of violent men and violent contexts does not really overcome this problem. Although he stresses how violence emerges in interaction, he assumes that only violence-prone men will react violently. According to him, men who lack the predisposition to violence construct their interactional sequences in a more peaceful manner. Toch contrasts his approach with game-theory, which begins with the assumption that men act rationally to maximize their self-interest. He notes that he wants to study the "perceptions and motives and needs of real players in concrete settings. We must study the psychological results of their motives, in the sense of finding out how one person's action affects the other person's feelings and perceptions, and how this second person acts as a result" (Toch 1972, 71). Through his emphasis on violence as a psychological process, Toch makes acts of violence epiphenomenal manifestations of inner urges and reduces such concepts as honour, self-esteem and identity to internalized norms. His approach complements the normative approach of Wolfgang and Ferracutti by showing how violence is functional for individuals as well as a basic cultural norm. He thereby vitiates what use he makes of interactional analysis and recasts the problem in terms of individual psychosis, not social interaction.

In his study of terror, E.V. Walters summarizes the major deficiencies of these approaches. "An inclination to identify violence with disorder leads many observers to think of repetitive violence exclusively as a product of disorganization, and they do not stop to inquire if it might be sometimes the principle of a certain kind of order" (Walters 1972, 245). Although Walters emphasizes the extent to which violence is a legitimate part of the Zulus' political culture under Shaka, unlike Wolfgang, Ferracutti and Toch, he focuses his analysis on how violence constructs the relationship between the rulers and the ruled. According to Walters, in terroristic regimes violence displays the omnipotence of the ruler and creates fear in subjects who witness it. Insofar as violence breaks the subject's resistance to the tyrant's rule, it actually helps create his power.

Walters also focuses on the relationship between violence and the structure of the broader context within which it occurs. He explains Shaka's terror, for example, as an instrument in his attempt to build a despotic state from a fragmentary society hitherto based on the domestic mode of production. The function of the terror was to undermine the ability of the smaller units in Zulu society to resist the demands of the state. In contrast to Wolfgang, Ferracutti and Toch, the precise relationship between violent transactions and the wider context of social control is problematic and defines different types of social systems.

Anton Blok (1974) also examines the relationship between interpersonal violence among the Mafiosi and systems of social control. In Sicily, however, violence does not create a tighter integration between the state and local populations. Rather, because violence forces peasants to depend upon local power brokers, it separates them from the state and binds them to its *de facto* representatives. The code of "omerta", moreover, enjoins local patterns of solidarity and secrecy that preclude peasants from appealing to high state functionaries and isolates them more from the state.

In spite of these ethnographic differences, Walter and Blok share two basic points in their approach to violence: they emphasize the extent to which local people consider violence a legitimate expression and technique of social control; and they emphasize the role of fear and the capacity of violence to intimidate people. For both writers, violence is a test of strength that constructs and legitimates systems of social control through its capacity to fragment local organization and minimize resistance. Men hold power if they can engender fear and physically defeat opposition. Hence, although particular leaders may rise and fall, violence reproduces fear and perpetuates the violent political order whenever men use it to resolve conflicts.

Neither Walters nor Blok has a very well-developed theory of emotional behaviour. Consequently, they use the concept "fear" in a very commonsense way. Because fear is a critical aspect in their interactional approach to violence, they fail, therefore, to provide a particularly concise picture of the means by which violence accomplishes its work. They also fail to specify the conditions under which some men become fearful and others not.

Hence, they miss a vital point in their analysis. Insofar as they stress the display element of violence, they emphasize the communicative aspects of violent interaction; yet their inadequate concept of fear prevents them from analysing the interdependence of the emotional, communicative and exchange dimensions of a violent confrontation.

In a flawed but highly suggestive analysis of feud, Black-Michaud (1975) attempts to do this. Following Gellner's critique of segmentary lineage theory, Black-Michaud suggests that fear of aggression is the "prime mover" in feuding societies. Although he does not make it explicit, he apparently considers fear as the experience of a political order in which total anarchy constantly threatens but is contained by alliances among local groups. He suggests that the feud is the means by which alliances are made and the tenuous order of these societies emerges (Black-Michaud 1975, 87, 120–21). Like Walters and Blok, Black-Michaud observes that violence is at the very centre of the social life of the communities he examined. Without the threat of unlimited violence and the judicious use of regulated violence, feuding societies would not exist in the form observed. Building on Peters's analysis, Black-Michaud also notes that feud not only creates relationships, it communicates or marks their nature. To say that two groups either do or do not feud is "to characterize their relationship to one another" (Black-Michaud 1975, 75; Peters 1967, 268). Feud is, therefore, a mechanism for developing social relationships and a language for talking about them.

Insofar as they maintain the unity of the constructive and the communicative aspects of feuding, the analyses of Black-Michaud and Peters are productive. When Black-Michaud argues that the feud is the total social system of feuding societies, however, he fragments the phenomenon and his analysis falls apart. He makes a particularly serious error when he tries to adapt Coser to his own purposes and to differentiate "realistic" from "non-realistic" conflict (Black-Michaud 1975, 184–90). His immediate problems are to explain why sedentary agricultural societies prosecute more violent and more lethal feuds than (mobile) pastoral societies and to relate these processes to the emergence of leadership. He ultimately explains the differences between the two types of societies with reference to their different ecological circumstances. Although pastoral societies experience "total scarcity" more comprehensively than sedentary agricultural societies, land is not scarce and pastoral groups are highly mobile. Consequently, neighbouring pastoral groups can "solve" basic conflicts over scarce resources by moving away from one another. Among sedentary agricultural groups, however, land and water are supremely scarce and groups cannot move. Hence, feuds are more frequent and intense. Black-Michaud does not say, however, that feuds in sedentary societies directly concern material resources. He asserts that because serious conflicts over material resources in settled communities "lead to the appropriation of the best and the most by the strongest and the complete disintegration of the community as such", sedentary people fight over non-realistic elements, in particular, honour (Black-Michaud 1975, 193). Fighting over honour acts as a safety-valve that ensures that some people but not all suffer. Tensions are released but the society remains intact. In spite of the array of sociological references he brings to his problem, therefore, Black-Michaud ends up with a psychological and functional explanation of violence.

He concludes his analysis of the feud by asserting that it is a ritual of social relations. However, his whole approach is undermined by the basic distinction between realistic and non-realistic conflict. He restates that distinction in different terms in his definition of ritual as inefficacious, symbolic behaviour that represents but does not act upon the social reality it mirrors. He finally destroys the unity between the constructive aspects of feud by arguing that the feud only communicates. The constructive elements of feuds lie not in the process of feuding but in the way power-seeking individuals exploit the ambiguities of what is, ultimately, non-realistic conflict.

Black-Michaud's analysis (his references to Mauss and total prestations notwithstanding) is a brand of what Bourdieu calls "economism". He fails to appreciate that feuds occur in social universes where economic (realistic) resources are interconvertible with symbolic (non-realistic) resources. Indeed, as Bourdieu says, far from being inefficacious or simply expressive, honour is "perhaps the most valuable form of accumulation" in feuding societies precisely because it can be so readily converted into absolutely essential resources (Bourdieu 1977, 179). The many inconsistencies in Black-Michaud's account emerge most clearly, however, when, at the very end of his analysis, he suggests that honour might be a "medium for 'conversion' between distinct spheres of value culminating in the sphere of prestige out of which no further conversion can be made" (Black-

Michaud 1975, 239). Had he made this point the beginning of his work instead of a speculative end, he might have made the analysis Bourdieu suggests and been more faithful to the integrity of his subject.

Although these various approaches to violence each have limitations, together they posit a number of questions about particular incidents of violence. These might be summarized in terms of three general questions.

What is the nature of the contexts within which violence emerges?

What does violence do to the contexts within which it emerges?

What are the consequences of violence for the ongoing relationship between the people concerned and for their relationship to the wider context?

The major points about violence in Mt Kelly will be developed with reference to three case studies. In general, violence emerges in Mt Kelly when key items in the exchanges between people become incommensurable or inconvertible. The process of rendering key items incommensurable makes people's total role identities relevant to the situation, makes the inconsistencies in those identities apparent and compromises those identities. As a result of these processes interaction becomes non-negotiable. If there is no way for the people involved to escape the situation, violence erupts. Violence erupts in what Gilsenan calls "situations of ultimate reference" (Gilsenan 1976). Violence acts upon the situations within which it emerges by suspending the relevance of the definitions that initially constituted them and made them non-negotiable. Violence thereby re-establishes the conditions for negotiable interaction and for the emergence of a new definition of the situation. The effect of violence upon the relationship of the people concerned and upon their relationship to the wider context varies and is part of what must be renegotiated after the violence. The more people depend upon one another prior to the violence, the more they work to deny its significance. Consequently, violence reproduces the conditions for its own re-emergence in the context of those relationships that are most intimate, most multiplex, and that are ultimately constituted by the greatest degree of interdependence.

Domestic Violence in Mt Kelly

I have already presented some data about the extent to which interpersonal violence is part of everyday Mt Kelly life. One major conclusion of my analysis of the significance of the domestic group is that interpersonal violence is thematic and crucial in articulating the Mt Kelly people with the outside world. This is true for interaction between domestic groups and for individual Aboriginal people in their relationships with whites. Interpersonal violence is equally thematic and crucial for relationships within domestic groups (particularly between men and women). The prevalence of violence in everyday domestic life is one index of the extent to which the contradictions emergent from Mt Kelly people's relationships with the outside world condition relationships within their own social groups.

Table 2 presents information on the number of violent incidents that occurred during my fieldwork in Mt Kelly. The purpose of this data is not to show that the Mt Kelly people are particularly violent; rather, it is to document the types of relationships within which violent encounters emerge. Although violence is certainly seen as a legitimate form of interaction on some occasions, the Mt Kelly people are not simply "violent persons" (Toch 1972). Violence is a phenomenon related to and emergent from the nature of the Mt Kelly people's social relationships with one another.

The figures document that interpersonal violence does not occur between everyone in Mt Kelly. It is substantially limited to

Table 2   Violent encounters at Mt Kelly, April 1975 to June 1976

Total number at Mt Kelly	58
People who	
Share domestic resources, including same camp	44
Share domestic resources, not same camp	9
Do not share domestic resources	5
	58
By Gender	
Male–Female	42
Male–male	13
Female–female	3
	58
Parent–children over 15 years old	7
Parent–children under 15 years old	3

adults, in particular to adults who share domestic resources. Although some people argue that an occasional good spanking makes children respectful, parents indulge children and rarely use physical violence as a means of child-rearing. Children witness many violent incidents between adults in Mt Kelly yet they do not emulate their parents in play or use much violence among themselves. Interpersonal violence is an adult activity and emerges in an individual's life career only when he or she becomes engaged in social relationships as an adult.

Although physical violence is infrequent between parents and children, it is most frequent among adults who share domestic resources, in particular adults who live in the same camp. More than half the number of violent incidents occurred between men and women living together as spouses. Although these data show only correlations, violence in Mt Kelly apparently emerges in the context of social relationships characterized by multiplex exchanges and great interdependency. Violence outside the context of domestic exchanges is rare.

The fact that children are so seldom involved in violence suggests a general explanation of the correlation between violence and the exchange of domestic resources. Gouldner notes that in the everyday world, some people get "something for nothing" in their transactions with others. These include people who, by virtue of some special characteristic, cannot reasonably be expected to reciprocate or can reciprocate only token gestures. Children and invalids are examples of such people (Gouldner 1975). Debts incurred by people who cannot reciprocate are rendered irrelevant for their wider relationships. I suggest that violence in Mt Kelly concerns the social meaning of debt and that it occurs in contexts where this meaning becomes problematic, particularly when people become unable or are not permitted to pay their debts. Because they are being cast into the role of getting something for nothing but are none the less still subject to the rules of reciprocity, they risk being defined as perpetually dependent, less than fully adult social identities and totally subject to their debtors' control. Violence constitutes a denial of such a definition of the situation. The fact that violence occurs so often in the context of the most multiplex relationships in Mt Kelly suggests that the social meaning of debt and exchange is highly problematic. Indeed, the Mt Kelly people do not readily recognize the commensurability of different items of exchange. They do not readily permit each other to escape debt and, therefore, attempt to control one another through the manipulation of the conditions of exchange.

There are two contradictory conditions operating on relationships between men and women in Mt Kelly. On the one hand, men and women each have access to separate sources of income: for the women a variety of pensions and welfare benefits, for the men, work, mostly in the cattle industry. These two sources of income are distinct and they separate men and women. Cattlework is physically distant from the urban area. Moreover, the conditions under which women acquire pensions encourage them to withdraw into their domestic groups and minimize their social relationships with men. On the other hand, men and women depend on each other to counteract the inadequacies of their respective incomes. As a result of the seasonal nature of cattlework and other factors, men must often rely on women's incomes to survive periods of unemployment. Because most women lose access to pensions when their children mature and the possibilities for domestic work are declining, women also rely on the men's incomes. Men and women are independent of each other under some circumstances and critically dependent on each other under others. The situation generates an essential indeterminacy and makes it difficult for men and women to agree upon the nature of their relationships. Indeed, under these circumstances long-term relationships between men and women are difficult to sustain.

Case One

The first case concerns a relationship that accounted for at least six violent incidents during my fieldwork. It involved Barry Corcoran and Gladys Williams, two young Mt Kelly people who established a kangaroo relationship for six months during my fieldwork. The case is interesting because it illustrates clearly the dynamics of the relationship between pastoral and welfare incomes, the conditions that generate "matricentric" domestic groups in Mt Kelly and the significance of violence in these other processes. The point is that Barry engaged in violent interaction with Gladys and her kinsmen as he suffered a decline in his rela-

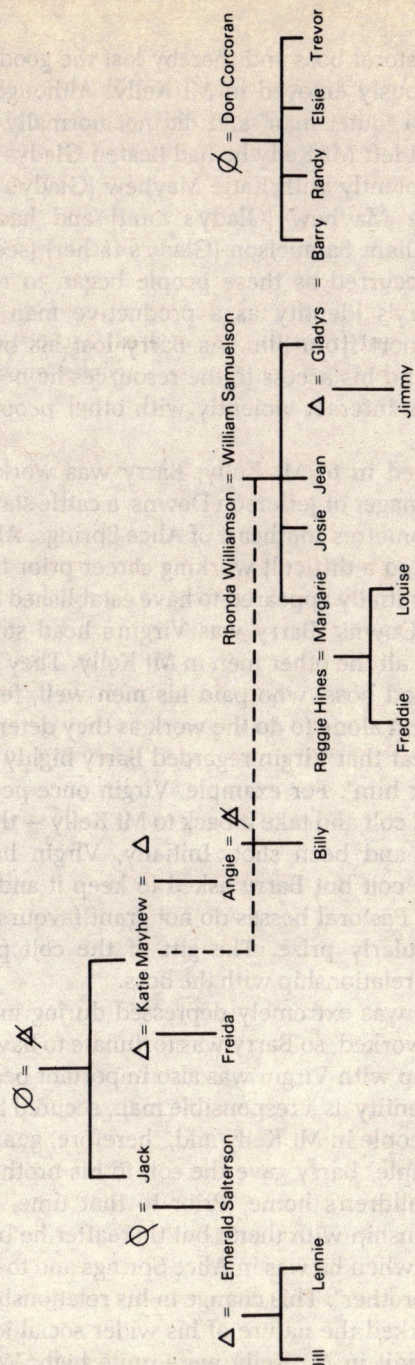

Figure 3 Case One: Extended family tree

Note: The dashed line indicates "foster children" – Margarie, Josie, Jean and Gladys were the "foster children" of Katie Mayhew.

tionship with his pastoral boss and thereby lost the good credit-rating he had previously enjoyed in Mt Kelly. Although Barry considered himself a "quiet man" and did not normally assault people, by the time I left Mt Kelly he had beaten Gladys several times, quarrelled violently with Katie Mayhew (Glady's "grand-mother") and Angie Mayhew (Glady's aunt) and had bitter arguments with William Samuelson (Glady's father) (see figure 3). The incidents occurred as these people began to redefine their image of Barry's identity as a productive man and to withdraw their support from him. As Barry lost his boss, his creditable identity and his access to the resources he needed to survive, he began to interact violently with other people (particularly his spouse).

When I first moved in to Mt Kelly, Barry was working for Clem Virgin, the manager of Jefferson Downs, a cattle station approximately 250 kilometres southeast of Alice Springs. Although Barry had experienced a difficult working career prior to being hired by Virgin, he initially appeared to have established himself nicely at Jefferson Downs. Barry was Virgin's head stockman and secured jobs for all the other men in Mt Kelly. They all considered Virgin a "good boss" who paid his men well, fed them properly and left them alone to do the work as they determined. Moreover, it was clear that Virgin regarded Barry highly and intended to "look after him". For example, Virgin once permitted Barry to save a small colt and take it back to Mt Kelly — the mare had broken its leg and been shot. Initially, Virgin had also wanted to shoot the colt but Barry asked to keep it and Virgin granted his request. Pastoral bosses do not grant favours except to men they particularly prize. The gift of the colt publicly documented Barry's relationship with the boss.

The cattle market was extremely depressed during my field-work and few men worked, so Barry was fortunate to have a job. His close relationship with Virgin was also important because it authenticated his identity as a responsible man, secured his relationship with key people in Mt Kelly and, therefore, guaranteed his credit. For example, Barry gave the colt to his brothers and sisters at a local children's home. Prior to that time, he had neglected his relationship with them; but thereafter he began to visit them regularly when he was in Alice Springs and to assume the identity of "big brother". This change in his relationship with his siblings also marked the nature of his wider social identity. His prestige and credit in Mt Kelly were quite high. When he returned from the bush, he threw great drinking sprees that were widely appreciated and well attended. Barry and Gladys also established their own household. During this period Katie Mayhew, Gladys's grandmother, and William Samuelson, Gladys's father, were foremost among Barry's supporters and creditors. Indeed, William considered Barry a very valuable man to have attracted as a "son-in-law".

It is impossible fully to understand either Barry's identity or his position in Mt Kelly without reference to Gladys. Although Barry was certainly a productive man and did not initially need Gladys to sustain him, his capacity to court her successfully and his access to the credit her kinsmen controlled were highly inter-related. In the light of what happened to Barry subsequently, the fact that Gladys's kinsmen approved of her living with Barry was a critical marker in their general appreciation of him. This is important because Gladys had a number of significant opportunities that might have enabled her to be independent of Barry and his income. For example, when I first moved into Mt Kelly Gladys lived with Katie Mayhew. Although William Samuelson was her father, Katie had raised her since she was very young. Katie received an extra supplement on her pension to support Gladys and Gladys enjoyed an unlimited call upon Katie's resources. Furthermore, Gladys had access to Mrs Douglas, a white lady who lived in a house a few hundred metres southeast of Mt Kelly. Mrs Douglas had fostered Gladys and her siblings for a short time and still maintained contact with the young people. They could go to her house at any time, had free access to her food and occasionally slept at her place. Mrs Douglas kept a keen interest in Gladys's affairs. As a result of her relationships with these other people, Gladys was able (and, at a certain point, compelled) to consider what Barry offered her in the context of other competing opportunities.

The value of her other opportunities was not constant to Gladys. In many respects, they were potential opportunities and became relevant only in the context of her changing relationship with Barry. When Barry and Gladys initially set up house, the couple spent most of their free time sitting in Katie's camp talking, drinking and occasionally eating. Although Katie was generous with them, Barry was able to support them both on his income. The same was true of their access to Mrs Douglas. They took advantage of what she offered them but did not need it to survive. They were secure and self-contained. When Gladys moved in with Barry, she certainly did not surrender access to these people. She shared her opportunities with Barry and relied upon his income to support them substantially. The significance of her choice emerges clearly with respect to her baby.

When Gladys and Barry initially established their household, she was pregnant. Although everyone in Mt Kelly knew that Barry was not the father, he announced on several occasions that he was planning to "grow up" the child as if it were his own. Gladys and her kinsmen did not question Barry's right to make this claim. On the contrary, they considered his remarks to be appropriate, manifesting his identity as an affluent, responsible man. Moreover, they interpreted his willingness to care for the child as an indication that Gladys herself was in good hands. By recognizing Barry's responsibility for the baby, however, Gladys surrendered access to resources she could have acquired through her own solitary control of the child, in particular a supporting mother's pension. In general, by giving Barry access to her own kinsmen and her baby, Gladys denied herself independent access to the resources she needed to support her domestic group. Insofar as everyone else concurred in Gladys's judgment, they accepted this arrangement, considered it part of Barry's creditable identity and supported the entire domestic group.

In spite of these facts, however, Gladys maintained some social distance from Barry and did not totally commit herself or her child to the relationship. She marked her reserve principally by keeping her own surname, Williams, and giving it to her child. Barry and Gladys kept a kangaroo relationship and denied they were married. Gladys did not initially make a public issue of her surname or their marital identity. It was only when Barry began to experience problems with Virgin, however, that she began to assert her autonomous identity and qualify her marital commitment publicly.

Barry first began to have problems with Virgin after the August 1975 rodeo. It is customary for stockmen to come into Alice Springs for a short break at rodeo time. Virgin brought the Mt Kelly men into town for the weekend and, although he was supposed to have returned on Monday, he did not return until mid September. Because Barry spent most of his money at the rodeo, he and Gladys depended on Donald Corcoran (Barry's father), Katie Mayhew and William Samuelson. After returning to Jefferson Downs, Virgin brought them back to Mt Kelly in November when Gladys's baby was due. Barry again expected

Virgin to collect him soon after the baby was born. However, he did not come until May 1976. During that six months, Barry's social world collapsed.

When Virgin did not appear, Barry began to search for him in Alice Springs and discovered that his boss had returned to the station. It was an unusually rainy period in Central Australia at this time and Barry publicly suggested that Virgin was marooned out bush: he would come for him after the road cleared. Virgin did not come. Indeed, another Mt Kelly man's boss (who lived further away from Alice Springs and travelled over worse roads than Virgin) did appear and took his workers out bush. One day Barry's father openly voiced his suspicions. He stated bluntly that Virgin had fired Barry and was never coming back. Barry denied his father's allegation and reasserted that Virgin would arrive any day. Barry's hopes were disappointed, however. He found Virgin in Alice Springs and asked him for a job and a loan. Virgin did not guarantee him the job and gave him only four dollars, not even a morning's wages.

In the months that followed Barry and Gladys began to have increasingly bitter and violent public quarrels. Gladys denied she was Barry's wife, stated publicly that she was "only living with him" and reasserted her control over her baby. She also tried to prevent Barry from going to town to drink with his workmates from Mt Kelly. Whenever he got in a car to accompany them, she swore at him and screamed for him to stay. Initially Barry acquiesced. He presented himself as a "quiet man" who did not hit women and was considerate of Gladys's wishes. As Gladys became more vitriolic in her remarks, he abandoned his pacific stance and struck her. When this happened Gladys screamed hysterically and called for her "uncles" to help her.

Gladys's uncles were Barry's working mates, the very same men with whom he tried to go drinking. Gladys's appeals put them in a difficult situation and they did not respond or come to Gladys's aid. On the contrary, they criticized Barry for letting Gladys influence him so much and began to say that she dominated him. They interpreted his efforts to please Gladys and his failure to beat her as a sign of weakness. In their view, Barry should go to town whenever he pleased and ignore his woman's wishes completely.

Barry commented to me that Gladys had jeopardized his relationships with his mates. He noted how they never came to see him at his camp any more and resented the way that Gladys tried to prevent him from drinking with them; he wished he were working out bush where he would not have these problems.

Barry's problems were not limited to Gladys and his work-mates. His conflicts with Gladys gradually engaged him in secondary conflicts with Katie Mayhew and William Samuelson. Although Gladys's uncles refused to come to her aid, Katie and William began to support her against Barry. Katie cut off her credit to Barry and eventually fought violently with him. Barry also had a fight with Angie, Katie's daughter. William Samuelson was less quick to interfere. Originally he had thought quite highly of Barry. As time went on, however, and the fights between Barry and Gladys became more violent, William started to take Gladys's side. He accused Barry of being a "bludger" and supported Gladys's disclaimers about the nature of their relationship. He began to disparage Barry in private conversations and compared him unfavourably with Greg Davidson, a young Mt Kelly man who was head stockman at Malapunya station.

During this long process Gladys began to take advantage of her other opportunities. Mrs Douglas took an active interest in Gladys, the baby and Barry. She insisted that Gladys wash the baby's nappies in her own automatic washing machine. She hired Barry to do weeding, raking and other small odd jobs, for which she paid him and fed the family. Although she tried to help Barry, Mrs Douglas's primary interest was in Gladys and her baby. Gladys finally moved into Mrs Douglas's house and left Barry in the camp. Sister Leslie Grey arranged for Gladys to receive a supporting mother's pension and the break with Barry was complete. Not long after Gladys received her first pension cheque, she, her baby and Mrs Douglas flew to New South Wales to live with Mrs Douglas's mother.

On 8 May 1976 Virgin came back. As a token of his relationship with Barry he gave him a new pair of working boots. He took Barry and several other Mt Kelly young people out to Jefferson Downs. I visited them before I left Alice Springs in June. Although he was again working, Barry's relationship with his boss was not clear. Barry criticized him extensively, saying he was a bad boss and an inept manager. Barry alleged that Virgin had made an error and lost a mob of wild horses the men had spent all day mustering. Virgin once rebuked Barry for having driven some bullocks so hard he crippled one. It was a young beast and too small to kill but, because it could not walk, Virgin had to shoot it. He held Barry responsible because he was the head stockman.

This case critically raises the question of the relationship between "non-economic" (or symbolic) and "economic" capital (Bourdieu 1977). On the one hand, a man's symbolic capital is crucial in establishing his access to material resources. For example, Barry's identity as a generous, responsible, productive man was critical in legitimating his access to credit. On the other hand, a man's symbolic capital is valuable only insofar as he can corroborate it with access to material resources. In this case, the value and authenticity of Barry's social identity was intimately tied to how other people assessed his relationship with Virgin and his chances for work. This conditioned Barry's capacity to convert symbolic resources into economic resources. Prior to his problems with Virgin, Barry was able to convert his symbolic capital and social identity into domestic credit. After Virgin apparently withdrew his support, Barry's identity changed and he lost his credit. There were two aspects to Barry's loss of credit. Because it appeared he would never work for Virgin again, other people refused to credit him for his possible future earnings; and he also lost the credit he had accumulated from his gifts to the community in the past. People denied that his past contributions to their welfare were relevant to his needs when he was out of work. When it was apparent that there was a discontinuity between Barry's past and his present, the Mt Kelly people redefined his identity and rendered their past debts to him irrelevant for his current exchanges with them. In this way, it became impossible for him to convert symbolic capital into economic resources.

Violence emerged in Barry's interaction with others only as his social identity and credit were being redefined. It was part of a transitional, ambiguous phase in his relationship with other Mt Kelly people and occurred only as people began to refuse to convert or render his past contributions to them commensurable with current exchanges. Moreover, Barry only fought with those people who were critical for the maintenance of his credit. He fought with Gladys more frequently because their relationship was the focus of the social field his credit needs defined. The violence also developed these processes more and actually contributed to Barry's "bankruptcy". Barry's mates insisted that for him to remain a man in their eyes, he had to beat and control his wife. Gladys's kinsmen did not agree. Had Barry maintained access to Virgin, they might have considered it legitimate for him to strike Gladys; but because Barry had apparently lost his boss, William and Katie considered the beatings illegitimate and justified their own interference in the affair as necessary to protect her. The violence that was necessary for Barry to keep face with his workmates undermined the support of Gladys's kinsmen. The violence finally stopped because Gladys established her own "matricentric" domestic group and destroyed the social field their relationship initially constituted.

Case Two

The second case considers a domestic situation that accounted for at least ten violent incidents during my fieldwork. It concerns Terry and Isabel Sharp and their family. The case contrasts with the preceding one in several important ways. First, the Sharps did not maintain a "matricentric" domestic organization. Rather, they are an example of the second major type of domestic organization current among contemporary Alice Springs Aborigines: Terry worked in the cattle industry and Isabel accompanied him throughout his career; their children each moved into institutions for part-Aboriginal children when they came of school age. Second, violence in this family was most common between the parents and the children. Of the ten violent incidents I recorded, only one occurred between Terry and Isabel and none occurred between the children. Nine occurred between a child and one parent. Two violent incidents between Isabel and George, the eldest son, will be examined in detail. Third, the violence occurred during a period of transition in the life of the family as a group and in George's life particularly. Unlike Barry's case, however, George's situation was improving and his identity was becoming more secure. Fourth, whereas Barry's creditors severed their links with him by altering their terms of exchange, Terry and Isabel manipulated norms of domestic reciprocity to maintain control over and access to their children. The children had to legitimate ways to limit their parent's demands. The violence occurred at moments when there were major disagreements about the significance of reciprocity and the limits of debt in the family's domestic relationships.

There were two images of the Sharps' domestic identity that were important in the family's development: the Welfare

Branch's image and the family's own self-image. At the centre of each image was the question of how adequately the Sharp parents (particularly Isabel) fulfilled their responsibilities toward their children. The Welfare Branch considered them irresponsible parents and insisted they put the children in institutions in Alice Springs. The Sharps maintained an image of themselves as a solidary family throughout their history. Yet, because the parents and children lived apart, they were not certain about the significance of the family's ideology of domestic reciprocity for their interpersonal relationships with Isabel. These problems emerged in an acute form during my fieldwork. When Terry and Isabel retired from active work and acquired pensions, the family began to reassemble at Mt Kelly. By this time, however, four of the children worked and received incomes of their own. Because Terry and Isabel tried to legitimate access to their children's resources by invoking the family's norms of domestic reciprocity, the significance of the family's past and its self-identity became the subject of intense discussion. The family objectified and scrutinized the ambiguities in their relationships with one another. The violence among them emerged in the context of this debate.

The key to the family's identity is the conflict between Terry's working career and his children's educational careers. Terry was a highly respected part-Aboriginal stockman who worked in the bush for most of his life. The Welfare Branch considered his children were part-Aborigines and consequented required them to attend school in Alice Springs. This situation created a major dilemma for the family, particularly for Isabel. Isabel could not accompany Terry in the bush and tend to her children in the manner the Welfare Branch demanded. Because she chose to stay with her husband, the children went to institutions and lived apart from their parents. The family only came together during school holidays and once for a brief period when Terry worked in town.

The Welfare Branch did not interpret the family in terms of the conflict it had created nor did it understand its own part in the development of the Sharps's domestic organization. The Welfare Branch interpreted the family's problems in terms of judgments about the moral identities of its members. I discussed the Sharps with Mrs Thatcher, the welfare officer who was responsible for them throughout this period. She observed that Terry had always been a poor worker and poor provider. She also considered Isabel an unfit mother. According to her, Terry and Isabel drank too much liquor and indulged themselves at the expense of their children. There had always been a problem with the children's schooling. Although the Sharps eventually chose to send their children to institutions in Alice Springs, the Welfare Branch had to threaten to commit the children to the care of the state before they would acquiesce. Had Terry and Isabel not responded to its pressure, the Welfare Branch would have taken formal court action against them. According to Mrs Thatcher, Terry was a good man out in the bush because he drank no liquor. The children too lived better when their parents were gone: they received educational allowances from the state and Grannie, Isabel's mother, looked after them. Indeed, Grannie was a responsible woman who nurtured her grandchildren tenderly. Unlike Terry and Isabel, she did not indulge herself at the children's expense. On the contrary, she took over responsibilities that should have been Isabel's.

The significance of Mrs Thatcher's comments is not that she liked or disliked particular members of the family. Her comments constitute the family's welfare identity and legitimated the Welfare Branch's action against it. The contrast between Isabel and Grannie was particularly important. Grannie worked in Alice Springs as a housekeeper for white families. Although she had a male friend with whom she associated, she lived alone and supported herself. The Sharp children lived with her every weekend. Isabel travelled with Terry, however, and refused to subordinate her relationship with her husband to the care of her children. These facts were the basis of the Welfare Branch's attitude toward the two women. Grannie's situation conformed to the Welfare Branch's family policy whereas Isabel's life did not. According to the Welfare Branch, therefore, Grannie was the responsible adult female and Isabel was a wastrel. Isabel's mistake was not that she drank, but that she committed herself to Terry. Because liquor and drinking were part of the deviant identity the Welfare Branch ascribed to most men, Isabel's identity as a drunk was a metaphorical representation of her life career and of her rejection of the Welfare Branch's plans for her family. Because Isabel's deviant identity legitimated the Welfare Branch's action against the family, this identity was crucially instrumental in reorganizing the family's domestic life, dispersing its members across the face of Central Australia and, therefore, contributing to the family's problematic self-identity.

In my analysis of Barry's case, I suggested that the Mt Kelly people assess the relevance of past transactions in the context of present circumstances. Although some exchanges proceed as if there were no problem converting particular exchange items or making them commensurable, relatively unproblematic transactions mask what is inherently uncertain in all exchanges. Because the Sharps were reconstituting their domestic group during my fieldwork, and had experienced the history outlined above, they encountered this problem dramatically. Of particular significance was the fact that their four eldest children had already established working careers and had independent access to the means of survival. Whereas Terry and Isabel previously had to subordinate their relationships with their children to the demands of their work, after having retired they had a major interest in reconstructing links with their children and in legitimating them as socially real and constraining. Although they had no long-term history of domestic exchanges, they nevertheless tried to obligate their children by invoking norms of kinship and domestic reciprocity.

The Sharps often discussed the norms of reciprocity that were meant to prevail in their family. They described their domestic transactions in terms reminiscent of Sahlin's "generalized reciprocity" (Sahlins 1974, 193–94). According to the Sharps, their transactions were motivated by the commitment of each member to the family and implied no debt or obligation to repay. As George explained it, "In our family, people don't lend money. They give it." The Sharps stressed that, insofar as they were a family, they helped one another when necessary. The "solidary extreme" of generalized reciprocity constituted the family's image of its own moral identity.

Sahlins (like the Sharps) stresses that the norms of generalized reciprocity typically leave debt "out of account" and that "the expectation of reciprocity is indefinite" (Sahlins 1974, 194). Nevertheless, I think Sahlins's point can be generalized so that it accounts for the Sharps' situation more accurately. In general, the power of generalized reciprocity stems from the fact that it is based upon permanent, ineradicable debt. Generalized reciprocity obscures the notion of "exchange" and treats all transactions in isolation. Because people gloss transactions as if they were unrelated (that is, as if they were not reciprocally motivated exchanges), no transactional items are interconverted or rendered commensurable. Consequently, no exchanges can ever be said to have occurred and no debts are ever extinguished. Debts grow with each transaction and constitute permanently binding obligations.

Insofar as the norms of generalized reciprocity specify no limits to the help expected and potentially required, they also make it difficult if not impossible for people to acquit themselves honourably and limit or terminate a relationship. People who, under the norms of generalized reciprocity, try to construct a "bill" or to "balance their accounts" are considered selfish, unsociable and perhaps even traitors to the group. From this perspective, the norms of generalized reciprocity contain the seeds of their own contradiction and are "altruistic" only if people disattend to the debts accumulated. Such studied disattention occurs only under some circumstances and constitutes a limiting case. Indeed, insofar as people deny that exchanges occur and isolate transactions from one another, the norms of generalized reciprocity can lead to real material imbalances, legitimate what some parties to the interaction consider unfair exchange and generate exploitative relationships. This is particularly likely to occur in the context of kin relationships in which certain kinds of obligations are conceived as natural and ineradicable in any case.

In the light of this analysis, Terry and Isabel tried to reconstruct the family's domestic relationships by manipulating the norms of generalized reciprocity so as to make their children recognize a permanent debt to them. There were several aspects to this process. First, they insisted their children were indebted to them simply because they were their children. Second, they denied that the children's contributions to the family's well-being (particularly that of Terry and Isabel) were commensurable with the items that constructed the kinship debt. Hence, they refused to recognize that the children had discharged any portions of their kin debt and even denied that the children honourably attempted to uphold the family's norms of solidarity and reciprocity. Third, by denying the significance of their domestic contributions, Terry and Isabel legitimated an unlimited call upon their children's resources.

The Sharp children accepted the basic legitimacy of their parents' demands and the norms of domestic reciprocity. However, as their parents manipulated the terms of their kin debt, the children began to feel that Terry and Isabel made unreasonable, exploitative demands and abused the norms of reciprocity. Within the terms of generalized reciprocity, however, they could not limit their parents' demands. On the contrary, as long as they glossed their relationships in those terms, the children were obligated to honour their kinship obligations. As Terry and Isabel's demands increased, the children began to reinterpret the terms of their domestic relationships. They began to "quantify" their debts to their parents and insist they had discharged them honourably; in other words, they began to deny the relevance of the norms of generalized reciprocity for their domestic transactions and assess them in terms of "balanced reciprocity" (Sahlins 1974). Only in this way could they limit their obligations and withdraw from their parents' control.

The children's efforts to accomplish this task, however, were seriously undermined by the fact that they periodically depended upon their parents for basic resources or other essential aid. Although Terry and Isabel valued the resources their children controlled, they received pensions and did not necessarily ever depend upon their children. These conditions meant the children were disadvantaged in their negotiations with their parents and regularly found themselves in totally inconsistent, compromising situations. Violence erupted between parents and children on these occasions.

Although several violent incidents occurred among members of the Sharp family during my fieldwork, the problems between the eldest son, George, and Isabel highlight the family's domestic situation. The problems between George and Isabel focused on Hope, George's two-year-old daughter. Several months prior to my arrival in Mt Kelly, George separated from Helen Leon, Hope's mother. Unlike most men in Alice Springs, George kept his daughter and threw his wife out of Mt Kelly. Because he worked and led an active social life, George asked Isabel to care for Hope and gave her money to support the child. Isabel accepted the money and agreed to mind her. Difficulties emerged, however, when George became dissatisfied with his mother's care of the child and began to demand she be more attentive. These processes established a complex domestic field with Hope as its central and fundamental resource. Her significance can be gauged by the fact that George struck his mother twice during conflicts over her.

At the time of my fieldwork George Sharp was beginning to re-establish himself in a relatively secure position. After having worked irregularly for several years, George obtained a full-time job as a field officer for a local Aboriginal organization. He was also elected president and public officer of the Mt Kelly Housing Association. In that capacity, he represented the camp and negotiated with the many outside bureaucrats who took an interest in it. These two new positions gave George access to important and valuable resources. He earned a good wage and was influential in the local politics concerned with Aboriginal affairs. These positions also enabled him to verify his longstanding but recently tarnished identity as a highly resourceful, self-sufficient man. George enjoyed great prestige in Mt Kelly as a result of his success in the Australian Army. He spent eight years in the army, fought in Vietnam, earned two medals for outstanding bravery under fire and retired with the rank of sergeant. After George left the army, however, his career declined. For the next five years, he moved from job to job and, in his own words, "wasted" his time. In the six months immediately prior to his appointment with the Aboriginal organization, he was unemployed and dependent upon his parents for survival. He expected his new job would begin an era in his life congruent with what he had experienced in the army. Hope was a significant part of his plans.

George and Helen established a kangaroo relationship in 1973. George explained that he threw Helen out of the camp because she was a negligent mother and bad wife. She drank too much, did not do her domestic work and failed to obey his orders. He represented her as the embodiment of the wastefulness he thought characterized his own life during the period of which she had been a part. George was unusual in Alice Springs in insisting that he keep Hope. Few men ever kept their children after separating from their spouses. However, George considered caring for Hope a major index of his revitalized social identity. In his capacity as her father and guardian, he documented his sense of responsibility and further heralded his changed circumstances.

George's new identity was not only significant in Mt Kelly. The Aboriginal organization for which he worked was attempting to become a vital, legitimate force in local and national Aboriginal affairs. It needed employees who had good public images and who represented Aborigines as self-determining, responsible people. It pressured its employees (including George) to control their drinking, dress well in public and look after their families.

Bad employees undermined the organization's tenuous legitimacy. Their pressure sometimes put George in an awkward position. It was difficult for him to stop drinking, for example, and still meet his obligations to the other young men in Mt Kelly. The important point was, however, that these pressures increased the significance of Hope. Insofar as George cared for her, he increased his value to, and helped secure his position with, the organization.

As an expression of George's new self, Hope was crucial in maintaining George's good standing both inside and outside Mt Kelly. None the less, George could not actually care for her: he had to depend upon Isabel. Isabel also realized some benefits from this transaction. She received a subsidy on her pension and child endowment for Hope. As these items indicate, the local welfare officers supported her. George too gave her extra money. More important than this, however, was the fact that her care for Hope legitimated a general claim upon George, his current resources and the resources he potentially controlled. George was becoming an increasingly valuable man. Isabel's control of Hope was the key to her long-term access to whatever George might produce, including quite substantial benefits from the new welfare programmes for Aborigines.

Hope was the key to George's and Isabel's efforts to control each other. George needed Isabel to help guarantee his emerging identity and new working career. Isabel wanted access to George's productivity. Hope was the fundamental item in this complex set of transactions. When Isabel neglected the child, the meaning of the transactions became unclear and the subject of intense debate between George and his mother. In particular, these problems posed the question of the significance of their norms of domestic reciprocity and of their mutual debts.

Incident A. George first struck his mother approximately seven weeks after he began work. Within the family, two stories competed as explanations for the incident. Kathy, George's sister, alleged that Isabel got very drunk and almost dropped Hope into the fire. George struck Isabel when he returned home from work and discovered what had happened. Isabel and Terry, on the other hand, insisted that George struck his mother after having discovered her suckling Hope. The incident occurred in the early hours after midnight and I did not witness it. The terms of both stories are highly significant and articulate basic themes that characterized much of the contemporary family gossip.

From the moment he first returned to work, George began to worry and criticize his mother for her care of Hope. He was particularly alarmed at the fact that Isabel drank heavily and often neglected the child. In the weeks prior to this incident, George had several arguments with his mother and urged her to reduce her drinking. Grannie, Isabel's two youngest daughters and the family's neighbours also commented that Isabel was "grog mad", "never satisfied" and abused her family's goodwill. They were particularly critical of her neglect of the children for whom she was responsible. Kathy's explanation of the beating was consistent with this line of criticism and she supported George in the quarrel.

Isabel's explanation was consistent with her efforts to refute the family's accusations. Isabel insisted that she had always been a solicitous mother whose care had ensured her children's current success. She pointed out that her children now held good jobs because she had sent them to institutions where they received good educations. She echoed George's criticisms of Helen, but insisted that she (not George) had rescued the child. When Hope's mother went drinking and left the child alone crying, it was Isabel who fed and calmed her. Finally, Isabel commented on George's ancestry. She claimed that George was not Terry's son. Rather, he was the son of Mervyn James, a white man of high prestige and authority in Alice Springs. George owed his own, high-quality constitution to her.

When Isabel's kinsmen complained that she was never satisfied, they were also criticizing her for constantly demanding more money from them. Although Terry and Isabel did not often fail to feed their family, they did spent most of their surplus money on invalid port. Moreover, when they exhausted their money, they pressed their children, Grannie or one of their neighbours for cash to buy more. If anyone refused, Terry and Isabel often abused them loudly. Although most of the arguments between George and Isabel occurred in this way, he did not object to Isabel's drinking as such. George drank heavily himself, often gave his parents the money they wanted and frequently shared their parties. What George did object to was the fact that Isabel seemed not to credit his efforts to satisfy her or to accept any obligations in return for his gifts. Her "greediness" was a mark of her unwillingness to limit her demands upon him and of her apparent attitude that he owed her everything he had. Moreover, when she neglected Hope, she compounded her "greediness" with a failure to honour her responsibilities toward George. She acted independently of George. The attacks on her identity as a responsible guardian of Hope and her own children summarized this critique.

Isabel's comments are equally interesting with respect to the family's norms of domestic reciprocity. In essence she argued that her children were permanently indebted to her because they owed her thanks for the jobs they now enjoyed. Without her care they could not possibly have achieved such creditable positions. Consequently, they owed her access to what they gained from their jobs. Her comments about George's father were particularly uncompromising. In part she was simply praising herself for having been so seductive that she attracted a white man. She was also basing her demands upon George even in his physical make-up. In Central Australia, most whites consider part-Aborigines inherently superior to "full-blood" Aborigines and give them better access to favourable opportunities, including good employment. Isabel was a "full-blood" Aborigine who, by attracting a white lover, made her son a superior man. George owed his superiority to her and the advantages it gave him. He could no more escape her debt than he could change his ancestry. Isabel rebutted George's criticism of her care of Hope by elaborating on this nurturing theme. Not only was Isabel responsible for having rescued Hope, but also by claiming George objected to her suckling the child and explaining the assault in these terms, she accused him of attacking the very foundation of Hope's development, that is, her attachment to a nurturing mother figure.

Incident B. George struck his mother a second time ten days after the preceding incident. The incident again occurred very late at night after George had returned from work. On this occasion, I was present.

George woke me and asked me to join him for a beer at his parents' camp. When I arrived, Terry, Isabel and Hope were lying on a mattress in front of their hut. George was standing in front of them with Percy O'Callaghan, a young man who was then sharing George's hut, and Garry Loveday, an old friend. We all chatted together, sipping from cans of beer. George asked his mother if she knew the whereabouts of a new pair of shoes his sister, Patricia, had just bought for Hope. Isabel answered that she did not know. George raised his voice angrily and said, "Patricia just spent fifty dollars buying new clothes for Hope and you have lost them before the week is out." He abused both his parents for being so careless. When he finished yelling, he turned and looked at me. Just at that moment, however, Percy said, "Look, she's teasing Hope", indicating Isabel. George turned, grabbed Hope and handed her to me. He then quickly kicked his mother twice in the chest. As his parents hurried to get out of his way, George abused them for being such ungrateful, irresponsible parents. He said that when he was in the army, he spent most of his money on them. They had wrecked two vehicles and squandered hundreds of dollars he had given them. He grabbed the foam mattress they had been sleeping on and took it to his own hut, all the while continuing to abuse them. While he was gone, I took Hope to Grannie's tent. George walked over to where I was standing. He held the medals he earned fighting in Vietnam in his hands. There were tears in his eyes and his face was contorted. He held out his medals and said, "Four of my best mates died while I was earning these". He then threw the medals into Grannie's fire and returned to his hut.

In this incident George balanced his accounts with his parents and symbolically destroyed his relationship with his mother. The lost shoes were significant because they documented that Isabel's carelessness and irresponsibility were an intrinsic part of her attitude toward George and Hope. The shoes were a gift from Patricia − a gift that Isabel squandered. Her act represented all aspects of what George considered her carelessness: she accepted gifts from her children, treated them as if they were insignificant and refused to honour her domestic obligations in return. When George criticized his parents for having squandered all the money he gave them earlier, he elaborated upon this theme and showed how it had been characteristic of their attitude for many years (McHugh 1968). The teasing added an extra dimension to this process. Although there is an institutionalized joking relationship between grandparents and grandchildren among Aborigines in Alice Springs (and I observed George enact it), the fact that Percy used the word "teasing" suggested that Isabel was actively and intentionally harming Hope, not merely neglecting her. Like the earlier incident with the fire, there was a risk of injuring Hope. Unlike the fire incident, however, Isabel was actively responsible for her actions because she was not drunk.

Isabel's carelessness and alleged hostility were radically inconsistent with the basis upon which George entrusted Hope to

Isabel, with how he interpreted his relationship with his mother and with his image of himself as Hope's father. It seemed as if by giving Isabel his daughter, George was actively endangering Hope. In spite of his efforts to meet Isabel's needs, to care for his daughter responsibly and to re-establish himself, George seemed to be wasting his time and to have failed to achieve his goals. Moreover, there did not seem to be anything he could do about it. Not even his own mother would respect his efforts. He was powerless.

The realization and objectification of these themes was disconcerting enough to George and may have been sufficient to cause him to strike his mother. However, it is quite important that these themes emerged in front of a critical audience. George lost face in front of men whose opinions were important to him. Although George would have had a difficult time redefining the significance of his mother's actions under any circumstances, the fact that these events occurred in public made the situation totally non-negotiable. George could neither escape the implications of his relationship with Isabel nor the public context within which they became apparent. George could escape the situation only by redefining it.

I suggest that this explains why he struck his mother. By hitting her, he acted directly upon the situation itself and began to restructure the prevailing definition of the overall context. When George kicked his mother, he made a metaphorical representation of his conflict with her. He suspended the immediately preceding definition of the situation by replacing the detailed themes of their conflict with a generalized expression of it. Having then expressed his idea of their relationship, he began to redefine it. His first act after kicking his mother was to remove the foam mattress. He had only recently given the mattress to his parents and it represented his efforts to meet their domestic needs and fulfil his obligations. When he took the mattress, he started to tally his accounts and deny any debt to his parents. The point of his reflection upon his past gifts and their carelessness was that he thereby freed himself of their debt. He showed that he had consistently tried to uphold the family's norms of reciprocity and be a good son, yet they had just as consistently neglected those norms, failed to authenticate his efforts and, finally, not reciprocated. In essence, George suspended the relevance of the norms of generalized reciprocity for his relationship with his parents, redefined it in terms of balanced reciprocity and emphatically asserted he was even with them.

By redefining his relationship with his parents in this way, George also denied his kinship identity with them. He kicked his mother in the chest. From where he was standing he could have kicked her practically anywhere. In light of the earlier breast-suckling episode, I suggest that George assaulted Isabel's very identity as a mother. The fact that George also destroyed his service medals strengthens this interpretation. As George threw the medals into the fire, he counted the dead who helped him earn them. George thought that he had been best able to fulfil his role as son while in the army. Insofar as the medals symbolized his army experiences, they linked the debt he owed the dead men with the debt he owed his parents. By burning the medals, he declared the men's lives wasted and denied his identity as a son. The heart of his conflicts with Isabel lay in his relationship with her as son to mother. By destroying the most fundamental symbols of their mother–son identity, he symbolically destroyed the relationship itself.

In the last analysis George could not escape the situation that had bred the violence with his mother. Although Grannie was willing to care for Hope for a short time, she would not assume long-term responsibility for the child. Hence, after a week George returned Hope to Isabel and gave his parents a gift of sixty dollars. More generally, George could not keep Hope and do without a woman. Approximately one month after the beatings, he took another spouse who agreed to care for the child. George never again hit his mother but he did hit his new spouse on two occasions. Later, after Isabel had died and George had moved out of Mt Kelly, he also hit Grannie. Because I did not witness these events I cannot analyse them in detail. Yet, I suggest they too were related to the ambiguities in the relationships George maintained with these women.

Domestic relationships, particularly between men and women, are fundamentally problematic in Mt Kelly, and I suggest that George's special problems revolved around his care of Hope. I once witnessed an event that epitomized the problems faced by George and other Mt Kelly men. One night I walked over to George's hut and stuck my head in through his window. Hope was sitting on the floor bawling loudly. George was sitting across from Glenda, his new spouse, with his head down. After I walked up, he leaned over, picked up Hope and put her on the bed. As she continued to cry, George said to me, "You know, she rules me. She's my boss instead of me being hers. She's got one up on me. She can bawl and expect me to pick her up and comfort her. I wish she were a boy. Then I could treat her more sternly."

Case Three

In the preceding chapters I have argued that Mt Kelly and the fringe-camps generally were places of relative structural flexibility in an otherwise highly determined context. The processes whereby fringe-campers exchange domestic resources are crucial to establishing and maintaining that flexibility and the advantages of fringe-camp life. The two cases just discussed document the difficulties fringe-campers (particularly men/women) have in determining the value and significance of domestic exchanges in their everyday life. I have explained how these conflicts are related to the fringe-campers' external relationships and how they emerge in social interaction. The general point is that, although the fringe-camps alter the conditions under which their residents must transact with the external, white-dominated world, they are also settings that condition how the outside world affects relationships among the fringe-campers themselves. Insofar as violence is related to conditions of domestic exchange, it documents the fact that fringe-camps do not isolate their residents but only change their mode of interaction with the world around them.

In the analysis of drinking it was argued that the Mt Kelly people must establish potential credit within the general community as well as obtain actual credit from specific individuals. In the preceding cases I have analysed violence between people who shared domestic resources. Although it was less frequent, violence also occurred between people who did not actually share domestic resources but who competed for access to the resources available in Mt Kelly. In the competition for the credit of the general community, an individual's chief resource is his social identity as a respectable, productive person. In Case One, it was shown how Barry suffered a decline in his relationships with his specific creditors as a result of the redefinition of his social identity. Individuals must also guard against being publicly disgraced in order to protect their access to potential credit and the community as a whole. This establishes the conditions for conflicts which are independent of particular domestic exchanges but which are none the less intimately associated with the conditions of everyday life in Mt Kelly.

I once observed a violent incident between William Samuelson and Donald Corcoran. The incident occurred at the camp of Henry Jacobs, a close friend and classificatory brother of William Samuelson. Henry, William, William's two nephews from Nirvana station and I were sitting around the fire trying to keep warm and talking quietly. Donald was sitting on the ground directly across from William. He was very drunk and appeared to be sleeping. In the midst of our talk, and for no apparent reason, Donald looked up at William and said angrily, "You fucking cunt!" William immediately tried to push the hot fire grill on to Donald's lap but was restrained by his nephews. He thereupon grabbed a table knife, yanked Donald's head back by the hair and drew the knife slowly across his exposed throat. William then jerked Donald to the ground. Because William did not apply any pressure, Donald's throat was not cut but he remained prone for several minutes. Henry, William and I looked away from the body. After an interval of silence, William assured me that he had only been "teasing".

William and Donald did not exchange domestic resources. Rather, they sometimes competed for access to the same individuals in Mt Kelly and always for command of the camp's store of honour. Both men independently exchanged liquor, domestic resources and time with Emerald Salterson, a lady pensioner in Mt Kelly. For several months while he was unemployed, Donald depended upon Emerald for what he needed to feed himself and his wife. Although William was a pensioner and did not depend upon anyone to live, he spent most of his time at Emerald's drinking port, eating and offering authoritative opinions about any subject that happened to come up for discussion. The particular nature of the relationship between William and Donald was marked by the fact that they could often be found sitting on opposite sides of Emerald's camp conducting separate conversations and exchanging only casual glances and scurrilous remarks between them. In general, they avoided one another.

For about six months William and Donald were affines. Barry Corcoran was Donald's son and Gladys Williams was William's daughter. The basis of the conflict between the two men, however, existed long before their children established their marital tie and continued well after they separated. William and Donald represented polar extremes in the possible life careers and social identities of Central Australian Aborigines. On the one hand, William was a "full-blood" Aborigine who had constructed a career conventionally associated only with part-Aborigines. Although retired, he still had a boss, Alfred Samuelson, who gave him money, food and the right to live on his cattle station at any time. Donald Corcoran, on the other hand, was a "half-caste" part-Aborigine who was gradually assuming the identity of a "blackfellow" in the eyes of other people, if not his own. He had lost his cattle boss and suffered a serious decline in his working career after having left pastoral work. Indeed, he was unemployed for approximately six months during my fieldwork in Mt Kelly. The social identities of both men, therefore, were constituted by inconsistent elements and were mutually incompatible. Normally, they avoided each other. Whenever they had to interact directly or even dispute, they focused on their identities. Donald did not recognize the relevance of William's work career for his overall identity: he considered William a "blackfellow". For his part, William considered Donald a hopeless drunk and a "cheeky" man who talked out of turn and acted above himself. It was impossible for these men actively to interact without quarrelling over their identities.

Their competition for Emerald's attention created a particular setting and sometimes specific reasons for conflict; but neither man limited his field of activities to Emerald. On the contrary, they each anticipated exploiting many resources (particularly those controlled by the camp's young men) which only existed potentially and in the form of generalized claims of kinship, friendship or indebtedness. The ambiguities in their respective identities and mutual identification were most significant at this level of camp life. Each man had to protect the authenticity of his identity so as to legitimate claims to these potential resources as they materialized.

The violent incident I have just described occurred in a public context in which their general identities were at stake. Although William shared his liquor with the men gathered around Henry's fire whenever they were all together, none regularly exchanged domestic resources. They were all highly productive men who gave William unsolicited gifts as expressions of their respect for his exceptional character and great prestige. None of these men recognized any particular debt, only a willingness to help each other if necessary. When Donald insulted William, William was compromised in front of the type of men he valued most and to whose general productivity he cultivated access. The composition and general significance of the immediate audience is crucial in understanding why William reacted so violently. It compares strikingly with a similar event earlier that same day but in front of a different audience.

Just before breakfast on the day of the mock knifing, I was sitting in Emerald Salterson's camp. William was next to me preparing his morning shave. Emerald was boiling tea at the fire. Donald sat across from us talking to Reggie Hines and his spouse, Margarie (see figure 3). Donald had only recently stopped drinking from his binge of the previous night. He had taken a shower and was preparing to visit his children at the children's institution in Alice Springs. Although his children had all grown up at the institution he was praising them and claiming credit for having made them such fine youngsters. After concluding his self-praise, he turned and asked Reggie why he had not presented the children with any gifts. Don claimed to have given Reggie's children several gifts in the past and accused him of being cheap. Reggie responded by saying that Donald's children did not even live in the camp, that their father did not care for them. He also asked Donald when he had ever made gifts to anyone other than himself.

Meanwhile, William continued to prepare his shave. As he soaped his face, he quietly mimicked Donald's distorted face and covered his face in mock shame. Emerald and Margarie chuckled at William's mime and rolled their eyes at Donald's extravagance. In the middle of this interchange, Donald became abusive. He told everyone to "shut up" and called them "myall blackfellows". William leaned over to me and asked for a pencil. When I gave it to him, he threw it at Donald and said, "If you are so smart, write your name". Donald stood up and left the camp still abusing everybody. As he left, Margarie commented, "He is a cheeky bastard when he's drunk".

What is interesting about this incident is the extent to which Donald was so thoroughly discredited without any physical violence. Although he certainly insulted everyone present, they simply dismissed his talk as the ravings of a drunken fool. This was typical of how people usually handled him. He was considered a man of so little worth that even his insults lacked import. In this incident he contributed to his own loss of face by invoking two critical aspects of the identity of a respectable man: the maintenance of his dependants and his knowledge of the white man's ways. The Mt Kelly people compare themselves favourably with "myall blackfellows" that is, with bush Aborigines who, they claim, lack the most rudimentary ideas about white civilization and even become ill if they eat white food (particularly sugar). Although there are "full-blood" Aborigines ("blackfellows") living in Mt Kelly, none consider themselves "myall". Moreover, they interpret their links with white men (particularly with cattle bosses) as major signs of their sophistication and knowledge of civilized living. They also think that a sophisticated individual with solid links into white society "looks after" himself and his dependants. He never depends upon the charity of others; rather, he stands on his credit as a productive man. Because he had lost his cattle boss and never raised his own children, Donald failed to live up to the essential criteria by which the Mt Kelly people judge others in everyday life. Yet, Donald did not accept their judgments and stood on his identity as a part-Aborigine to elevate himself above his neighbours. They all knew the facts of his life and had no difficulty dismissing his claims. When he rebuked Reggie and called everybody "myall blackfellows" he made the contrasts in their respective identities relevant and invited a response. Insofar as a pencil and writing one's name (a feat Donald could not perform) signified the white man's culture (as well as their own understanding of my identity), William could not have discredited Donald's claims more thoroughly. Donald was an obsequious man when sober: he curried favour and called his intended benefactor "boss" and "lovely man". The Mt Kelly people greeted these displays of affection with as little sympathy as his fits of anger. When Margarie commented that Donald was cheeky when drunk, she denied he had any self at all worth crediting.

Bourdieu notes that an honourable man responds only to the challenge of an equally honourable man (Bourdieu 1977, 12). When William and the others gathered at Emerald's camp and humorously dismissed Donald's ravings, they were treating Donald with the contempt he warranted as an inferior in honour. Why then did William respond so vigorously later that evening? The composition of the two audiences was, as I suggested earlier, critical. Although everyone in Emerald 's camp treated Donald as an inferior, except for William and me, their identities were not in fact as secure as they appeared. Two of the people were women and Reggie was no more of an independent man than Donald. Indeed, at the time, he and Margarie were living with Emerald and depending on her gifts to survive. William risked losing no face with these people even though he shared liquor and domestic resources with them regularly. He did risk losing face with the evening audience of male equals. Donald's morning insults were unfocused. They encompassed everyone in Emerald's camp. That night, it was apparent that he intended his insult to apply only to William. Hence, although Donald was drunk, it was difficult to redefine his actions as humorous, irresponsible or out of his control. William was more seriously compromised and the situation less negotiable. The evening also followed the morning and perhaps William was willing to tolerate nothing more that day. A full explanation of William's later response, however, must consider his act.

William pretended to cut Donald's throat. He was "teasing". Had he so wished, however, he could have killed Donald without resistance. By only pretending to cut his throat, William responded to the insult but in a manner that emphasized Donald's worthlessness. He showed just how incapable Donald was of offering a genuine challenge. William restored the balance of honour without having to recognize the existence of a significant debt. Finally, Donald now owed William his life, and is, therefore, forever in his debt. Before the mock knifing Donald had a real if worthless social self. After the knifing, Donald's body was alive but his social self was dead.

8

Burning Mt Kelly

An important matter that remains to be considered is the question of how the fringe-campers in Alice Springs perceived and reacted to the changes in Aboriginal administration during my fieldwork. The points made in previous chapters are crucial to the understanding of their reactions to the new programmes initiated most visibly by the DAA. By living in the fringe-camps Aborigines minimize their debt and involvement with whites and thereby substantially suspend the general features of Central Australian society they necessarily face as Aborigines. It has been stressed that fringe-camps emerged as Aborigines responded to the increased power and involvement in their lives of the Commonwealth government. Throughout its participation in Aboriginal affairs, the Commonwealth government has legitimated its activities by arguing they mitigate the effects of "culture contact" and help prevent detribalization. Although whites commonly understand fringe-camps as the most manifest examples of the effects of detribalization, they are in fact responses to the increased penetration of Aboriginal society by the Commonwealth government. Because fringe-camps have been seen as symptoms of detribalization they have legitimated increases in the power of the Commonwealth government over Aborigines – power that has in turn generated more fringe-camps.

Consequently, although the DAA offered Aborigines many new benefits it also represented and wielded great power over them. Indeed, as Aborigines understood quite clearly, the benefits themselves were means by which the DAA and the white administration generally established their power at the local level. Moreover, the mandate of "self-determination" as well as the competition among white administrators for black clients encouraged them to seek out Aborigines and actively incorporate them in administrative processes. The DAA's new programmes and active approach, therefore, raised yet again the critical question for Aborigines of how to maintain access to, but withdraw from, white agents. They raised very special problems for fringe-dwellers, who make a virtue out of withdrawing from interaction with whites as much as possible; they have rejected quite explicitly many social welfare benefits in their efforts to keep their debts to whites low.

Of special interest is the fact that the racial tension crisis legitimated an increase in the power of the local DAA, primarily in terms of problems emergent most visibly from the fringe-camps (see chapter 2). Both the public safety issue and the alternative images of detribalization pictured the fringe-dwellers as the most conspicuous threats to local order and the most obvious signs of detribalization. Practically everyone in the town agreed that something had to be done to help improve conditions in the fringe-camps if relations between Aborigines and whites in Central Australia were to improve or develop peacefully. Indeed, among Senator Cavanaugh's earliest efforts to improve the situation were the pick-up service for drunks and the tent programme, both of which were aimed primarily at the fringe-campers. As efforts to help prevent detribalization, these moves were in the classic mould of increasing the power and involvement of the administration in Aborigines' everyday life under the gloss of helping them improve their living conditions – only this time fringe-dwellers were officially supposed to help themselves in this process.

The fringe-campers followed the progress of the racial tension crisis as closely as did most local white people. Indeed, they too were worried about the state of public safety and felt threatened when they went to town. They were alarmed at how "myalls" or Aborigines from the settlements were getting out of control and bashing Aborigines who lived in town. The Mt Kelly people told me stories of violent incidents in which men from Papunya bashed camp residents and were generally making life difficult. They too worried about the state of public order in the Todd River and considered it a very dangerous place. The Mt Kelly people were also vividly aware of what local white people were saying about life in the fringe-camps, and they denied the relevance of such comments to Mt Kelly. Their eagerness to distinguish themselves from the Todd River people, although a long-standing feature of their self-perceptions, may have acquired special salience as a result of local white people's tendency to describe all fringe-campers as if they were part of the situation in the river.

In general, many white administrators considered the Mt Kelly people a "better class" of fringe-dweller than most. The camp was large, relatively cohesive and had existed for many years. Even so, whites still considered its people degenerate – alcoholic failures for the most part. Moreover, Mt Kelly was the subject of particular identification in the racial tension crisis as a fringe-camp with special problems with land tenure, health, facilities, and general living conditions. Some local white administrators singled out the camp as a classic example of how bureaucratic bungling and local powerlessness had measurably contributed to the misery of Aborigines. In spite of their own views of themselves, the Mt Kelly people were publicly represented as exemplifying all the various kinds of problems different local whites portrayed as threats to local stability and peaceful relations between Aborigines and whites. Their reactions to the events that flowed from the racial tension crisis, therefore, have particular significance to the understanding of fringe-campers in the context of contemporary administrative efforts to solve the problems of Aborigines.

Burning the Bush

On 21 and 22 May 1975, George Sharp burnt the bush around the eastern half of Mt Kelly. His action was typical in some respects of the autumn housecleaning conducted annually by all Mt Kelly domestic groups. Each year when the grass becomes dry, the Mt Kelly people burn areas around their domestic camps in order to clean them and eliminate cover for the many poisonous snakes that inhabit the vicinity. In addition, people rake the burnt areas free of cans and other non-flammable rubbish left disentangled by the fire. They often wash their blankets and, in general, rehabilitate their living environment for the coming year. Because burning the bush is understood as an expression and extension of each domestic group's responsibility for, and control of, its own camp, the people usually burn only that area immediately adjacent to their camp, which everyone conventionally recognizes as their land. Indeed, bush-burning is the most dramatic expression of the Mt Kelly people's identification of their personal independence with their occupation of space outside the control of anybody else.

Unquestionably George Sharp burnt the bush for these reasons. He told me that he wanted to clean the region, rake the rubbish and make the area safe from snakes. It had been a very rainy summer, the grass was quite high and snakes were crawling through the camp in alarmingly high numbers. In a manner appropriate for, and typical of, the head of his domestic group, George was reordering and making safe the environment for them. The scope, timing and particular circumstances of George's bush-burning in this case lent additional significance to his action. George burnt an area many times larger than what was necessary simply to clean his own camp. Indeed, the area he burnt covered one-half of Mt Kelly's total area and enclosed the camps of seven domestic groups. Because he also burnt the grass a little earlier than normal, it was still somewhat green and he had to use kerosene to help ignite it. The central point is that George burnt the bush around Mt Kelly when the basic assumptions of power, responsibility and independence, which underlie bushburning and the identities of the Mt Kelly domestic groups as a whole, were under assault and subject to grave compromise from outside forces. Indeed, the very capacity for the Mt Kelly people to maintain their positions and identities as fringe-dwellers were being undermined. As president of the Mt Kelly Housing Association and chief camp spokesman, George occupied an inter-hierarchical role which made him personally aware of, and subject to, the ambiguities of Mt Kelly's relationship to the wider setting (Gluckman 1968, 69). As a symbolic act of personal responsibility and power, George's bush-burning was a response to the dilemmas arising from these conditions.

The Land

When I first arrived in Mt Kelly in April 1975, Mr Justice Woodward had submitted both his reports and legislation was being prepared in the federal Parliament to grant Aborigines land rights. The main thrust of the land rights movement was to grant Aborigines on settlements and missions in the Northern Territory ownership of their tribal "countries" (Woodward 1974,

1-3). Woodward also recognized that Aborigines who lived in the urban areas, in particular the fringe-dwellers, also had needs that the provision of land would help satisfy. Hence, although such people rarely could establish traditional claims on land, their land rights should be recognized as a first step in resolving a situation which (quoting the submission of the Central Lands Council) he described as "totally unsatisfactory to both themselves, to the white population of these towns and to Australian society as a whole" (Woodward 1974, 50). He also made a number of stipulations about how urban land claims should be handled: special planning for Aborigines' living areas should be an "integral part of all town planning", Aborigines should be involved at all stages of such planning, they should be allowed to live where they were used to living at the time of the report, "tribal differences" should be respected so as to avoid tensions, and these areas should not be seen as "convenient sites" for white development. In summary Woodward said, "It is quite unacceptable that Aborigines should be pushed farther and farther away from the centre of towns by the apparently inevitable urban sprawl" (Woodward 1974, 51).

Mt Kelly was one of the fringe-camps about which Woodward (and the Central Lands Council that pressed the needs of the urban people upon him) was most concerned. Although the Mt Kelly residents identified themselves as Arunta, Kaiditja, or Anmatijira people, none could claim that Mt Kelly was their traditional country. Moreover, many were part-Aborigines who, according to the conventional views of most white Central Australians, had no right to make claims to traditional land. None the less they had occupied the land around Mt Kelly for over twenty years and were most definitely threatened by the expansion of Alice Springs. In particular, the Mt Kelly people were engaged in major disputes with the Department of Housing and Construction the Department of the Northern Territory (DNT) Lands and Survey Branch and the DNT Urban Development and Town Planning Branch, about a proposed open sewerage drain which was to have run through Mt Kelly from a new subdivision to the Charles River. Had the drain been built according to the original plans it would have bisected the camp, occupied over a quarter of its land and in general made Mt Kelly uninhabitable. Indeed, in September 1974 it appeared that these three departments expected the Mt Kelly people to move their camp to another site.

During the first half of 1974, the Mt Kelly people lodged an application for a special title lease to the land on which the camp was located, incorporated themselves into the Mt Kelly Housing Association and objected to the plans for the drain through their DAA community adviser. However, plans for the drain continued. On 3 September 1974, a representative of the DNT Urban Development and Town Planning Branch, held a meeting in Alice Springs with several local people including George Sharp, other Mt Kelly men and representatives of the DAA, CAALAS and the CAAC. The DNT representative explained that alternatives to the drain route through Mt Kelly would be considerably more expensive than the original proposal and, moreover, that rerouting would delay the drain for a year and make the affected area less attractive. He further suggested that these objections would encourage other people affected by the drain to object to Mt Kelly's lease application and to their development plans. After more thought the Mt Kelly people still refused to agree to move. The DNT made no public decisions about the drain or about the Mt Kelly lease application for several months. This was so in spite of numerous letters, unofficial inquiries and public demands for the DNT to act.

In the meantime, the Mt Kelly people (in particular, George Sharp) began to participate in the efforts to press their case and the cases of all the fringe-dwellers around Alice Springs. For example, he attended the monthly meetings of the Tungatjira Association, a group of fringe-camp representatives who, under the encouragement of the Institute of Aboriginal Development (IAD), met to discuss their individual and joint problems. Although people from the IAD, CAALAS and the CAAC attended the meetings, Tungatjira was represented as the body through which the fringe-dwellers could effectively participate in the mechanism of self-determination. In effect, it was a lobbying group that pressured the government in the name of the fringe-campers. More specifically, the Mt Kelly people began to plan how to upgrade the camp's living conditions. They contacted an architect and made preliminary plans for development. The problem was that without a decision from the DNT, the DAA could not fund the Mt Kelly Housing Association. Nor could the architect make any firm plans or prepare useful drawings for the people. Without a lease, the Mt Kelly people had no right to any of the resources the DAA had available for it.

Nothing had happened by March 1975 and the problem with

the Mt Kelly drain was raised during the racial tension crisis. Indeed, it was cited as an example of how bureaucratic delays measurably contributed to the decline in local race relations in spite of Aboriginal and white efforts to improve conditions. The problem was specifically discussed with Dr H.C. Coombs at a public hearing of the Royal Commission into the Public Service on 16 March,[1] two weeks after Cavanaugh's visit. Dr Coombs agreed that the situation was unsatisfactory and passed on the information he received to the regional coordinator of the DNT.[2] On 21 March the regional coordinator met with representatives of the Department of Housing and Construction, the drain contractors, Mt Kelly's architects and the DAA's community adviser for the Alice Springs fringe-camps. At that meeting the regional coordinator announced the drain would be rerouted and constructed north of Mt Kelly. He met with the Mt Kelly people at the camp on 27 March and explained the new plans. He also noted that he had not found any evidence of their first lease application and suggested they lodge a new one. Later I learned from him that the Department of Housing and Construction had always favoured the northern route and the extra cost was no longer significant.

In consultation with their architects, the Mt Kelly people prepared a preliminary development plan and submitted it to the DNT with a new lease application. In the letter accompanying the application, however, George Sharp noted, "As the people have been disappointed in their hopes, e.g. the drain, it is felt that very little serious planning can be expected from them" (Sharp, unpublished manuscript). Although George received acknowledgment of the application from the DNT on 16 April, nothing had happened by the time he burnt the bush. Indeed, the decision to grant the lease was not finally made until June 1976 after many months of pressure, public hearings and delay.

There can be no doubt that the Mt Kelly people wanted the lease to their land. Indeed, title to the land was perfectly consistent with their fringe-dwelling identity and would have created the legal conditions necessary to secure their position in perpetuity. What was important about their land claim, however, was that in order to secure their withdrawal from the outside world, they (and particularly George Sharp) had to enter into negotiations with powerful whites. They had to offer themselves and their "problems" as resources in political competition among whites if they were to gain access to what they needed. In this respect, the land claim not only promised to secure their fringe-dwelling identity but it also highlighted the basic ambiguities in that identity. These ambiguities emerge quite clearly in consideration of the people's efforts to upgrade their living conditions and improve the camp's health.

The Facilities

The Mt Kelly peoples' first priority for the development of their camp was a stout fence around its perimeter. The camp was on the north side of a dirt track connecting the Stuart Highway to a tourist attraction east of the Charles River. Whenever tourist buses travelled the road, the drivers slowed down when passing the camp and the passengers stared inquisitively. Tourists in private cars often "got lost" and drove into the camp. Nothing shamed and angered the Mt Kelly people more than the inquisitiveness of the tourists. As they often angrily told them, they did not consider themselves "animals" or "tourist attractions". The police also commonly drove into the camp inquiring about this or that. Because they could not readily abuse the police, the people usually turned away or walked off. Occasionally strangers visited the camp at night shining flashlights into people's eyes or doing "wheelies" in the dirt in their cars. The proposed fence, as well as a line of trees the people hoped to plant along the road, was designed to obscure the view, protect the camp and in general keep outsiders out. Indeed, the fence was the clearest marker of the reason for the land claim: the hope to avoid interaction with the external world.

It is important to note that a general condition for a special title lease at this time was that the lessee agree to develop the land. Preliminary statements about how the prospective lessee planned to use the land were necessary parts of the application. As pointed out already, the Mt Kelly people included such plans in their second lease application. Moreover, Woodward reinforced this condition by linking the fringe-dwellers' rights to land to the provision of social welfare programmes designed to upgrade their general living standard. Indeed, he saw this as the primary reason for granting land to fringe-dwellers (Woodward 1974, 52). In order to legitimate their land claims, the Mt Kelly people had to "develop" the camp. An unwelcome consequence of their campaign to upgrade camp facilities, however, was a relatively constant parade of officials inspecting the camp's "problems". Of particular concern to the officials were the substandard housing and ablution facilities and the poor state of health in the camp.

Although many officials presented themselves as interested in "helping" the Mt Kelly people, it was not always easy for the camp's residents to distinguish between the inquisitive stares of tourists and of officials. Indeed, the "shocked" reactions were often identical. I witnessed a Commonwealth minister "visit" the camp by driving in, with car windows up, and driving out again without having stopped. If it was possible, the Mt Kelly people ignored the visitors. The men would turn their backs and the women would often disappear inside. The problem was, however, that the new administrative style of "self-determination" encouraged visitors to enlist the aid of the fringe-campers as guides and informants about local problems. Consequently, someone (usually George Sharp) had to confront them directly, tour the camp explaining its difficulties and listen to the visitor's observations. In order to present the camp's case and perhaps enlist the visitor's support in the campaign, George had to forgo the strategy of avoidance.

The Mt Kelly people's awareness of what whites typically thought of them and their style of living was closely linked to these avoidance patterns. Given the expansion of local Aboriginal administration and the diversity of views that were current about how it should be run, not all the whites who visit Mt Kelly presented themselves in the same way. In fact, there was tremendous disagreement among whites about how the camps came to be the way they were; in particular, people disagreed on how much the fringe-campers were responsible for their condition. One school of thought (usually associated with erstwhile officials of the Welfare Branch) argued that the people themselves were responsible for their condition. Because of their ingrained tribal customs, many fringe-campers did not "want" the material goods of white culture. As the welfare officer, Mrs Thatcher, put it in a letter to the local newspaper, "Why try to change the life of the older and itinerant Aborigines who have from birth slept in the open round a camp fire with their dogs and with temperatures at freezing point and want nothing else?" On the other hand, it was argued that many fringe-dwellers were irresponsible drunks who abused what was given to them. Another, conflicting school of thought maintained that the people were victims of poor administration and powerless to control the outside forces that afflicted them. Supporters of the self-determination policy were most often of this view.

In the context of local administrative politics these views were usually interpreted as antagonistic; however, from the Mt Kelly people's perspective, they shared one crucial feature. They both suggested that the Mt Kelly people were incapable of looking after their own interests and well-being; because the fringe-dwellers were not self-reliant, they argued, they had to have the assistance of white administrators.

The Mt Kelly people unilaterally rejected the view of themselves as helpless and dependent. Indeed, their general identities as fringe-dwellers, as well as regular aspects of camp life such as drinking, emphasized the extent to which they were independent, sophisticated people able to support themselves without the government's assistance. Insofar as they avoided whites, they denied their dependence upon them and the importance of the conventional images of fringe-camp life. When George attended meetings or guided people around the camp, he surrendered the strategy of avoidance and confronted the images of his people as dependent wastrels. More fundamentally, by co-operating with whites, he validated their images of Mt Kelly and reinforced the very perspectives he denied.

The racial tension crisis raised all these issues and made them public, but Mt Kelly experienced some particular troubles that focused the issues on itself. The state of the camp's health was especially important. A number of outspoken white people in Alice Springs considered the fringe-camps a major risk to the health and the public safety of the community at large. The conventional image of the fringe-camp was of a filthy, disease-ridden place full of drunken, debauched people. However, there were also people in Alice Springs who were worried about how conditions in the fringe-camps harmed their residents' health, particularly the children. Evidence from both formal and informal surveys of Aboriginal physical health indicated that trachoma, scabies, salmonella, shigella, various pulmo-respiratory diseases and chronic colds as well as malnutrition contributed to a high rate of infant mortality and general ill-health among Aborigines, particularly the fringe-dwellers (Kirke 1974, 81–87). These facts as well as criticisms of the health care provided to Aborigines were used to legitimate attempts to upgrade the health care services and to establish a separate medical service for Aborigines.

The Central Australian Aborigines Congress (CAAC) took an active role in this issue and eventually received Commonwealth funds to create an Aboriginal Medical Service in Alice Springs. At the time of the racial tension crisis, however, it had received no support for its ideas. Soon after the crisis, the CAAC employed a young doctor from Melbourne to conduct a study of the prevalent illnesses in the fringe-camps. He concluded that the conditions in Alice Springs were as poor as any he had found in the slums and shanty towns of Africa and Melanesia. Most fringe-dwellers wanted decent housing ablution facilities, he noted, but what they had could only be considered disgracefully inadequate and unhygienic. As a result of these public health conditions and the high rate of unemployment in the fringe-camps, the fringe-dwellers (in particular, children) suffered serious risks to their health and to their chances to receive an adequate education.

The CAAC followed this study with a number of other assessments of health conditions in the fringe-camps. Its field officers gathered additional data. Moreover, the leading CAAC officers were well known to the national media. On several occasions, they brought major news reporters and film teams to Alice Springs to record conditions in the camps. They tried to document the close relationship between disease and poor living conditions. In their efforts to gather detailed, convincing evidence of the problems, the reporters filmed people who showed signs of scabies, trachoma and other diseases. They also filmed shacks and, at Mt Kelly, the toilet facilities. Throughout these exercises, the reporters explained to the fringe-campers that they wanted to show all of Australia just how badly Aborigines were forced to live in Alice Springs.

Mt Kelly became involved in the health surveys in a most comprehensive way. Early in the camp's campaign to upgrade its facilities, the people applied to the DAA for money to build new ablution amenities, including toilets, showers and a laundry. As an interim measure until the lease application was approved, however, the DAA decided to install three mobile privies. Although the order was submitted to an Aboriginal construction company in December 1974, the privies were not installed until June 1975, several months after they were due. The delay meant that the old latrines had filled and become unusable. Although the Mt Kelly people had always dug their own latrines, they had anticipated the installation of the new privies and had not replaced the old ones. Moreover, the DAA promised to dig deep, new holes with a mechanical post-hole digger. This, too, was delayed, but in any case the holes were unusable without the new privy sheds. When the situation became critical, the Mt Kelly people stopped using the old latrines and walked to an unused area of bushland in the small hills immediately north of the camp. The open, unusable privies and the exposed waste posed a specific health menace to the camp.

As the situation became worse, several people began to put pressure on the DAA and the Department of Public Health (DPH). George Sharp regularly complained to the DAA's community adviser about the urgency of the situation. The community adviser, in turn, wrote reports on the situation, pressured her superiors and sent letters to the DPH. The CAAC also sent letters to the DAA and, as I mentioned, paid special attention to Mt Kelly's toilet problems in their films and surveys. The senior nursing sister who visited Mt Kelly everyday and was a close friend of Grannie, George Sharp's grandmother, personally lobbied senior officials of the DPH. In response to all this, the DAA assured the Mt Kelly people that the privies would arrive soon. Six months passed.

The DPH started to become officially worried and sent several health inspectors to examine the situation, occasionally accompanied by the senior nursing sister or the DAA community adviser. The inspectors were introduced to George Sharp who took them around the camp examining the available ablution facilities and the old latrines. The regular DPH health inspectors, Mr Ajax and Mr Dingo, however, usually visited the camp alone and unannounced. They tended to drive into Mt Kelly, wander around asking questions and make notes about the latrines without explaining themselves to anyone. Although they made several trips to the camp, they always asked the same questions. George Sharp once caught them hiding in the hills surreptitiously taking photos of the camp.

Although the Mt Kelly people realized that the health inspections, the endless visits from outsiders, the films, and so on were part of efforts to improve their living conditions, they felt compromised by the process. No matter who inspected the camp, how justified their activities, or how sympathetically expressed their findings, all came to the same conclusion: Mt Kelly was unhygienic and unhealthy. Such a judgment always cut two ways. Implicit in statements that the camp was filthy and diseased were judgments about the people and the way they lived; of particular salience was the common knowledge that most Mt Kelly people drank what were considered large amounts of alcohol. The ironic thing was that the Mt Kelly people's drinking habits, their willingness to live in shacks, to tolerate less than adequate ablution facilities and their exposure to disease were all consequences of their identity as fringe-dwellers, of their assertion of their capacity to care for themselves and remain relatively independent of whites. The public image of the fringe-dwellers as degenerate and dependent was not only politically unacceptable and "impolite", but also it contradicted the people's self-image and misrepresented the general significance of fringe-camps.

George Sharp's Role

George Sharp was uniquely placed to confront systematically all the ambiguities of this process. Although not a "tribal elder", he was the president of the Mt Kelly Housing Association and was primarily responsible for handling Mt Kelly's business with the DAA and its associates. Occasionally, he brought his father or William Samuelson along to meetings or referred his authority for their approval but he did most of the work. He was also a field officer for the CAAC. Indeed, he worked closely with the young Melbourne doctor on the health survey. In this capacity as well as his role of camp spokesman, George was closely associated with the CAAC's efforts to publicize the problems of the fringe-camps and use them to legitimate the expansion of the CAAC's programmes. George plainly experienced the problems of how to gain access to, but withdraw from, the white bureaucracy.

George's relationship with the Mt Kelly people as a whole was not perfectly straightforward either. On the contrary, Mt Kelly's domestic economy undermined the capacity of anyone in his position to claim authority over the entire camp. Indeed, he restricted his active role as spokesman to the eastern half of the camp. Whenever he had to produce an opinion for the western half of the camp, he either referred the inquisitor directly to Katie Mayhew or asked William Samuelson to find out Katie's views. George furthermore maintained ambiguous relationships with his own family. At the time he was having to negotiate with the endless stream of health inspectors, he was also engaged in major conflicts with his mother. He first hit his mother on 21 May, the night of the first day of the bush-burning. The bush-burning occurred, in fact, at a moment when all the conflicts in George's identity as camp spokesman, head of his domestic group and son of his mother collided.

On Monday morning, 20 May, I was preparing breakfast on my fire when Mr Ajax, the health inspector, arrived. He informed me that, because my daughter had salmonella, a "reportable" disease, he had to ask me some questions, such as where I purchased my food, how I stored and cooked it and how I kept my home. He also asked about the toilet and sanitation facilities I used. He wrote on his health form that my sanitation facilities were unsatisfactory and my home kept poorly. While Mr Ajax was interviewing me, the senior nursing sister drove up with another unknown health inspector. They stopped at Isabel Sharp's camp. Hope, George's daughter, also had salmonella and the other health inspector had to acquire the same information as Mr Ajax.

After Mr Ajax finished interviewing me, he asked Terry Sharp to take him up to examine one of the old privies. The unknown inspector finished his discussion with Isabel and also looked around Mt Kelly. He very soon crossed over to my camp and said that he could not believe what he saw: the conditions in Mt Kelly were absolutely intolerable. He could not understand how the government could permit such a situation to exist. He noted that when he got back to his office he would write some angry letters and thump on a few people's desks. After he had finished speaking, I saw that Terry Sharp and Mr Ajax were coming down from the old privy. The new health inspector and I crossed over to Terry's camp where George, William Samuelson and Donald Corcoran were seated, watching. Mr Ajax got into his car and left. The inspector repeated to the men what he had told me. He assured them that he would speak to his superiors and complain about how they had permitted such an outrageous situation to have developed. The senior nursing sister drove up and he then left.

Terry Sharp told us all about his trip to the privy with Mr Ajax. He said that Ajax had asked why the Mt Kelly people did not dig their own privies and build their own sheds. The men all laughed and made scornful remarks about Mr Ajax. George remarked, "Ajax gives me the shits".

George burnt the small area of bush behind his own tent the next morning. As the bush burned and the flames died down, George, two young men living with him and I raked the rubbish into piles, loaded it into a trailer and took it to the city dump. The grass was not yet dry enough to burn easily. Consequently, George poured kerosene on the bush in order to help it ignite. Around sunset the young CAAC doctor who conducted the health survey came out to the camp. George had mentioned the unsatisfactory condition of a pan toilet near Emerald Salterson's camp and the doctor came to inspect it. George, the doctor and I walked over to examine the toilet and the doctor noted it was indeed useless. The results of the survey had been announced for the first time over the radio while we were raking the grass that morning. As we walked back from the toilet, the young doctor commented upon his survey. He noted how they had discovered that shigella, salmonella and trachoma were far too prevalent in the fringe-camps. He traced the disease to just the kinds of sanitation problems Mt Kelly was experiencing. Although such diseases were common among the earlier white pioneers, he noted, they disappeared with the adoption of modern sanitation facilities. He said that everyone in Mt Kelly probably had trachoma, and then he examined Isabel Sharp, Hope Sharp, and Kristina, my daughter. Isabel showed scars of earlier attacks of trachoma. Both Hope and Kristina showed symptoms of trachoma on the wane. Because they were taking a penicillin solution that was effective against both salmonella and trachoma, their eyes were improving.

After the doctor finished examining for trachoma, George told him that he had burned a small area of bush just behind his tent that morning and planned to burn a much larger area the next day. When I asked George why he burned it, he asked us to accompany him to the top of the small hill north of the camp. From there he pointed to one of the old, disused privies. He said that the Mt Kelly people had dug privies in this area ever since they first moved in. This old outhouse was only the latest of a series of such sheds. He then led us another fifty metres beyond a small rise just to the north of the old privy. He pointed out that because the old privies were full, many people (particularly the children) use the bush just over the rise. It was obvious from the waste about that he was correct. In addition the area was littered with cans and other more flammable waste. George said that he would burn all of this area in order to dispose of the flammable waste and make the rest easier to rake away.

The doctor then asked George where the boundary of Mt Kelly's current land application ran. George indicated that the proposed line ran from the Stuart Highway to the Charles River along a nearby crest of hills. He noted, however, that he wanted to expand the camp's area to include more land to the north. The doctor suggested that George wait until the first application was approved; otherwise, he said, the DNT would use the supplementary application as another excuse to delay action on the initial claim. George agreed with the suggestion. After this we walked back to the main camp, where I returned to my caravan. After a short talk with the doctor, George went to work.

The next morning, Wednesday 22 May, George burnt the rest of the bush around the eastern half of Mt Kelly. The final dimensions of the burnt area are crucial for understanding the significance of the bush-burning. George burnt south and east to the roads that were to have become the camp's boundaries in those directions. However, he burnt north beyond the boundary of Mt Kelly's first land application to a small tree at the base of the hills. This cleared an area approximately to the place where George had said he wanted to extend the camp on Tuesday night. He burnt west to a road that effectively divided Mt Kelly into eastern and western halves. The eastern (burnt) region included only those people for whom George felt responsible. The western (unburnt) half included those people George considered were under the influence of Katie Mayhew. The burnt line stopped just short of William Samuelson's tent. Again, the bush was really too green to burn and George had to use kerosene to ignite it. However, once some of the denser bush ignited, it burned furiously and sent great waves of flames and heat into the sky. At one point most of the camp's northeastern corner was in flames and the whole area shimmered.

In between the times when George was lighting the bush, he washed his daughter's clothes. Although Isabel normally washed Hope's clothes, she gave up her care of Hope after the beating. She and Terry spent the morning "hiding" from George in Don Corcoran's tent. In addition to their remarks about the beating, Terry and Isabel commented on George's bush-burning. Isabel had been worried for some time about snakes crawling through the camp. In the early morning she often called out to people and had them look at the fresh snake tracks made during the night.

When I asked her what she thought of the burning, she said she approved: it was good and would keep the snakes away. The other people in the tent agreed and did not dispute George's right to burn the large area.

George extended the significance of bush-burning as much as he extended the area he had the right to burn. He was cleaning the area and thereby expressing his identity as the head of his domestic group. Yet, there was very much more to clean in Mt Kelly's total environment at that time. Practically everything was out of place and the camp was subject to multiple threats. George's own daughter was sick. Significantly, she had the types of diseases the CAAC traced to the camp's poor living conditions, which, they argued, were outside the Mt Kelly people's control. Moreover, these threats had been exacerbated by bureaucratic delays that were also beyond the people's influence. As a result of the delays, the privies were full and the exposed human waste created a further disease threat. In the name of bureaucratic intervention, however, outsiders poured through the camp, intentionally or unintentionally condemning the people who lived there and threatening their identity as fringe-dwellers. These processes were themselves part of wider conflicts between Aborigines and whites that were often expressed in terms condemning the fringe-dwellers. When George burnt the bush around Mt Kelly he tried to free the camp of all these sources of contamination.

The Bushfire as Symbol

Bushfires commonly evoke two contradictory images in Central Australia. The most common is of an uncontrolled, destructive force. Bushfires are capable of sweeping through vast regions of the country, killing livestock and destroying property. If followed by a period of insufficient rain, a bushfire can even lead to major drought. The sign of the koala reminds the public that bushfires are to be avoided.

The bushfire also evokes an image of regrowth and the generation of new life. After lots of rain, the grass grows tall in Central Australia. As time passes and the rain stops, however, the grass dries and goes brown; it sustains cattle but does not fatten them. Trees shed their leaves and branches break. Stakes and fallen branches make the bush hazardous for man and beast. Bushfires burn the fallen limbs and the dry grass tops. If rain follows, new grass sprouts from the roots of the burnt tussocks. Cattle and horses wander safe from dangerous stakes and grow fat on the nutritious herbage.

George burnt the bush and cleaned Mt Kelly. He also told me quite explicitly that he burned the old grass to allow the roots to sprout new growth on the next rain. I do not stretch the point, therefore, by saying that the bush-burning was a symbol of George's hope for the rebirth and renewed health of his family and Mt Kelly. The fact that he extended the burnt area beyond the boundaries of Mt Kelly's first land application out to where he hoped the boundary might one day lie attests to one dimension of his aspirations. However, the bushfire was also a fundamental manifestation of George's impotence. Although the burning expressed his identity as the head of an autonomous domestic group, he had little control over his domestic affairs, the bureaucracy or disease. Indeed, he depended upon members of his domestic group (most notably his mother) and the bureaucracy to protect his daughter and his people from disease. The fact that George did not burn Katie's area signifies that the bush-burning was a limited act even in its own terms.

Burning the grass could not eradicate the camp's health problems or compel the bureaucracy to grant Mt Kelly's needs. Indeed, insofar as the action was a response to conditions imposed on George by the outside world, it shows how he was controlled by and depended upon others, even in an act of utmost cultural expression. In this respect the bushfire was most fully a fundamental expression of the overall position of the fringe-campers. In the same way as white people commonly misunderstand and misrepresent fringe-camps, they also failed to grasp the meaning of the fire. The senior nursing sister drove up just as the flames were reaching their peak and were dancing hotly around most of the northeast segments of the camp. I asked her what she thought of the cleansing. She responded that if George was not careful, a spark would ignite the tents and burn them all down.

Notes

1. Dr Coombs was one of the Labor government's chief advisers on Aboriginal affairs, a close confidant of several local white administrators in Aboriginal affairs and chairman of the Royal Commission into the Public Service.
2. This position was established after Cyclone Tracy in an effort to minimize the disruption the cyclone caused to local administration in general.

Epilogue:
The Bureaucratic Expropriation of Aboriginal Culture

I first encountered Australian Aborigines in a BBC TV documentary on the Gurrindji's struggle to gain title to their sacred lands at Wattie Creek. In addition to exploring the personalities and efforts of Vincent Lingiari, Captain Major, Dexter Daniel and other Gurrindji, the documentary presented white Australian writer Frank Hardy. Hardy had become personally involved with the Gurrindji during a journey around Australia in which, as he says, he tried "to rediscover Australia, to think about what I'm going to write next, to have a look inside myself" and ultimately "to get some strength out of the earth". (Hardy 1978, 16). A book, the documentary and, perhaps, the great strike at Wave Hill Station in 1966 were among the results of Hardy's journey. He also revivified his writer's sense. Indeed, as he tells it, there was a twin rebirth in the outback of Hardy the writer and of the Gurrindji, the archetypal Aborigines, who moved back to Wattie Creek, the ancient source of their being.

The key to Hardy's story and its interest to anthropologists is how it handles the significance of the Australians' link to the land. Hardy announced in advance that he looked to the harsh land of the outback to nurture him back to emotional, financial and creative health. He confirms that force in *The Unlucky Australians*. In the first chapter, "The Impact of the Ancient Land", he tells of the discipline the land imposes on all who approach it "for the land has always held something in reserve and imposed its habit on the black man, then the white" (Hardy 1978, 17). Retracing the steps of the early explorers, Hardy hops a truck and travels across the Blue Mountains through Bourke to the outback, waiting "for the impact of the ancient land to shatter self-doubt" (Hardy 1978, 17). As Donald Horne (Hardy, 1978, 7) points out in the Foreword, however, *The Unlucky Australians* is a book about Hardy and the Aborigines. Both feel the impact of the ancient land as the story unfolds. Clearly, Hardy feels that impact not directly but through the Aborigines, most notably through the Gurrindji as they struggle to return to Wattie Creek.

One can hardly avoid understanding Hardy's point that the Australian soul is impoverished insofar as it breaks with the earth. Unifying with the earth means coming to terms with the Aborigines and, more particularly, letting the Aborigines re-establish their cosmological ties with the earth and the Dreamtime it embodies. At this point Hardy the writer is Hardy the Australian. At once he identifies himself with what he describes as the shame of Australia and speaks in unambiguously Australian terms. We meet the Gurrindji as they acted in a historical moment and as Hardy the Australian interprets them acting. For all his Communist sympathies and learning, Hardy gives us the Aborigines and his experiences with them in cultural terms. It is appropriate now, at the end of this analysis, that I should attempt to understand Hardy's book, which presaged my own experiences with the Aborigines.

Who Is an Aborigine?

The town of Bourke is the symbolic gateway to the Australian outback. "Back of Bourke" is a colloquial phrase signifying the far reaches of the desert as it unfolds endlessly in the heat. To Hardy, Bourke also meant "memories of Lawson" and the unionization of the shearers. He goes through the pubs searching for an old timer who may have remembered Lawson or his poetry. He finds none of Lawson's mates but, more significantly, on the edge of the ancient land, he finds the first of the many Aborigines he was to meet during his journey.

She was "an old Aboriginal woman, drunk and flabby, [coming] out of the ladies'. She flowed into a chair beside a round table in the yard, mumbling. In her eyes dwelt the mystery and the defeat − and a dozen flies. She sat forlorn and disgusting − a symbol of white Australia's guilt" (Hardy 1978, 19). Hardy's mind travels away to his time as a soldier in Mataranka, a town far up the track in the Northern Territory. There he had known "black people who had once mastered this pitiless land" (Hardy 1978,

19). In the face of images of Aboriginal degradation and white ig-
norance of its past, Hardy reboards the truck and heads into the
dying centre.

His contrast of the drunken Aborigine with the Aboriginal
masters of the land defines the two poles of a continuum by
which Australians typically interpret all Aboriginal experience.
The founding metaphor of this continuum, moreover, is Hardy's
theme of the Aborigine's relationship to the ancient land. There
in Bourke, on the boundary between urban Australia and its outback, sat an Aborigine representing the inevitable fate of all
Aborigines who forcibly or otherwise severed their essential tie
to the earth.

To Hardy, white Australians had to bear responsibility for the
Aborigines' fate because they had initiated the train of events
that severed their natural tie. The expropriation of the land, the
shameless exploitation of Aboriginal bodies and labour, and pre-
judice had pushed most, perhaps all, Aborigines into Bourkian
netherlands all across the continent. If an Aborigine is only an
Aborigine when tied to his natal land, perhaps there were none
left. By travelling into the dead centre of Australia Hardy tried to
discover if anything could be done to save the Aborigines and his
own soul – and, by implication, the soul of the Australian
nation.

Representations of the kind of Aborigine for which Hardy
searched are ubiquitous in Australia. Postcards depicting a semi-
clothed Aboriginal hunter staring intently into the distance may
be found in any Australian airport. Souvenir shops throughout
the country sell boomerangs and totemically decorated teatowels
as well as more authentic Aboriginal works of art; rulers for sale
in the Northern Territory picture Aborigines dancing a cor-
roboree, a water buffalo, a sunset and a Darwin church. The
average Australian associates Aborigines with the natural
exotica of the landscape. They represent a natural Australia few
Australians ever encounter directly. Hardy may be correct in
saying that the average Australian cannot tolerate having
Aborigines close at hand, yet the symbolic terms of his analysis,
if not its moral vectors, have helped define general understanding about Aborigines since the earliest days.

It may be more contentious to argue that these symbolic terms
also structure anthropological interpretations of Aboriginal life.
One may object, for example, that Durkheim, Fortes, Levi-
Strauss, Sahlins, Scheffler and the countless other foreign an-

thropologists who have made such marvellous use of the
Australian ethnography can hardly be said to see Aborigines
through Australian eyes. One may also properly condemn
Baldwin-Spencer's Social Darwinism and his belief that
Aborigines were doomed in the face of a superior civilization.
The metaphysical assumptions of his ethnography may have as
little to do with modern analyses as the average man's pre-
judices. Moreover, it could be argued that, as trained social
scientists, anthropologists, particularly those who have done extensive fieldwork among Aborigines, have shed their own
cultural assumptions and come to describe Aboriginal reality as
it must be. Can one really argue that those thousands of pages of
ethnography have been structured by the cultural assumptions
of white Australians?

At many levels, the anthropological debates about Aborigines
have lives of their own within the context of scholarly work. It
can hardly be denied that the disputes about Aboriginal
cosmology, kinship, local group composition, territorialty and
so forth derive at least some of their force from within the
academic community and are primarily relevant to it. In addition, although many of the best ethnographers of Aboriginal life
have been Australians (example, Baldwin-Spencer, Berndt,
Elkins, Meggitt), a few have been foreigners, most notably
Radcliffe-Brown. Accepting that these scholars entered the field
with their own preconceptions, can one believe they have sustained them in the face of the professional scrutiny of an international community of scientists? Because the anthropological
debates about Aboriginal life take their fundamental assumptions for granted and develop within the context of the shared
assumptions of which I write, these questions may be answered
affirmatively, without questioning the professionalism of
Australian ethnographers or the veracity of their research
reports (Barnes 1977). For Australian and foreign scholars alike,
the assumptions structure anthropological debate at a level
which is almost never examined itself.

The division of the field is basic evidence for this proposition.
The anthropological literature as well as most courses about
Aborigines in Australian universities tend to divide the field of
study into two parts: a "tribal" part, which addresses such hoary
issues as Aboriginal customary kinship and local group composition, and an "urban" or "non-tribal" part, which addresses the
much smaller and less well-known literature on Aborigines liv-

ing in white society. The astonishing point is that the anthropologists tend to share the commonsense view that these two parts of the Aboriginal literature have nothing to do with each other. At best they agree with most lay analysts that there is an evolutionary relation between them in that the "urban" people mark an inevitable falling away from the condition of the tribal people because of uncontrolled contact between Aborigines and Europeans. These points are true in spite of the fact that all information about the Australian Aborigines has been gathered in the colonial context, often by anthropologists, missionaries and others who were directly involved in the development of the colonial infrastructure.

By focusing on the information about tribal Aborigines and their allegedly customary life, foreign anthropologists have adopted this framework of analysis and endowed the relevant literature with a theoretical significance rivalled by few other ethnographic areas in anthropology. Australian and non-Australian anthropologists have learnt, responded to and developed the rich debates in the literature always within this wider, unexamined framework. Instead of questioning the division of the Aboriginal field (a division, incidentally, that answers comfortably to many anthropologists' assumptions about tribal cultures generally), the international debates have entrenched and legitimated it. When new approaches to Aboriginal life from France, England or the United States arrive in Australia, the Australian assumptions that have helped structure them return home "laundered".

One important consequence of the tendency to treat urban and tribal Aborigines as distinct and unrelated categories is that anthropologists generally ignore the wider Australian colonial context when analysing customary social life. The long debates about local group organization, for example, are famous in the anthropological literature and continue unabated to this day. What is striking about this literature is the sustained effort to treat all data gathered in the last hundred years as comparable and equivalent. The wider historical processes that have totally reorganized Aboriginal residence and work patterns in the twentieth century are used only as analytic screens through which to filter the modern data in order to sift their impact and leave an authentic customary residue. Then proceeds the analysis on the residue which is treated as the golden grain in the sand.

Nowhere else has the "ethnographic present" been more misleading as a model for anthropological thought.

Sansom's recent analysis of the fringe-camps around Darwin is a curious example of this process. Almost no one denies that the Aboriginal squatter settlements that have developed around small cities and country towns in the outback are somehow related to the coming of white Australians. Given the orgiastic lifestyle of most fringe-camps, anthropologists usually outdo the average layperson in labelling these places as aberrrant, manifestly deviant expressions of cultural decay. I have tried to develop an alternative interpretation in this book. None the less, I do agree that the fringe-camps have emerged as part of the Aboriginal adaptation to the colonial order. After Sansom devotes most of his book to the analysis of the kind of behaviour that earns fringe-camps their unsavoury reputations, he concludes by asserting that one may understand them as self-contained, self-reproducing social units (Sansom 1980). If it is mystifying to treat tribal Aborigines in this way, one can only marvel at the obscurantism of anthropologists who must deny the reality they perceive in an effort to legitimate its analysis.

In light of recent structuralist and Marxist efforts to theorize about the relative autonomy of various domains of social life, my points may seem irrelevant. One must understand, however, that anthropologists have not asked these kinds of questions about patterns of Aboriginal local organization. By separating the study of urban Aborigines from the analysis of customary culture, anthropologists beg the question and miss the opportunity ever to raise it. The evidence suggests that anthropologists share the assumptions that the boundary between tribal and urban Aborigines as well as between authentic Aborigines and whites is absolute. There would appear to be no chance for any autonomy of Aboriginal culture life within the wider Australian society. Consequently, it is implied that the two societies and their analyses must be kept apart.

Land Rights and the Expropriation of Aboriginal Culture

When Frank Hardy arrived in Wattie Creek for the first time, he stepped into a long-established role in the Northern Territory, that of the white broker. His reflections on his participation in the Gurrindji's struggle and the dilemmas it posed for him are valuable sources of information about how the role is imposed on, and played by, whites. I analysed the broker's role in the first chapter and briefly suggested that the issue of Aboriginal land rights is a generalization of the transactions in secret, sacred information between Aborigines and whites that have long been part of it. Because the Gurrindji's struggle at Wattie Creek and Hardy's publicity campaign about it thrust the land rights issue on to the national scene for the first time, Hardy's own career as the Gurrindji's broker provides some support for my proposition. What is crucial for this chapter, however, is how only particular aspects of the Gurrindji's situation came to be defined as socially relevant in their dispute. What began as a strike about wages and working conditions eventually became defined as a crisis in the maintenance of customary Aboriginal culture. Against Hardy's initial perceptions and, perhaps, better judgment, he came to accept and actively promote this redefinition of the Gurrindji's situation.

Hardy is a well-known Communist activist in Australia. When he first encountered Aborigines in the Northern Territory he was appalled at their miserable wages and working conditions. Although he did not go to the Northern Territory to become involved in Aboriginal political issues, he arrived in Darwin during a strike at Newcastle Waters, one of the oldest cattle stations in the region, and immediately became interested. He first made the acquaintance of the Aboriginal activists living in Darwin, one of whom, Dexter Daniels, was to play a vital role in both the Newcastle Waters and Wattie Creek disputes. During this early period Hardy focused on the wages and working conditions issues. In addition to being interested in the strike at Newcastle Waters, he was concerned about the failure of national negotiations to guarantee all Aboriginal stockmen the award wage paid to white cattleworkers. Nevertheless, Hardy did not stay long in Darwin: continuing his search for the Australian land, he visited some homesteader friends in the bush and there eventually encountered the Gurrindji.

The Gurrindji were not urban activists; on the contrary, they were a perfect blend of tribal Aborigine and Aboriginal stockman. As stockmen, they sympathized with striking Aborigines at Newcastle Waters and were prepared to walk out. They were also concerned that white men abused their women and that their children grew up unhealthy and poorly educated. As tribal Aborigines, however, they were worried, above all, about their land, most notably their sacred sites at Wattie Creek. The more Hardy became involved with the Gurrindji, the more convinced he became that land rights and the preservation of Aboriginal cultural identity were the fundamental issues. Like the lawyers of CAALAS whom I knew in Alice Springs and who represented the Gurrindji in their final negotiations with Vesteys,[1] the more Hardy became a broker for the Gurrindji and the more he emphasized the cultural component of their situation. He never surrendered his concern for their material well-being, but began to emphasize that solving their cultural problem was of primary importance; in particular, he began to stress that the Gurrindji themselves were preoccupied with the cultural implications of gaining title to their sacred land and with securing the mythological source of their being. In the Gurrindji and their struggle for Wattie Creek, Hardy found the Australian land (Hardy 1978, 220).

He very actively promoted the Gurrindji's land claim. As he describes in his book, he helped organize tours of the southern capitals by the Gurrindji leaders, wrote many articles describing their situation and personally lobbied trade unionists, politicians, public servants and others on their behalf. The BBC documentary shown in England was perhaps the highlight of the campaign. As a result of this publicity, the Gurrindji land claim became an international *cause célèbre* and the wider issues of Aboriginal welfare in the Northern Territory once again drew the public eye.

Hardy (1978, 319) expresses disgust at the fact that it took ten years for any positive action on the Gurrindji claim to happen. The delay, as well as the Gurrindji's success, occurred because of major cleavages in the administration of Aboriginal affairs throughout the country. There were increasing demands that the Welfare Branch and its venerable "assimilation policy" that had commanded Aboriginal administration in the Northern Territory since the early 1950s be replaced with a more enlightened regime. More generally, the Commonwealth government began gradually to assert its responsibility for all Aborigines in the country and to usurp the dominance state governments had previously enjoyed in Aboriginal administration.

The success of the 1967 referendum enjoining the Commonwealth government to assume control of Aboriginal affairs was the first milestone in this new effort. In preparation for assuming its new responsibilities, the then Liberal government established an office of Aboriginal Affairs in the Prime Minister's Department. When Gough Whitlam became prime minister in 1972, he established the Department of Aboriginal Affairs and announced the new "self-determination policy", thereby establishing the organizational and philosophical foundations for the new regime. Land rights and the particular emphasis on the cultural significance of the issue to Aborigines were political cornerstones of the young governments.

On 8 February 1973, Mr Justice A.E. Woodward formally received his commission to conduct an inquiry into how best to recognize and establish traditional land rights for Northern Territory Aborigines. The Woodward Commission institutionalized the land rights issue and created an organizational edifice through which to process it. In the customary style of Australian government inquiries, Judge Woodward called for written submissions from all interested persons and select experts, including anthropologists. He extended his formal procedure and tried to incorporate Aborigines into the inquiry process. His successful recommendation was that the government establish and fund two Aboriginal land councils in the Northern Territory, in Darwin and in Alice Springs. In addition to requiring the solicitors from the lands councils to take evidence from Aborigines, Woodward himself visited most of the major settlements, some cattle communities and other Aboriginal groups (Woodward 1973).

A list of the individuals and organizations who made submissions to the Aboriginal Land Rights Commission form an appendix to the final report (Woodward 1974). It includes Aboriginal activist groups, missionaries, government officials from all states and the Commonwealth, anthropologists, mining companies, cattle organizations, individual Aborigines and Aboriginal councils. One would be hard pressed to find a more definitive list of the people who regularly interact with Aborigines or who regularly help define the social significance of being an Aborigine for the wider Australian public.

In placing a high priority on Aboriginal opinion, Woodward's approach was consistent with the Labor government's "self-determination" policy. More significantly, the list of contributors documents how Woodward incorporated into his investigation the brokerage relationships that existed among Aborigines and whites in the Northern Territory — brokerage relationships that, as in Frank Hardy's case, had initially helped define land rights as an issue for Aborigines. Not only did Woodward officially recognize and legitimate the cultural significance of land rights to Aborigines, but he also attempted to insert his commission and the new administration into the very heart of the social structure of the Northern Territory. Indeed, the primary significance of the commission was that it began to establish the administration of the Commonwealth government as the grounds upon which debate and conflict over this key issue would occur.

The very fact that the land rights issue warranted such close attention from the new government helps substantiate my points about the cultural and political significance for the wider Australian public of the Aborigines' link to the land. The details of Woodward's charge and his recommendations extends the analysis. Initially, Woodward's charge was to investigate "the appropriate means to recognize and establish the *traditional* rights and interests of the Aborigines in and in relation to land and to satisfy in other ways the reasonable aspirations of Aborigines to rights in and in relation to land . . . (Woodward 1974, 1, my emphasis). By phrasing the charge in this way, the government did not restrict Woodward to investigating only customary Aboriginal land tenure, although that was his primary responsibility. He was to address "other reasonable aspirations" but he was to find means "to vest title to land in the Northern Territory" for Aborigines living in their customary way on reserves. The fundamental distinction between Aborigines who have maintained their link to the land and those who have not was built into the terms of the inquiry.

It is interesting to note that the Gurrindji at Wattie Creek were a problematic case within the terms of the commission. Although they certainly had continued to live in the area of their customary territory and to maintain their links to its sacred ground, they lived on a cattle station, not a reserve. Their claims to land on traditional grounds conflicted patently with the claims of the white leaseholder who occupied it on terms defined by European law. There were many such cases in the Northern Territory, all of which document how the land rights commission was not an inquiry into how to reform the land tenure system. When there were clear conflicts between the customary rights of Aborigines and the legal rights of others, the basic terms of the inquiry did not apply.

Special measures had to be found to address such cases. For

example, in spite of the fact that some contributors argued that Aborigines like the Gurrindji should be given the same title as those on reserves, Woodward demurred. He was willing to excise small areas for their use and/or the protection of their sacred sites, and he supported the purchase of leases lying on the land of large residential Aboriginal communities. However, he recommended that such groups receive conventional title to the land which did not depend upon their ethnic identity or invest them with any special rights (Woodward 1974, 33–37).

This argument also applied to the fringe-dwellers and other Aborigines whose links to their sacred land, their "country", were interpreted as broken or moribund. Woodward approved providing them with land and with the means to make it habitable, but it was not to be the same as on reserves. "Aboriginal title", as he came to call it, was to be restricted to Aborigines whose traditional links to their land did not appear to have been altered by the coming of the white man. Hence, even the Gurrindji were a problem (Woodward 1974, 63–64).

The implication of these positions is that real Aborigines are Aborigines who have both maintained their links to their sacred land and apparently remained independent of the white colonization process. If one realizes that the most institutionalized of all Aborigines – those living on the settlements and missions – were the primary candidates for this designation, its cultural foundation and ideological consequences become transparently clear.

As discussed in chapter one, Woodward suggested a procedure for verifying land claims that was modelled on a ubiquitous type of transaction between whites and Aborigines in the Northern Territory and that reaffirmed the salience of the customary criteria differentiating one category of Aborigine from another. To verify a claim, outside investigators should consult the male tribal elders, who, as trustees of the group's sacred lore, objects and sites, have exclusive and definitive knowledge of the land. The investigators must record the information so obtained, plot it on a map and thereby delineate the boundaries of the particular group's land. This translation of Aboriginal cultural knowledge into terms relevant to Australian law was to have been the basis for any group's land claim.

The implication of this procedure for the incorporation of whites into "middler"-type brokerage roles between local Aboriginal groups and the wider bureaucratic context was emphasized in chapter one and alluded to in the discussion of Hardy's gradual incorporation into Gurrindji society. Clearly, Aborigines are constructing their political relationships with critical whites using these cultural terms. To this extent, they are indeed defining or "self-determining" their interaction with white bureaucrats, politicians, anthropologists, and so on. The key point for now, however, is that the white analysis of these transactions (whether anthropological or otherwise) generally portrays them as unproblematic expressions of traditional Aboriginal custom. They ignore the fact that Aborigines are participating in brokerage relationships, are trying to manage an overarching bureaucracy and are helping construct images of themselves that will modify their life chances in the wider political context.

When Woodward turned his attention to the Aboriginal land rights issue, he was not an expert in Aboriginal affairs anymore than Frank Hardy. Unlike Hardy, he consulted people who were experts and became involved with Aborigines as a major administrative power. As he was becoming a broker, he consulted other white brokers and Aborigines who appreciated the role of the white broker in their social life. He absorbed the broker's definition of the situation and institutionalized it in the verification of land claims.

Appropriately, he presented his judgments as consistent with the most informed opinions on the subject. In an extended discussion of the thorny issues of traditional Aboriginal custom (1974, 141–46), he drew upon anthropological and other reliable sources that were relatively unimpeachable in the context. None the less, like his sources, he failed to contextualize the social significance of the cultural practices he was invoking. As anthropologists, politicians, missionaries, bureaucrats and others had done before him, he expropriated Aboriginal culture, reinvested it in the emerging political arena and used it to reproduce the wider political context within which it was embedded.

Conclusion

Analysts commonly assert that, because many Aborigines still observe their customary religious and kinship practices, they must be understood apart from white society. On the one hand, they say that tribal Aborigines have their own culture which is free of white influence. On the other hand, they argue that Aboriginal norms and values conflict with white values and prevent their adherents from participating fully in white society. My analysis of the fringe-campers suggests that neither of these views is particularly satisfactory. For many years whites have legitimated particular administrative practices on the basis of Aboriginal custom. Under the Welfare Branch, Aborigines who followed "the law" were subject to systematic controls and suffered major political and economic disadvantages. Under the current regime, principles allegedly derived from Aboriginal custom itself (most notably, principles of land tenure and political authority) overtly guide administration. These facts have meant that for at least twenty-five years Aborigines have had to consider their culture as well as their political and economic position in the context of white administration. Even practices as fundamental to Aboriginal customary life as boys' initiation ceremonies cannot occur independently of the scrutiny and, more importantly, the judgment of whites. On the contrary, if Aborigines are to control whites at all, they must bring them close to such occasions and try to bind them within the boundaries of Aboriginal society. Hence, far from inhibiting the participation of Aborigines in white society, Aborigines use their customs to adapt to whites and force whites to adapt to them.

Tribal Aborigines share with fringe-dwellers, therefore, the necessity of having to come to terms with the power of white agents. For this reason the meaning of their culture has been as dramatically transformed (even where it appears to have remained untouched or stable) as that of any fringe-dweller. By this remark I do not mean that all Aborigines share the same values or social interests; on the contrary, Aborigines are now fragmented more than ever before in their history. Aborigines in Central Australia must all take account of the fact that whites (particularly white social-welfare administrators) monopolize most political and economic resources. The autonomy that many claim tribal people enjoy is, therefore, as distorted a representation of their social life as is the "detribalized" image of the fringe-dwellers. Neither image represents accurately the fact that Aborigines must interact with and try to control whites if they are to accomplish their goals or to survive.

Although the bush-burning at Mt Kelly was the act of one individual in one small fringe-camp on the edge of Alice Springs, it expressed the ambiguities faced by all Aborigines in Central

Australia in their everyday life. The analysis of Aborigines must come to grips with this kind of situation if it is to progress in the future. Contemporary Aboriginal social life will continue to be misread as long as it is considered in isolation from the wider society in which Aborigines must live.

It was suggested in the Introduction that anthropologists tend to treat the transformation of Aboriginal society in the colonial context as a moral crisis and mourn the loss. If Hardy is any indication, perhaps the anthropologists are also mourning themselves. As long as Aborigines appear to remain intact, some kind of secular salvation is possible for white Australians and regular interaction with them a purificatory process. I have also hinted, however, that deeper political issues also remain only partially hidden in all this intellectual flagellation: anthropologists are political and bureaucratic activists in the welfare arena encompassing the Aborigines. By defining who Aborigines are, they wield definitive power in all senses of the term. If anthropologists, missionaries, bureaucrats and politicians were to recognize the validity of the newly emerging Aboriginal ways of life, they would have to surrender a primary resource in their efforts to dominate Aboriginal people.

What of the Australian soul? Perhaps that is the final issue after all. As guardian of the Aborigines, these intellectuals present themselves as the guardians of the Australian national consciousness. Hardy could not be more explicit even as he articulates his objections in a political language many Australians would reject. One need only observe that those who guard a nation's soul rule its people, Aborigines and whites alike.

Notes

1. Vesteys is the common name of the British multinational company that held the lease to Wave Hill station and against which the Gurrindji went on strike.

Appendix 1:

The Central Australian Cattle Industry

The Northern Territory has been divided into four districts for the purposes of the administration of the pastoral industry: the Alice Springs District in the south; the Victoria River District in the northwest; the Barkly Tableland District in the northeast; and the Darwin and Gulf District in the far north. Stories about the Victoria River District and the Barkly Tableland tend to dominate the public image of the great nothern pastoral industry. The large company stations and great cattle drives are in these two regions. Vesteys, the Victoria River District and the Gurrindji have been so important and so visible to the Australian public that the important and real differences among the districts tend to be lost. The Bureau of Agricultural Economics (BAE), however, introduced its 1968 report on the Northern Territory pastoral industry with these words (BAE 1968, i).

> The information in this report is on a district basis; because of the heterogeneity of characteristics such as land types, rainfall and station size, no attempt has been made to amalgamate district figures into averages for the Northern Territory as a whole.

These other differences have produced major sociological differences. For that reason, I wish to preface my particular discussion of the structure and development of the Central Australian (Alice Springs Pastoral District) pastoral industry with some discussion of the four together.

The annual average rainfall for the Northern Territory varies from 130 millimetres at Charlotte Waters, Central Australia, to over 1520 millimetres on the north coast. The annual average rainfall for each district is: Alice Springs, 130–380 millimetres; Barkly Tableland, 180–510 millimetres; Victoria River District,

510–1020 millimetres; the Darwin and Gulf District, 760–1520 millimetres. Rain is also more reliable in the Victoria River District and the Darwin and Gulf Region. The Alice Springs and Barkly Tableland districts have erratic rainfall, few permanent waterholes and no permanent rivers. Although the Tanami Desert occupies the southern half of the Victoria River District, the Victoria River provides a much greater amount of natural surface water than in the centre or on the Barkly Tableland. The Darwin and Gulf District has the highest proportion of natural waters in the Territory.

The Alice Springs District is, of course, the driest of the four. It is also the largest, covering approximately 549,100 square kilometres of which 283,600 square kilometres were under pastoral lease in 1965. The Darwin and Gulf District covers 320,000 square kilometres. The Barkly Tableland is third with 243,500 square kilometres and 182,600 square kilometres under pastoral lease. The Victoria River District is the smallest with 235,700 square kilometres and 116,500 square kilometres under pastoral lease (BAE 1968, 7–14).

The Alice Springs District and Darwin and Gulf District have a greater number of smaller stations than either of the other two. The Barkly Tableland and the Victoria River District are characterized by relatively few, quite large leases (BAE 1968, 15) (see table 3). It is significant that the long east–west belt of plain and tableland that crosses the Victoria River District and Barkly District have the big stations. They also carry the most cattle and

Table 3 Average station area and percentage distribution of stations by district: as at 30 June 1965

Area in sq. miles (sq. km)	Alice Springs (%)	Barkly Tableland (%)	Victoria River (%)	Darwin and Gulf (%)
Under 501 (1,298)	6	–	–	8
501–1,000 (1,298–2,590)	37	10	–	30
1,001–1,500 (2,592–3,885)	24	25	25	38
1,501–2,000 (3,887–5,180)	18	35	25	8
2,001–2,500 (5,182–6,475)	6	10	31	–
2,501–3,000 (6,477–7,770)	6	10	13	–
Over 3,000 (7,770)	3	10	13	16
Total	100	100	100	100
Average	1,359 sq. miles (3,520 sq. km)	2,064 sq. miles (5,346 sq. km)	2,239 sq. miles (5,799 sq. km)	1,412 sq. miles (3,757 sq. km)

Source: BAE 1968, 15 (metric conversions added)

the biggest herds, even though they have the lowest areas under lease.

The districts with more cattle also have more men working per station. The Alice Springs District has the fewest people working, the lowest number of labour weeks per year and the fewest number of labour weeks per 259 square kilometres (100 square miles). However, it has the most labour weeks per one hundred head of cattle. The Victoria River District leads in all these categories but the last.

There appears to be a rough correlation among the size of the stations, the average herd size, the total number of cattle in the region and the size of the labour force. The bigger the stations, the larger the herds, the greater the total number of cattle in the region, the greater the size of the labour force (BAE 1968: 2–21) (see tables 4 and 5). This produces a scale with the Victoria River District in the top position, followed by the Barkly Tableland, the Darwin and Gulf District, and the Alice Springs District.

Table 4 Average herd size per station, by district: 1963 to 1965 (as at 30 June)

Year	Alice Springs (no.)	Barkly Tableland (no.)	Victoria River (no.)	Darwin and Gulf (no.)
1962–63	2,401	13,119	18,983	10,047
1963–64	2,490	13,694	18,035	9,979
1964–65	2,040	13,696	17,597	10,312
Average	2,310	13,503	18,205	10,113

Source: BAE 1968, 20

Table 5 Percentage distribution of stations by herd size: three-year average, 1962–63 to 1964–65

Herd Size	Alice Springs (%)	Barkly Tableland (%)	Victoria River (%)	Darwin and Gulf (%)
Under 2,501	67	15	6	15
2,501– 5,000	27	15	–	23
5,000– 7,500	6	20	–	31
7,501–10,000	–	5	19	–
10,001–12,500	–	–	25	8
12,501–15,000	–	–	–	8
Over 15,000	–	45	50	15
Total	100	100	100	100

Source: BAE 1968, 21

These variations correlate roughly with the distribution of types of ownership from region to region (BAE 1968, 17) (see table 6). The most important point is that in 1968 not a single pastoral lease in the Alice Springs District was owned by a company. Sixty-seven per cent were owned by individuals and 33 per cent were held by partnerships. In contrast, the majority (56 per cent) of the stations in the Victoria River District were held by companies. Only 19 per cent were held by individuals. Eighty-eight per cent of the owners in the Alice Springs District lived on their stations: only 39 per cent of the owners in the Victoria River District did so. A similar pattern emerges in the distribution of stations by management type (BAE 1968, 18) (see table 7). Only 15 per cent of the Alice Springs leases had paid managers. On 85 per cent of the stations either the owner or a partner managed the station. In the Victoria River District, 62 per cent of the leases had paid managers. Owners or partners managed 38 per cent of the leases in the Victoria River District.

Table 6 Percentage distribution of stations by ownership type: as at 30 June 1965

Ownership type	Alice Springs (%)	Barkly Tableland (%)	Victoria River (%)	Darwin and Gulf (%)
Individual				
Resident	61	45	19	23
Non-resident	6	5	6	8
Partnerships				
Resident	27	15	19	31
Non-resident	6	0	0	0
Company	0	35	56	38
Total	100	100	100	100

Source: BAE 1968, 17

Table 7 Percentage distribution of stations by management type: as at 30 June 1965

Management type	Alice Springs (%)	Barkly Tableland (%)	Victoria River (%)	Darwin and Gulf (%)
Sole owner	58	45	19	15
Partner	27	15	19	31
Paid manager	15	40	62	54
Total	100	100	100	100

Source: BAE 1968, 18

These features of the four regions have established different structures of industrial relations between the pastoral workers and their bosses. The stations in the Victoria River District, for example, have much larger, more stable Aboriginal communities than are generally found in Central Australia. This is in part connected with the greater demand for labourers in the Victoria River District. The Gurrindji are a famous example of the relatively large communities living on these expansive stations. It is rare to find communities of more than twenty people on Central Australian properties,[1] and the demand for labour in the Alice Springs District is much smaller than anywhere else in the Northern Territory (BAE 1968, 53) (see table 6).

These differences in the size of resident populations in each district make for differences in the scale of operations and the structure of industrial relations. The majority of properties in Central Australia are managed by resident owners. Some owners live on their properties but employ a manager (BAE 1968, 17) (see table 7). These men and women have often lived on their stations for many years and recruited their labourers from among the same groups of Aborigines. Relations among pastoralists and their workers tend to be highly personalized. In the Victoria River and Barkly Tableland districts, however, the structure of boss–worker relations is more formal and characteristic of industrial settings. Although a significant number of properties are managed by owner-residents, large companies dominate these two regions and hire managers to operate their properties. The workers are segregated according to task, skill and social prestige. There is a much clearer hierarchy of authority and prestige than in Central Australia.

One final point about the four regions. They have developed different markets for their cattle and, until the governments of the United Kingdom and the Commonwealth of Australia signed a meat agreement in 1951, the fortunes of the four districts varied independently of one another. The Alice Springs District sold its cattle to South Australia; in 1965, for example, 98 per cent of the beef sold from there went to South Australia. Occasionally pastoralists sold cattle for fattening in Queensland. There has also always been a small market for local cattle in Alice Springs. Pastoralists on the Barkly Tableland have historically sent their cattle to Queensland; most go to the Channel Country for fattening, and some go to abattoirs in Brisbane and, in recent years, Katherine or Darwin. This pattern

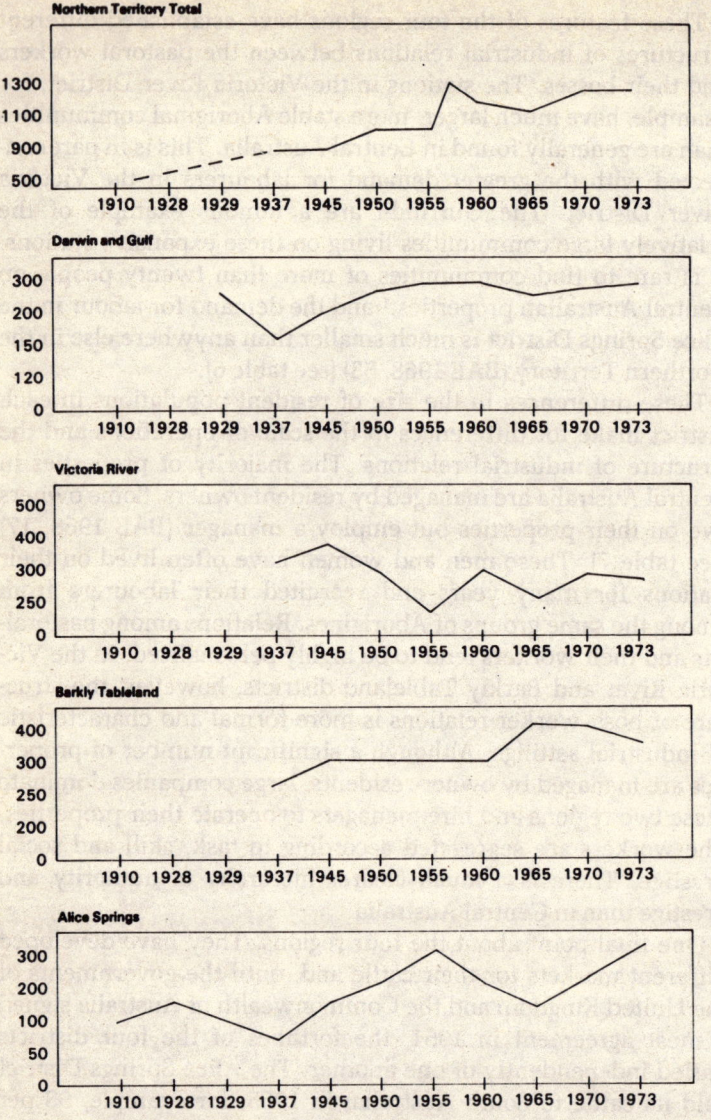

Figure 4 Northern Territory cattle numbers (in thousands): By districts, 1910 to 1973

Sources: BAE 1959, 2; 1968 5
Northern Territory Administration, Administrator's *Annual Report*, relevant years
Central Australian Administration, Administrator's *Annual Report*, relevant years

encouraged companies such as Vesteys to establish a series of properties along the east–west stock route. They bred cattle in the most western properties (such as Victoria River Downs or Wave Hill) and moved them along to the eastern properties for gradual fattening. The Victoria River District divided its cattle between the Wyndham meatworks in Western Australia and Queensland and Southeast Asia. In recent years it has also sent cattle to the abattoirs at Katherine and Darwin. The Darwin and Gulf District earlier relied upon the trade in live cattle to the Philippines. Since that ended it sends cattle to Queensland, Darwin and Katherine. As described in detail below, the market for none of these regions was secure until 1951. Moreover, because of the diversity of the demand in earlier times, plans that helped one region did not always affect the others (see figure 4).

The Alice Springs Pastoral District

Central Australia is an arid region. Average annual rainfall varies between 50 millimetres a year at Charlotte Waters in the south to over 380 millimetres a year at Tennant Creek in the north. Alice Springs and the MacDonnell Ranges average about 250 millimetres per year (Perry 1962). Most Central Australian rain comes from the north in the summer as a remnant of the great summer monsoons that water the Top End. Autumn usually marks a drop in the expected rainfall. Rain falls only occasionally in the winter when the wind and the weather blow from the south. In spite of these regularities, both local areas and the region as a whole are subject to wide variations. Heavy monsoons and severe droughts disrupt the normal curve. Rainfall varies from year to year. When it falls within given years is also variable. Moreover, it sometimes happens that some small, local areas enjoy surplus rain while others only a few kilometres away perish. Variability is the key to Central Australian natural rhythms (Davidson 1972, 38–39).

According to the agricultural economists, Central Australia has no particular growing season (Davidson 1972, 32–33). Plants germinate whenever there is enough water. Vegetation varies according to the amount of water plants need to germinate, mature and go to seed again. Normal years provide enough water in the summer to germinate and sustain natural sorghums. Winter rains nourish forbs. These require fairly heavy rainfall followed by secondary falls to sustain growth. It sometimes happens that rain is so widely dispersed in time and area that not enough falls at once to initiate germination. This can happen even if there has been sufficient total annual rainfall. Plants sometimes germinate but die from lack of follow-up rain. Hence, normal total rainfall can produce and has produced droughts.

Although the whole region is arid, the key is microecological variations within a set of conditions. Compared with regions in the southern parts of Australia, Central Australia is uniformly harsh, yet the prevailing conditions vary from season to season and region to region. These variations are important to the people and animals that live there. The mountains, for example, provide opportunities that do not exist in the desert. The Mac-Donnell Ranges bisect Central Australia from east to west. There are also smaller sets of foothills clustered to the northeast, northwest and southwest of the main ranges. The major rivers of the region have their sources in these mountain ranges and flood on to the plains below. Although the ranges are somewhat formidable, the countryside around them is the richest in the region. The rivers and mountain crevices store water. The soil provides nutrients necessary to sustain a varied, succulent plant life and varied animal life. Deserts surround the mountains on the east, south, west and northwest. Life is possible here but conditions are harsher than in the mountains. Rain falls less frequently and is more irregular; water is not stored well; the grasses that survive are hardy perennials with deep roots, such as spinifex; and fewer animals survive per unit of land.

The Aborigines appreciated the vagaries of the climate and lived accordingly (Meggitt 1962, 49–50; Sahlins 1974, 1–40). The history of pastoral settlement, however, testifies to the fact that few whites in the early days understood the region's character. Perhaps the majority underestimated its capriciousness (Duncan 1967). Before the turn of the century, however, there was abundant evidence that the settlers had to adapt their ways of living if they were to survive. The problem was that the cattle market did not warrant the cost of installing the technical devices necessary for large-scale pastoralism; bores were quite expensive. Several investors went broke trying to develop the region. They withdrew from the field and either sold or surrendered their leases (Duncan 1967, 47–77). The pastoralists who followed had to limit the size of their herds and the scope of their activities to what the natural resources would carry. This meant they ran small herds on large tracts of land among the mountains and along the rivers. This was the only way they could obtain sufficient natural water to keep stock alive.

The earliest settlement of Central Australia occurred along the telegraph line, the MacDonnell Ranges and south of Alice Springs. From 1910 to 1930 settlers slowly occupied the mountain regions to the northeast and northwest of Alice Springs. Although at least one settler brought sheep in from Queensland, many of the new pastoralists originally entered the area for other purposes. For example, Arltunga, a small goldfield northeast of Alice Springs, sparked a minor goldrush from the 1890s to about 1910. During the peak mining period Arltunga had a larger population than Alice Springs and stimulated some local commerce and demand for meat. After the gold ran out most of the miners left, but a few who had run businesses or held minor government posts moved on to the land. At least six pastoral leases in the region around Arltunga were opened by such men up to 1920. There were similar minor mineral rushes at Hatches Creek, Mt Doreen and the Granites (Meggitt 1964, 25).

This settlement did not mark steady development in the cattle industry. The number of cattle, for example, apparently either decreased or remained roughly the same throughout this period. Duncan estimates that there were about 100,000 head of cattle in Central Australia in 1910. By 1937 the number is estimated to have been less than 80,000 (Duncan 1967, 140; BAE 1959, 17). Although there was a severe drought in 1928–29, it does not seem likely that its effects were felt for so long or can account completely for the low cattle population. The small herds indicate the nature of pastoralism at the time and reflect the absence of a market.

It is apparent that the settlement of the region during this period was a piecemeal process and developed in response to the needs of individual settlers. Some settlers, for example, ran cattle and operated other enterprises at the same time. The horse market provided many with an income based on pastoral pursuits. Mining engaged others, and others subsisted. Although the settlers had leases, rents were low and not properly enforced in the centre. Payne and Jackson report, for example, that in 1937 arrears in rent were £19,650. Of that £9,492 was on Central Australian properties. Rather than pressure the pastoralists, the government made efforts to stimulate pastoral development: it offered to subsidize the construction of bores and fences and to subsidize the freight charges on hybrid bulls. The pastoralists failed to respond because the cost was too great (Payne and Jackson 1937). There were no credit facilities open. The pastoralists either had little reserve capital, spent what they had on costly imports or saved it. They did not use it to develop their station equipment. The point is that the pastoralists did not over-commit themselves to cattle husbandry. Pastoralism was not an industry but rather a tactic some men used to provision what was essentially a domestic economy.

In technical terms, the pastoralists used the "open-range" technique of cattle husbandry. This term refers to a broad spectrum of husbandry practices that employ natural pastures and permit animals virtually to run wild. It contrasts with techniques involving management of animals and the use of hybrid, cultivated pastures or feed lots. The two techniques have different capital, land and labour requirements. Open-range husbandry uses large areas of undeveloped land, large amounts of cheap labour sporadically and little capital. Intensive use of any or all of these three resources marks a more closed technique. Davidson remarks that, given a market, the most efficient and profitable approach in Australia employs large areas of cheap land, small amounts of expensive labour and, consequently, intensive use of capital (Davidson 1972, 64). Under the circumstances, anything other than a completely open-range approach was economically unjustified and inimical to the pastoralists' interests. There were certain consequences.

The pastoralists settled in the region that supported the most bountiful game and were otherwise ecologically the most favourable. They introduced a species of animal that consumed great quantities of the same natural resources as the fauna the Aboriginal hunted. In this way, they directly threatened the Aborigines' ecological base and, consequently, their ability to survive.

It was nevertheless true that cattle did not necessarily undermine the Aborigines' economy. Cattle are far simpler to hunt than many other animals and could have made the region more bountiful. The problem was that not all pastoralists appreciated having their cattle speared. Aborigines were regularly gaoled for cattle spearing and police and some pastoralists took more drastic action. In many areas, therefore, the pastoralists and the Aborigines competed over the rights to use the land and its resources.

During this period, however, local Aboriginal groups and individual pastoralists could negotiate private settlements. I have no idea how common such agreements were, nor do I really know if anything so formal as a verbal or other explicit agreement ever existed. However, it seems certain that tacit agreements developed. I have been told, for example, that some men always had trouble with "the natives" because they did not treat them properly. Duncan observes that "native depredations" were said to cause great hardship in the herds and often seriously depleted them (Duncan 1967, 70–73). Not all pastoralists suffered the incursions. Aborigines describe pastoralists as "cheeky" or not, according to the extent to which they fulfil certain expectations. The early pastoralists had a relatively uniform reputation for being cheeky, although some are remembered with greater distaste than others. The extent to which pastoral settlement undermined the capacity for the Aborigines to live and, consequently, seemed inimical to the Aborigines' interests varied and was a matter for negotiation. This must have been especially true when cattle were relatively worthless and their numbers low.

The point is that the open-range technique of cattle herding required a lot of cheap labour for short but crucial periods during the year. White labourers could not be hired in Central Australia, Davidson notes that during the time the Northern Territory was being settled the urban economy of southern Australia offered greater opportunities for work than it had in the mid nineteenth century. Hence, white labour was quite expensive (Davidson 1972, 65). Aborigines were the only alternative source of labour and the pastoralists had to procure them. The pastoralists did not often pay Aborigines in cash (Rose 1965, 34), and nor was there a minimum set wage. Aborigines gave their labour as part of their agreement and set of exchanges with pastoralists. They gave labour and access to their land in exchange for being "looked after" by the pastoralists. Exactly what they received in return varied. Some men were known as "good bosses" and were "generous"; others were not. The point was that, prior to the Second World War, the Aborigines and the white settlers managed to sustain linked but functionally autonomous domestic economies in many areas. The conflict between their modes of production and their wider social interests was not yet manifest. During this period, the dynamics of interaction between the two societies developed in the context of personal, local relationships between particular Aboriginal groups and local white settlers.

In 1929 the railway arrived in Alice Springs. This meant that Central Australian cattle could be trucked and sold as fats on the Adelaide market. Notwithstanding, the demand was sporadic and still insufficient to make the industry flourish. Pastoralists near the railheads benefitted most. By 1937, Payne and Jackson still complained that the industry was underdeveloped and largely unprofitable (Payne and Jackson 1937, 40).

The early encroachment of white settlers on the pasturelands of Central Australia created a different set of circumstances from those that existed in the Victoria River District or the Barkly Tableland. The local ecology, the absence of a market for cattle and the consequent scale and organization of pastoralism established conditions inimical to the emergence of an industrial structure proper. The pastoralists were not over-committed to pastoralism: they were free and often engaged in other activities in order to sustain their livelihood. Pastoralism was one tactic among others for survival in the relatively sparse and loosely organized field of the time.

These conditions affected the pastoralists' relations with the local Aboriginal people. It was clear the pastoralists occupied the Aborigines' land and introduced a new animal into the local ecology. The scale of operations and the low value of cattle, however, meant there was no necessary conflict of short-term interests. On the contrary, there were reasons for mutual interaction and localized cooperation. The fact and possibility of violent encounters between the Aborigines and the pastoralists or police loomed always in the background. Yet, the Aborigines' need for a secure food supply and the pastoralists' need for land and labour provided the opportunity for local agreements. The field was open to and characterized by negotiations between particular pastoralists and particular bands of Aborigines. Given the nature of this process, the results went both ways.

There is evidence that the Central Australian industry began to pick up during and immediately after the Second World War. The administrator for the Northern Territory Administration mentioned in a wartime report that the pastoralists were enjoying a buoyant market. Central Australian beef was drawing top prices and top prizes in Adelaide. The administrator also noted that there were no rents outstanding (Annual Report 1948). This contrasts with Payne and Jackson's observations ten years earlier

(Payne and Jackson 1937, 16). The soldiers stationed up and down the track between Alice Springs and Darwin during the war provided quite a significant local demand. In 1942–43, for example, it was reported that they consumed the beef of 2768 bullocks in Alice Springs, all of which was supplied by local pastoralists. This was more than 10 per cent of the total demand for the year. In addition, 20,525 bullocks were shipped to Adelaide during the same period (Annual Report 1944). The local demand collapsed when the war ended, but the Adelaide demand doubled immediately. Approximately 43,900 head of cattle were shipped to Adelaide in 1946–47, and 41,200 the next year (Annual Report 1948). In order to secure this demand for northern and Central Australian beef the Commonwealth government entered into negotiations with the United Kingdom for a long-term meat agreement.

On 11 October 1951, the United Kingdom and Australia signed a meat agreement and thereby transformed the Central Australian pastoral industry. The agreement covered the fifteen-year period from 1 July 1952 to 31 September 1967. In the treaty the governments agreed

> to develop further the production of meat in Australia, to increase the export of meat to the United Kingdom, and to provide a satisfactory market in the United Kingdom for the whole of the exportable surplus of meat from Australia during the term of the agreement.

The terms included a schedule of prices and a method by which to adjust prices in accordance with changes in the Australian industry's cost structure (BAE 1953, 1–7). This agreement temporarily solved two problems the Central Australian pastoralists had always faced: the absence of a regular market for cattle and a stable price structure. In the late 1950s a demand for manufacturing quality beef emerged in the United States and by 1961 the Australian government had agreed to help supply it. The United Kingdom agreement was not renegotiated and ended on schedule. In 1974 the United States imposed quotas on Australian beef: it claimed the Australians had surpassed their allotted amount. Once again Central Australian pastoralists were left without a market. In the meantime the nature of the industry and of Central Australian society had been completely transformed.

Prior to 1940 Central Australian settlers were not wholly committed to pastoralism: they could not afford to invest what limited capital they had in developing their properties. They marketed in response to their own immediate needs and the current demand and the volume of their production depended on the weather. They were not heavily in debt nor were they pressured by outside agencies to produce more. Although they endeavoured to produce and sell cattle for a market, they did not depend upon it in order to remain viable. The weather could break them, but market fluctuations could not.

The rise of an expanded market in Adelaide, the United Kingdom and the United States, however, stimulated them to expand production. In order to do so, they had to increase the relative carrying capacity of the land: they had to sink bores. Bores, however, were expensive and demanded the pastoralists invest capital in their properties. The government encouraged them to do so by granting tax concessions on capital improvements. There were no credit facilities available and pastoralists had to reinvest the profits from their cattle sales. Consequently, they became more dependent upon the existence of a cattle market than before 1940. In order to meet the market demands, in other words, the Central Australian pastoralists had to increase their commitment to pastoralism and cease operating only in terms of a domestic economy.

Many pastoralists did invest heavily in their properties and some settlers who had previously occupied land incapable of sustaining cattle on natural water supplies also sank bores and started new operations. The industry expanded to include all land of any value for grazing. Only the most worthless, inhospitable desert land remained vacant.

By 1965 there was an average of ten bores per property in the Alice Springs Pastoral District; there were also an average of two wells, four earth tanks and one dam. The pastoralists dug wells from the earliest days, but they were usually shallow and produced comparatively meagre supplies of water. As the soil of the Alice Springs District is not suitable for dams, bores are the best form of man-made watering point. Unfortunately, they are also the most expensive. There were almost no bores in the district prior to 1940. Only the government had the cash to sink them and then they existed only along some stretches of the north–south stock route. Although some pastoral experts insist the Central Australian pastoralists have failed to develop their properties sufficiently, the important point is that they have increased considerably the overall level of capital investment in the land.

Because their investment and commitment to the industry has

increased, pastoralists can no longer afford to allow Aborigines free reign on the properties and with stock. Even those men who had previously struck reasonable agreements with one or more local domestic groups can no longer withstand the cost of stock speared or slaughtered. Moreover, Aborigines, pastoralists and government officials all informed me that the change in the cattle market fundamentally altered the demand for Aboriginal labour. Uniformly they said that the demand for Aboriginal stockmen has decreased considerably in the last several years. Because the demand was minimal and sporadic before 1951, the further contraction of the job opportunities on the stations has left many Aborigines with no means to support themselves. There now exists a manifest and fundamental conflict of interests between the pastoralists and the Aborigines.

Pastoral experts insist that the Central Australian settlers still employ the open-range technique of animal husbandry. Some criticize pastoralists for not having erected a sufficient number of yards and fences (Kelly 1971, 146); others demand that they use more hybrid forms of pasture. Compared with southern parts of Australia where the climate favours intensive animal husbandry, Central Australia is indeed relatively undeveloped. Although some pastoralists in the region grow lucerne, a hybrid pasture, the climate in general does not favour it. It requires more water than is generally available and has remained a minor supplementary feed for drought relief and fattening purposes. It is also true that, compared to some southern regions, Central Australian paddocks are large and that cattle are left to wander unmanaged within them. Nevertheless, pastoralists have built fences and yards. In 1965, for example, there was an average of 70 kilometres of boundary fence and 78 kilometres of internal fencing per station in the Alice Springs District. There were, in addition, an average of nine bronco yards, two drafting yards and five miscellaneous-type yards per station (BAE 1968, 29) (see table 8). According to my informants, this process has continued since 1965. Although these figures are low relative to southern Australia, they have had some important effects on the demand for Aboriginal labour.

Prior to 1940 there were few fences or yards of any kind in Central Australia. Consequently, the cattle wandered anywhere, according to the quality of natural conditions. Beasts belonging to different pastoralists became mixed up in the process. In order to sort them for branding and sale, pastoralists and

Table 8 Structural improvements – station average by district: as at 30 June 1965

Item	Alice Springs (no.)	Barkly Tableland (no.)	Victoria River (no.)	Darwin and Gulf (no.)
Made waters				
Bores	10	23	9	2
Wells	2	–	–	–
Earth tanks	4	2	–	–
Dams	1	2	1	–
Total made waters	17	27	10	2
	miles (km)	miles (km)	miles (km)	miles (km)
Boundary*	44 (70)	80 (128)	30 (48)	19 (30)
Internal	49 (78)	127 (203)	151 (241)	92 (147)
Total fencing	93 (148)	207 (331)	181 (289)	111 (177)
	(no.)	(no.)	(no.)	(no.)
Yards				
Bronco	9	16	11	11
Drafting	2	3	5	3
Other	5	1	5	7
Total yards	16	20	21	21

* In the case of a "shared" boundary fence, half has been attributed to each.
Source: BAE 1968, 29 (metric conversions added)

stockmen from adjoining properties established mustering camps at central points. They spent several months each autumn and winter mustering, culling and branding. Each pastoralist hired eight to ten ringers for the muster and brought along his head stockman and supplementary ringers. Most of these men were, of course, Aborigines.

Boundary fences eliminate the need for the big autumn muster because cattle remain on the property. It now takes fewer men less time to muster them. They no longer have to search another pastoralist's property or spend time sorting one person's cattle from another's. The pastoralists can therefore do without many supplementary ringers. Before 1940 the mustering season extended from April to October, a period of seven months. In 1965, the Bureau of Agricultural Economics estimated that in the Alice Springs District an average of 7.6 Aboriginal men worked twenty-two weeks a year on each station and that 3.8 white or part-Aboriginal men worked twenty-six weeks a year (BAE 1968, 53) (see table 9).

By suggesting that only the time men work has been reduced, these figures contradict what people in Alice Springs told me. The point is that there is considerably less work now than before 1940. The precise way individual pastoralists choose to allocate

Table 9 Annual number of employees and average duration of employment – station average by district: two-year average, 1963–64 to 1964–65

Labour type	Alice Springs		Barkly Tableland		Victoria River		Darwin and Gulf	
	No.	Av. wks worked	No.	Av. wks worked	No.	Av. wks worked	No.	Av. wks worked
Male								
Aboriginal	7.6	22	13.3	30	23.3	26	19.2	31
Other	3.8	26	14.4	25	19.1	19	7.9	29
Total	11.4	23	27.7	27	42.4	23	27.1	30
Female								
Aboriginal	1.5	23	5.2	36	11.0	34	5.6	37
Total all labour	12.9	23	32.9	29	53.4	25	32.7	31

Source: BAE 1968, 53

it no doubt varies according to particular circumstances. It is clear, for example, that not all pastoralists erected fences at the same rate or to the same extent. The process took a number of years and proceeded unevenly throughout the district. In general, however, the pastoralists have erected fences and thereby reduced the demand for men to staff the large muster camps.

Pastoral work has always been seasonal in Central Australia, with the demand for Aboriginal workers always greatest during the autumn and winter. The point is that the number of men and the length of time they work during the mustering season has dropped with the construction of fences. This has been generally true in spite of the fact that the overall productivity of the stations has increased.[2] Because the pastoralists put their profits from cattle sales back into their stations, the expanded market financed the process that has reduced the demand for Aboriginal workers. It took a number of years to erect fences over the Central Australian countryside, but the change from overland droving to cattle trucking was fairly rapid and dramatic. Cattle droving, particularly in the Top End, has an unassailable place in the mythology of pastoralism. Within the industry, the drovers and their men occupy the top rung in the occupational prestige hierarchy. Aborigines who worked regularly for boss drovers had great prestige among their fellows and even among white bosses. Those who worked on the great routes in the Top End regarded themselves and were often regarded by others as especially skilled.

A skilled drover was essential. Droving occurred during the dry season when grass was normally less nutritious and often in short supply. In the early days water was in acutely short supply on almost all the great stock routes in the Northern Territory (Duncan 1967, 55). The condition and often simply the lives of the cattle upon delivery at the market depended upon a drover's capacity to drive the mob properly. If he made errors the cattle might lose condition or die. Skilled drovers are reputed to have defied even the worst weather.

In the mid 1950s men began to experiment with large trucks known as roadtrains. Nowadays all cattle in Central Australia are transported from station to the market or railroad in Alice Springs by roadtrain. Initially roadtrains were rather expensive but it was not long before the cost dropped. The advantages of roadtrains have put drovers out of business (BAE 1968, 4) (see table 10). They eliminate almost all the uncertainty attendant upon droving; and they are safer and quicker. Pastoralists no longer have to consider the condition of the stock routes in order to decide whether to drove cattle. Roadtrains travel from almost anywhere in Central Australia to either Alice Springs or Mt Isa in a matter of hours. Cattle hardly have time to get thirsty, let alone die from lack of water or insufficient grass. Although cattle may be bruised upon arrival, they do not lose condition as badly as on droves and arrive in much the same condition as when they left.

Table 10 Road transport of cattle in Northern Territory: 1958–59 to 1964–65

Year	Cattle moved off stations	Cattle carried by road transport	Percentage by road transport
1958–59	205,873	41,996	20
1959–60	209,871	48,276	23
1960–61	209,226	93,151	45
1961–62	186,379	85,823	46
1962–63	160,430	67,045	42
1963–64	180,265	101,151	56
1964–65	149,802	113,292	76

Source: BAE 1968, 4

This change further reduced the labour demand, particularly for the most skilled Aboriginal stockmen. In conjunction with the decline in work on the stations, the death of droving seriously constricted Aboriginal employment opportunities. Some pastoralists also became reluctant to support non-working Aboriginal populations or permit them to exploit the land's resources freely. Those that had previously been only unnecessary and part of the local scene were transformed into a dispossessed and dependent people.

The Central Australian cattle industry is now relatively capital intensive (see tables 11 and 12). Whereas before 1951 most pastoralists relied upon many cheap Aboriginal labourers, they now use relatively fewer men who are more highly paid. In the early days pastoralists could be ruined by the weather or fires. They were, however, relatively impervious to the vagaries of the cattle market. Because they sought in the first instance to provision themselves, sold cattle only when the demand permitted and did not invest heavily in their operations, they had no debts. Banks could not foreclose and the market could not injure them. The relatively intense capital investment in their properties since 1951, however, has changed that situation. Pastoralists

Table 11 Capital structure – station average by district: three-year average, 1962–63 to 1964–65

Capital item	Alice Springs		Barkly Tableland		Victoria River		Darwin and Gulf	
	$	%	$	%	$	%	$	%
Made waters	37,274	22	100,089	14	46,596	6	9,652	2
Fencing	23,450	13	51,511	7	55,970	8	36,102	9
Yards	9,628	5	12,962	2	18,178	3	15,861	4
Buildings	7,922	5	29,530	4	29,760	4	11,158	3
Plant and machinery	9,936	6	20,060	3	24,854	3	18,728	5
Total excl. cattle	88,210	51	214,152	30	175,358	24	91,501	23
Cattle	84,436	49	488,447	70	542,024	76	298,561	77
Total	172,646	100	702,599	100	717,382	100	390,062	100

Source: BAE 1968, 33

Table 12 Gross annual investment – station average by district: three-year average, 1962–63 to 1964–65

Capital item	Alice Springs		Barkly Tableland		Victoria River		Darwin and Gulf	
	$	%	$	%	$	%	$	%
Waters	2,816	23	14,550	28	10,946	26	2,108	7
Fencing	1,392	11	5,004	10	8,098	19	8,838	32
Yards	454	4	1,482	3	2,706	7	2,190	8
Buildings	980	8	3,664	7	5,916	14	3,408	12
Plant and machinery	2,226	18	7,232	14	7,934	19	7,712	28
Total excl. livestock	7,868	64	31,932	62	35,600	85	24,256	87
Livestock*	4,394	36	19,510	38	6,198	15	3,518	13
Total	12,262	100	51,442	100	41,798	100	27,774	100

* Includes horses, and transfers of cattle between stations.

Source: BAE 1968, 37

Table 13 Net income structure – station average by district: three-year average, 1962–63 to 1964–65

Item	Alice Springs ($)	Barkly Tableland ($)	Victoria River ($)	Darwin and Gulf ($)
A. Cash income	24,994	92,096	80,349	42,226
B. Cash cost	23,780	70,959	60,971	40,486
C. Net cash income (A − B)	1,214	21,137	19,378	1,740
D. Interest paid	2,280	1,641	2,480	2,364
E. Cattle investory change	1,427	47,794	36,763	27,739
F. Depreciation	9,030	22,228	24,428	12,184
G. Net farm income (C + D + E − F)	−4,109	48,344	34,193	19,659
H. Operator's labour allowance	1,903	1,903	1,903	1,903
I. Capital and management income (G − H)	−6,012	46,441	32,290	17,756
J. Total capital	172,646	702,599	717,382	390,062
Percentage return to capital and management (100 I ÷ J)	−3.5%	6.6%	4.5%	4.6%

Source: BAE 1968, 49

now depend critically upon the market simply in order to keep themselves solvent. Indeed, in Central Australia very few pastoralists make a living at all (see table 13).

Aborigines have suffered in the course of this process. One basic condition for their continued ability to maintain their domestic economy and have some control over the effects of white settlement was eliminated. It is now absolutely impossible for them to wander back and forth between their own domestic economy and that of the white settler. The white settler has given away his own domestic economy and thereby made it impossible for Aborigines also to sustain one.

Notes

1. The major exception is the group of properties three hundred kilometres northeast of Alice Springs near the headwaters of the Sandover River.
2. The construction and maintenance of bores and fences created new jobs, of course. However, the evidence suggests that men who already had fairly permanent jobs were assigned the new tasks during the off-season; hence, the new jobs did not offset the decrease in demand for ringers. It was also the case that specialists emerged: some men formed small companies that took contracts for fencing, boring and even mustering.

Appendix 2:

Work Careers of Mt Kelly Adults

Name*	Sex	Urban	Rural
Blake, L.	F		•
Cooper, J.	M	•	•
Corcoran, B.	M	•	•
Corcoran, D.	M	•	•
Corcoran, R.	M	•	•
George, H.	M	•	•
Hines, M.	F		•
Hines, R.	M	•	•
Jackson, J.	M		•
Jackson, L.	F		•
Jackson, P.	M		•
Mayhew, A.	F		•
Mayhew, K.	F	•	•
Peters, A.	M	•	•
Richardson, B.	M	•	•
Richardson, C.	F	•	•
Richardson, D.	M	•	•
Richardson, G.	M	•	•
Richardson, M.	F	•	•
Richardson, N.	M	•	•
Richardson, P.	F		•
Richardson, T.	M		•
Salterson, E.	F		•
Samuelson, W.	M	•	•
Sharp, C.	M	•	•
Sharp, G.	M	•	•
Sharp, G.	F	•	•
Sharp, I.	F	•	•
Sharp, P.	F	•	•
Sharp, T.	M	•	•
Taylor, N.	F		•
Williams, G.	F	•	•
Williams, J.	F		•

* All of these adults were considered residents of Mt Kelly at some time during my fieldwork from April 1975 to June 1976. They do not represent the total adult population at any single time.

Bibliography

Adams, Richard N. 1970. Brokers and career mobility systems in the structure of complex societies. *Southwestern Journal of Anthropology.* 26: 315–27.

Albrecht, P.G.E. 1969. The social and psychological reasons for the alcohol problem among Aborigines. In *Better health for Aborigines?*, ed. B.S. Hetzel, M. Dobbin, L. Lippmann, and E. Eggleston, 36–41. St Lucia: University of Queensland Press.

Alice Springs Citizens Association. 1975. Minutes.

Australian Bureau of Statistics. 1971. *Census of population and housing.* Commonwealth Bureau of Census and Statistics. Canberra: Australian Government Printing Service.

BAE. 1953. *Beef cattle production: An index of cost movements.* Canberra: Australian Government Printing Service.

———. 1959. *Economics of the road transport of beef cattle: Northern Territory and Queensland channel country.* Canberra: Australian Government Printing Service.

———. 1968. *The Northern Territory beef cattle industry: An economic survey 1942–43 and 1964–65.* Canberra: Australian Government Printing Service.

Bain, M.S. 1969. Alcohol use and traditional social control in Aboriginal society. In *Better health for Aborigines?*, ed. B.S. Hetzel, M. Dobbin, L. Lippmann, and E. Eggleston, 42–52. St Lucia: University of Queensland Press.

Barnes, J.A., J.C. Mitchell, and M. Gluckman. [1949] 1963. The village headman in British Central Africa. *Africa* 19 (2). Republished in M. Gluckman, *Order and Rebellion in Tribal Africa.* London: Cohen and West.

Barwick, D.E. 1974. And the lubras are ladies now. *Women's role in Aboriginal society*, ed. F. Gale, 51–64. Canberra: Australian Institute of Aboriginal Studies.

Becker, H. 1973. *Outsiders*. New York: Free Press.

Beckett, J. 1964. Aborigines, alcohol and assimilation. In *Aborigines now*, ed. M. Reay, 32–47. Sydney: Angus and Robertson.

———. 1977. The Torres Strait Islanders and the pearling industry: a case of internal colonialism. *Aboriginal History* 1: 77–104.

Berger, P., and T. Luckman. 1966. *The social construction of reality*. Ringwood: Pelican.

Berkowitz, L. 1972. *Aggression: A social psychological analysis*. New York: McGraw-Hill.

Berndt, R.M. 1977. Aboriginal identity: reality or mirage. In *Aborigines and change: Australia in the '70s*, ed. R.M. Berndt, 1–13. Canberra: Australian Institute of Aboriginal Studies.

———. and C.H. Berndt. 1977. *The world of the first Australians*. Sydney: Ure Smith.

Black-Michaud, Jacob. 1975. *Cohesive force*. Oxford: Basil Blackwell.

Blau, P. 1964. *Exchange and power in social life*. New York: Wiley.

Bleakley, J.W. 1928. *The Aboriginals and Half-Castes of Central Australia and North Australia*. Commonwealth Parliamentary Paper 21. Canberra: Australian Government Printing Service.

Blok, A. 1974. *The Mafia of a Sicilian village 1860–1960: A study of violent peasant entrepreneurs*. New York: Harper Torchbacks.

Bourdieu, P. 1977. *Outline of a theory of practice*. Cambridge: Cambridge University Press.

Bureau of Agricultural Economics, see BAE.

CAALAS (Central Australian Aboriginal Legal Aid Service). 1975. Press release.

Cawte, J.E. 1972. *Cruel, poor, and brutal nations*. Honolulu: University Press.

Cohen, A.P., and J.L. Comaroff. 1976. The management of meaning: On the phenomenology of political transactions. In *Transaction and meaning: Directions in the anthropology of exchange and symbolic behaviour*, ed. B. Kapferer, 87–108. Philadelphia: Institute for the Study of Human Issues.

Collmann, Jeff. 1981. Clients, cooptation and bureaucratic

discipline. *Administrative frameworks and clients*. Special issue. *Social Analysis*, ed. Jeff Collmann and Don Handelmann, 48–62.

Coombs, H.C. 1972a. The future of the Australian Aboriginal. *The George Judah Cohen Memorial Lectures*. Sydney: University of Sydney.

———. 1972b. Decisions by Aborigines. *Anthropological Forum III* (2): 136–45.

———. 1973. Decentralization trends among Aboriginal communities. Unpublished manuscript.

DAA. 1974. *Annual report 1973–74*. Canberra: Australian Government Printing Service.

———. 1976. *Annual report 1975–76*. Canberra: Australian Government Printing Service.

DAA, Northern Territory Division. 1973. *Annual report 1972–73*. Canberra: Australian Government Printing Service.

Davidson, B.R. 1972. *The northern myth*. Melbourne: Melbourne University Press.

Department of Aboriginal Affairs, see DAA.

Department of the Northern Territory, Welfare Branch. 1953. Bungalow File. 49/90.

———. 1954. Bungalow File. G.E. 32/127.

———. 1958. Bungalow File. G,E, 38/22.

Dollard, J. 1967. *Frustration and aggression*. New Haven: Yale University Press.

Downing, J. 1968. Communication. Unpublished manuscript.

———. 1971a. Report on a trip to Kunamata and requests from the Aboriginal people associated with the Fig totem site. Unpublished manuscript.

———. 1971b. Consultation and self-determination in the social development of Aborigines. In *A question of choice: An Australian Aboriginal dilemma*, ed. R.M. Berndt. Nedlands: University of Western Australia Press.

———.n.d. *Aboriginal "Dreamings" and town plans*. Alice Springs: Institute for Aboriginal Development.

Duncan, R. 1967. *The Northern Territory pastoral industry: 1863–1910*. Melbourne: Melbourne University Press.

Elkin, A.P. 1951. Reaction and interaction: A food-gathering people and european settlement in Australia. *American Anthropologist*, 53: 164–86.

Epstein, A.L. 1958. *Politics in an urban African community*. Manchester: Manchester University Press.

Esterson, A. 1972. *The leaves of spring: Schizophrenia, family and Sacrifice*. Ringwood: Penguin.

Fanon, F. 1967. *The wretched of the earth*. Ringwood: Penguin.

————. 1970. *Black skin white masks*. London: Paladin.

Fink, R.A. 1957. The caste barrier: An obstacle to the assimilation of Part-Aborigines in North-west New South Wales. *Oceania* 28: 103.

————. 1960. *The changing status and cultural identity of Western Australian Aborigines*. Unpublished Ph.D. Thesis in Anthropology. New York: Columbia University.

Frank, A. Gundar, 1967. *Capitalism and underdevelopment in Latin America*. New York: Monthly Review Press.

Gale, F. 1970. The impact of urbanization on Aboriginal marriage patterns. In *Australian Aboriginal Anthropology*, ed. R.M. Berndt, 303–25. Nedlands: University of Western Australia Press.

Garbett, G. K. n.d. Graph theory and the analysis of multiplex and manifold relationships. *Numerical analysis in social anthropology*, ed. J.C. Mitchell. Philadelphia: Institute for the Study of Human Issues.

Gilbert, Kevin J. 1973. *Because a white man'll never do it*. Sydney: Angus and Robertson.

————. 1978. *Living black: Blacks talk to Kevin Gilbert*. Ringwood: Penguin.

Gilsenan, M. 1976. Lying, honour and contradiction. In *Transaction and meaning: Directions in the anthropology of exchange and symbolic behaviour*, ed. B. Kapferer, 191–219. Philadelphia: Institute for the Study of Human Issues.

Gluckman, M. 1958. *Analysis of a social situation in modern Zululand*. Rhodes-Livingston Paper no. 28. Manchester: Manchester University Press.

————. 1968. Interhierarchical roles: Professional and party ethics in the tribal areas in South and Central Africa. In *Local-level politics*, ed. M. Swartz. Chicago: Aldine.

————. 1971. Tribalism, ruralism and urbanism in South and Central Africa. In *Profiles of change: African society and colonial rule*, ed. V.W. Turner, 127–66. Cambridge: Cambridge University Press.

Goffman, E. 1967. *Interaction ritual*. Garden City: Anchor Books.

Gouldner, A.W. 1957–58. Cosmopolitans and locals: Toward an

analysis of latent social roles – I and II. *Administrativ~
Science Quarterly* 2: 281–306, 444–80.

_____. 1975. *For sociology.* Ringwood: Penguin.

Gray, W.J. 1977. Decentralisation trends in Arnhem Land. In *Aborigines and change: Australia in the '70s,* ed. R.M. Berndt, 114–123. Canberra: Australian Institute of Aboriginal Studies.

Graves, T.D. 1967. Acculturation, access, and alcohol in a tri-ethnic community. *American Anthropologist,* 69: 306–21.

Grey, L. The needs of the half-caste community exempt from Aboriginal ordinance. Unpublished manuscript.

_____. and H. Thatcher. 1967. Annual report of work of female welfare officers to 30th June, 1958. Unpublished manuscript.

Handelman, D. 1976. Bureaucratic transactions: The development of official–client relationships in Israel. In *Transaction and meaning: Directions in the anthropology of exchange and symbolic behaviour,* ed. B. Kapferer. Philadelphia: Institute for the Study of Human Issues.

Hannerz, U. 1969. *Soulside: Inquiries into ghetto culture and community.* New York: Colombia University Press.

Hardy, F. 1978. *The Unlucky Australians.* Sydney: Pan Books.

Hartwig, M. 1977. Capitalism and Aborigines: The theory of internal colonialism and its rivals. In *Political economy of Australian capitalism,* Vol. 3, ed. E.L. Wheelwright and K. Buckley, 119–41. Sydney: Australia and New Zealand Book Company.

Hay, D. 1976. *The delivery of services financed by the Department of Aboriginal Affairs.* Canberra: Australian Government Printing Service.

Honigmann, J.J. 1973. Alcohol in its cultural context. In *Proceedings of the Annual Alcoholism Conference of the National Institute on Alcohol and Alcoholism.* Springfield, Virginia: National Technical Information Service.

House of Representatives Standing Committee on Aboriginal Affairs. 1976. *Alcohol problems of Aboriginals, Northern Territory aspects.* Canberra: Australian Government Printing Service.

_____. 1977. *Alcohol problems of Aboriginals, final report.* Canberra: Australian Government Printing Service.

Kapferer, B. 1972. *Strategy and transaction in an African factory:*

African workers and Indian management in a Zambian Town.
Manchester: Manchester University Press.

———. 1976. Introduction. In *Transaction and meaning: Directions in the anthropology of exchange and symbolic behaviour,* ed. B. Kapferer, 1–22. Philadelphia: Institute for the Study of Human Issues.

Kelly, J.H. 1971. *Beef in Northern Australia.* Canberra: Australian National University Press.

Kirke, D. 1974. The traditionally oriented community. In *Better health for Aborigines?,* ed. B.S. Hetzel, M. Dobbin, L. Lippmann, and E. Eggleston, 81–87. St Lucia: University of Queensland Press.

Klockars, C.B. 1974. *The professional fence: Thirty years of "wheelin' and dealin' " in stolen goods.* New York: Free Press.

Laing, R.D. 1972. *The politics of the family and other essays.* New York: Vintage Books.

Langer, S.K. 1978. *Philosophy in a new key.* Cambridge: Harvard University Press.

Larbalastier, J. 1977. Black women in colonial Australia. *Refractory Girl* 6: 43–53.

Levy, S. and S.J. Kunitz. Indian drinking: Problems of data collection and interpretation. In *Proceedings of the Annual Alcoholism Conference of the National Institute on Alcohol and Alcoholism,* 217–36. Springfield, Virginia: National Technical Information Service.

Long, J.P.M. 1964. Papunya: Westernization in an Aboriginal community. *Aborigines now,* ed M. Reay, 48–58. Sydney: Angus and Robertson.

———. 1967. The administration and the Part-Aboriginals of the Northern Territory. *Oceania* 37(3): 186–201.

———. 1970a. Polygyny, acculturation, and contact: Aspects of Aboriginal marriage in Central Australia. In *Australian Aboriginal Anthropology,* ed. R.M. Berndt, 292–304. Nedlands: University of Western Australia Press.

———. 1970b. *Aboriginal settlements: A survey of institutional communities in eastern Australia.* Canberra: Australian National University Press.

Mauss, M. 1969. *The gift.* London: Cohen and West.

McHugh, P. 1968. *Defining the situation: The organization of meaning in social interaction.* New York: Bobbs-Merrill Company.

Meggitt, M.J. 1962. *Desert people: A study of the Walbiri Aborigines of Central Australia*. Sydney: Angus and Robertson.

———. 1964. Indigenous forms of government among the Australian Aborigines. *Bijdragen tot der taalland, en volkenkunde* 120 (1): 163–80.

———. 1965. Marriage among the Walbiri of Central Australia: A statistical examination. In *Aboriginal man in Australia*, ed. R.M. and C.H. Berndt, 146–66. Canberra: Australian Institute of Aboriginal Studies.

Milhouse, J., et al. 1975. *Petition*. Unpublished manuscript.

Millar, C.H., and J.M.S. Leung. 1974. Aboriginal alcohol consumption in South Australia. In *A Question of choice: An Australian Aboriginal dilemma*, ed. R.M. Berndt, 91–95. Nedlands: University of Western Australia Press.

Mills, C. Wright. 1940. Situated actions and vocabularies of motive. *American Sociological Review* 5: 904–13.

Mitchell, J. Clyde. 1956. *The Kalela dance: Aspects of social relationships among urban Africans in northern Rhodesia*. Manchester: Manchester University Press.

———. 1961. Social change and the stability of African marriage in northern Rhodesia. In *Social change in Modern Africa*, ed. A. Southall, 316–29. London: Oxford University Press.

———. 1966. Theoretical orientations in African urban studies. In *Social anthropology of complex societies*, ed. M. Banton, ASA Monograph 4, 37–68. London: Tavistock.

———. 1974. Perceptions of ethnicity and ethnic behaviour: An empirical exploration. In *Urban ethnicity*, ed. Abner Cohen, ASA Monograph 12, 1–35. London: Tavistock.

Mullard, C. 1974. *Aborigines in Australia today*. Phillip, ACT: National Aboriginal Forum.

Northern Territory, Administration. 1944. Annual report. Canberra: Australian Government Printing Service.

——— 1948. Annual report. Canberra: Australian Government Printing Service.

Payne, W.L., and J.W. Fletcher. 1937. Report of the Board of Inquiry into the land and land industries of the Northern Territory of Australia. Canberra.

Perkins, C. 1975. *A bastard like me*. Sydney: Ure Smith.

Perry, R.A. 1962. General report on the lands of the Alice Springs area, Northern Territory, 1956–1957. Melbourne: CSIRO.

Peters, E. 1967. Some structural aspects of the feud among the camelherding Bedouin of Cyrenaica. *Africa* 37 (3): 261–82.

Radcliffe-Brown, A. R. 1952. *Structure and function in primitive society.* London: Cohen and West.

Reay, M. 1945. A half-caste aboriginal community in north-western New South Wales. *Oceania* 15 (4): 296–323.

Reay, M., and G. Sitlington. 1948. Class and status in a mixed blood community (Moree, NSW), *Oceania* 18 (3): 177–207.

Riches, D. 1975. Cash, credit and gambling in a modern Eskimo economy: Speculations on origins of spheres of exchange. *Man* n.s. 10: 21–33.

Robbins, R.H. 1973. Alcohol and the identity struggle: Some effects of economic change on interpersonal relations. *American Anthropologist* 75: 99–122.

Rose, F.G.G. 1965. *The winds of change in Central Australia.* Berlin: Akademie-Verlag.

Rowley, C.D. 1972. *The Remote Aborigines.* Ringwood: Penguin.

———. 1973. *Outcastes in white Australia.* Ringwood: Penguin.

———. 1974. *The destruction of Aboriginal society.* Ringwood: Penguin.

Sackett, L. 1977. Liquor and the law. In *Aborigines and change: Australia in the 70's,* ed. R.M. Berndt, 90–99. Canberra: Australian Institute of Aboriginal Studies.

———. 1978. Clinging to the law: Leadership at Wiluna. In *Whitefella business: Aborigines in Australian politics,* ed. M. Howard, 37–48. Philadelphia: Institute for the Study of Human Issues.

Sahlins, M. 1961. The segmentary lineage: An organization of predatory expansion. *American Anthropologist* (63): 322–45.

———. 1974. *Stone Age economics.* London: Tavistock.

Schutz, A. 1976. *The phenomenology of the social world.* London: Heinemann.

Senate Select Committee on Aborigines and Torres Strait Islanders. 1976. The environmental condition of Aborigines and Torres Strait Islanders and the preservation of their sacred sites. Canberra: Australian Government Publishing Service.

Simmell, G. 1964. *The Sociology of George Simmel.* Trans., ed., and with an introduction by Kurt H. Wolff. New York: Free Press.

Smith, M.G. 1974. *West Indian family structure.* Seattle: University of Washington Press.

Smith, R.T. 1956. *The Negro family in British Guiana*. London: Routledge & Kegan Paul.

Solien de Gonzalez, N.L. 1961. Family organization in five types of migratory wage labor. *American Anthropologist* 63: 1264-79.

––––––. 1965. The consanguinal household and matrifocality. *American Anthropologist* 67: 1541-48.

––––––. 1969. *Black Carib house structure*. Seattle: University of Washington Press.

Spencer, W. Baldwin. 1913. Preliminary report of the Aboriginals of the Northern Territory. Commonwealth Parliamentary Papers, 36-52. In Report of the Administrator for the year 1912.

––––––. and F. Gillen. 1968. *The native tribes of Central Australia*. New York: Dover.

Stanner, W.E.H. 1974. *After the Dreaming*. Sydney: Australian Broadcasting Commission.

Stein, M. 1964. *The eclipse of community*. Princeton: Princeton University Press.

Stevens, F. 1974. *Aborigines in the Northern Territory cattle industry*. Canberra: Australian National University Press.

Strehlow, T.G.H. 1947. *Aranda tradition*. Melbourne: Melbourne University Press.

––––––. 1970. Geography and the totemic landscape in Central Australia: A functional study. In *Australian Aboriginal Anthropology*, ed. R.M. Berndt, 92-140. Nedlands: University of Western Australia Press.

Szwed, J.F. 1966. Gossip, drinking and social control: Consensus and communication in a Newfoundland parish. *Ethnology* 5: 434-41.

Tatz, C.M. 1964. Aboriginal administration in the Northern Territory of Australia. Unpublished Ph.D. thesis, Department of Anthropology and Sociology, Australian National University.

Toch, H. 1972. *Violent men: An inquiry into the psychology of violence*. Ringwood: Penguin.

Waddell, J.O. 1973. "Drink Friend!": Social contexts of convivial drinking and drunkenness among Papago Indians in an urban setting. In *Proceedings of the Annual Alcoholism Conference of the National Institute on Alcohol and Alcoholism*. Springfield, Virginia: National Technical Information Service.

Wallace, N.M. 1977. Pitjantjatjara decentralisation in north-west South Australia. In *Aborigines and Change: Australia in the '70s*, ed. R.M. Berndt, 124–35. Canberra: Australian Institute of Aboriginal Studies.

Walters, E.V. 1972. *Terror and Resistance*. London: Oxford University Press.

White, W.F. 1955. *Street-corner Society*. Chicago: Chicago University Press.

Wolfgang, M., and F. Ferracutti. 1967. *The subculture of violence: Toward an integrated theory of Criminology*. London: Tavistock.

Wolpe, H. 1975. The theory of internal colonialism: The South African case. In *Beyond the Sociology of Development*, ed. I. Oxall, T. Barnett, and D. Booth, 229–52. London: Routledge & Kegan Paul.

Woodward, A.E. 1973. Aboriginal Land Rights Commission, First Report. Canberra: Australian Government Printing Service.

Woodward, A.E. 1974. Aboriginal Land Rights Commission, Second Report. Commonwealth Parliamentary Papers 69.

Index

Aboriginal culture, 8, 9
  and land rights, 228-34
  decline of, 1-3, 36
  expropriation of, 223-36
Aboriginal Hostels, 27, 37 n 5, 60
Aboriginal Land Rights Bill, 38 n 6
  CLP's concern over, 43
Aboriginal Land Rights Commission, 231
Aboriginal Legal Service (ALS), 19-20
Aboriginal Medical Service, 215
Aborigines
  adaption to new settings, 4
  administration of, 42, 74-81
    by Commonwealth, 12, 39, 43, 75
    prior to 1953, 75-76
  Anmatjira, 127, 164, 209
  anthropological debates about, 226-27
  Arunta, 127, 164, 209
  basic rights, 13
  and cattle industry, 247, 248, 251
  competition for resources among, 7
  controlling white administrators, 16, 30, 234
  ingenuity of, 8-9
  Kaiditja, 127, 209
  Labor government policies for, 41-43, 231-34
  local control of, 51, 52
  organizations for, 19
    DAA subsidized, 25
    threat to, 53
  part (urban), 34, 85-86, 226, 227-28

  distinction from tribal, 18, 22, 195
  job opportunities for, 80, 132, 134
  range of opportunities for, 81-82
  relations with DAA and CAALAS, 34
  as political resources, 31-32, 34, 40, 234
  and welfare agencies, 5, 12, 14, 40
  and white police, 52, 53
  and whites, 4, 28-29, 41, 49, 81-88, 105-6
  ties to the earth, 225
  tribal (full-blood), 18, 22, 34, 195, 226, 227-28, 235
administrators, white, 5, 11-13
  impinging upon Aborigines, 16
  relationships with Aborigines, 36, 40, 233-34
adult education, 18
Africans, 4, 5
Ajax, 216, 218
alcohol. See liquor
Alice Springs
  area of, 238
  cattle stations in, 238, 240
  Cavanaugh's visit to, 61-70
  Citizen's Association, 59
  housing programme, 111, 112
  Legislative Assembly for, 58-59
  Memorial Club, 46
  pastoral district, 243-57
  petition against drunkenness, 49
  racial tension crisis in, 41-70
  rainfall at, 237, 238

Tourist Promotion Board
(ASTPB), 66-67, 68
Town Council, 100
Amoonguna settlement, 67, 91, 93
Anglican Church
St Margaret's and St Anthony's,
134
Anmatjira. *See* Aborigines
Anzac Oval, 89
area, condition of structural
involvement, 83
Arltunga, 90, 245
Arunta. *See* Aborigines
assimilation policy, 15, 16, 17, 77,
118
implementation of, 110-11
inauguration of, 40
major aims of, 111
replacement of, 230
repudiation of, 25
women as key to, 119
Australian Labor Party (ALP), 16,
43
criticized by CLP, 42, 43
defeat of, 43
subsidizing of railroads by,
164-65
award wages, 136, 137, 167, 229

Bankside (pub), 44
Berndt, R.M., 1-2
binge drinking. *See* drinking
"blackfellows", 132, 133, 137, 138,
139
Black-Michaud, Jacob, 173, 174
Bleakley, J.W., 88-89
Blok, Anton, 141, 172
bosses, "good" and "bad", 130, 137,
140, 144, 145
Bourdieu, P., 174, 203
"boys", "good" and "bad", 144, 145
Bourke, 224
brokers, 16, 30, 32, 35, 37 n 1
help to define land rights,
231-32
"middler" type of, 233
role of, 24
transactions in sacred materials,
32
Bungalow, the, 89, 91, 113, 134
banishment from, 116
closing of, 91
escapees from, 91
as labor camp, 91
rationing at, 114-15
shift to Jay Creek, 89

bush-burning, Mt Kelly, 218, 235
extent of, 219-20
reasons for, 207-8, 219
significance of, 208, 221-22

cattle droving, use of, 254, 255
cattle industry, Central Australian,
237-57
boss-worker relationship in,
180-81, 184
employment opportunities in,
126-48
fencing of ranges by, 251-52
markets for, 130, 241, 249, 257
recruitment into, 80, 82, 98,
113, 131-36, 142
from institutions, 134
relations with Aborigines, 246,
248
United Kingdom's meat
agreement with, 249
violence against workers in,
137-39, 141-42
as recruiting technique, 142
work in, 117, 129-42
cattle stations, 14, 75, 76-77, 81,
238
authority over people, 86
Bullion, 127
distribution of, 240
early settlers on, 106
Gumtree, 127
Jefferson Downs, 180, 182
labor from fringe-camps on, 96
Malapunya, 184
Nijambah, 138
residents of, 22, 78-79, 86
right to live on, 80
right to work on, 80
subsidies for, 18, 78
Central Australian Aboriginal
Congress (CAAC), 37 n 5, 57
role in health care, 215
Central Australian Aboriginal Legal
Aid Service (CAALAS), 34-35, 96
Alice Springs' interpretation of,
56-57
dependence upon
Commonwealth support, 44
establishment of, 25-26, 33-34
rebuttal to drunkenness petition,
50
social order, position on, 51-52
work of, 25-27
Central Land Council (CLC), 28,
37 n 5, 209

Centralian Advocate (newspaper),
    45, 49
children
    conflicts with parents, 186-99
    control of, 120, 165-66
    health risks of, 215
    in institutions, 118, 134, 187-88
    naming of, 122-23
    neglect of, 118
    reciprocity to parents, 189-90
    as a resource, 167, 191, 193
    violence against, 176-77
Coombs, H.C., 24, 211, 222n 2
Corcoran, Barry, 140-41, 200
    problems with Virgin, 182-83
    relationship with Gladys
        Williams, 178-86
    relationship with workmates,
        183-84
Corcoran, Donald, 138, 139-40,
    164, 182
    relationship with William
        Samuelson, 202-4
cosmopolitans
    distinction from locals, 55
Country Liberal Party (CLP), 41-42,
    43
    victory of, 43
credit, 126
    extended, 108
    funds of, 149
    granting of, 152
    grantors of, 152-53
    potential, 152, 154-55, 155-56
    realized, 152, 154
    sharing liquor for, 151-59
    symbolic capital as, 168
    types of, 152
creditors
    general collectivities as, 152,
        154, 155-56
    specific persons as, 154-55
    types of, 152
Cross-Culture Group, 59
crown land, 100
Cyclone Tracy, 222 n 2

Department of Aboriginal Affairs
    (DAA), 12, 17-21
    Aboriginal Hostels, funding for,
        27
    ALS programme, 19-20
    establishment of, 17, 231
    involvement with Mt Kelly,
        205-16
    power over Aborigines, 70, 205,
        206

purchasing and subsidizing
        Aboriginal cattle stations, 18
    staffing of, 25
    subsidizing cattle stations, 18
    support for CAALAS, 35
Department of Housing and
    Construction, 211
Department of Public Health, 12,
    75, 216, 218
Department of Social Security, 96,
    103 n 3
    detoxification centres, 50, 51
    detribalization, 3, 5, 6, 7
        politics of, 39-72
    reaction against, 36
    symptoms of, 70-71
domestic economy, Aboriginal, 107
    pensions as basis of, 109
    significance of, 107
    women controlling, 109
domestic groups, Aboriginal
    interpersonal violence in, 176-78
    isolation of, 121
    matricentric, 178
    penetration by bureaucracy, 106
    significance of, 107, 124-25
    types of, 125
    women as heads of, 119
Douglas, Mrs, 181, 184
Downing, Rev J., 23-24
drinking
    among North American Indians,
        150
    among women, 165-66
    associated with white urban life,
        163
    as "social problem", 149-50
    sprees, 108, 128, 153-59
        to acquire credit, 155-56
        in Arnhem Land, 168
        attendees of, 157
        refusing to attend, 156-57,
            158
    to repay debits, 156
    tastes, 160, 162
    and violence, 170
drunkenness
    cause of racial tension, 44-48, 51
    Centralian Advocate (newspaper),
        45
    decriminalization of, 46, 47, 49,
        51
    as expression of personal power,
        165
    to lose shame, 164
    personal control of, 167
    petition against, 49

rebuttal of, 50
as reflection of white society,
    165
Elliotson, Ronnie, 162
employment, 5, 80
    in cattle industry, 129-42
    types of, 11, 129
    with government departments,
        79, 80
Enderby, Kep, attorney-general, 52
Enga, 168, 168 n 2
ethnic models, 132, 133, 136
    motivational structures of, 136,
        137

"fair exchange", 82, 104 n 6
families,
    matricentric, 119-20
    in United States black ghettos,
        119-20
fear, 172-73
federalism policy, 42
feuds, 173-74
flagons, 46
fringe-camp, 6, 73-104. *See also*
        Todd River fringe-camp
    as access to employment, 127
    as access to resources, 74
    to avoid welfare controls, 74
    as means to control mobility, 84
    composition of, 101
    contemporary situation of,
        94-101
    emergence of, 88-94
    location of, 100
    observations about, 87
    significance of, 71
    white men living in, 101-2
fringe-dwellers, 3, 22
    access to urban employment,
        95-96, 98
    controlled by whites, 6
    development of, 3
    ingenuity of, 8
    links to settlements and
        missions, 97
    mobility of, 84, 99-100
    rejection of welfare benefits, 10,
        206
    relationships with whites, 9
    as symptom of detribalization,
        205
    and Tungatjira Association, 210
Frontiers Conference, 60

goldrush, 245

good faith
    Cavanaugh's refusal to affirm,
        65
    as condition for political
        negotiation, 54, 55
    denied, 57, 58
Gouldner, A.W., 53-54
government, local
    control of Aboriginal affairs, 53
    threat to Aboriginal
        organizations, 53
grandmothers, 166
Grey, Sister Leslie, 93, 111, 112,
    117
Gurrindji, 35, 223, 228-29
    land claims, 230, 232

Haasts Bluff, 79, 113
Hardy, Frank, 223
    as a broker, 228-29, 230
    and land rights, 228-30
    at Wattie Creek, 228
health and sanitation, 219
    at Mt Kelly, 213, 214, 215-16,
        218
honour, 174
Hooker Creek, 5, 79, 116
horsewhipping (stockwhipping),
    138-39
housing
    Aboriginal Hostels, 27
    DAA efforts, 18
    by Housing Commission, 77
    regulation of, 107
    for tribal communities, 23, 24
    by Welfare Branch, 77
humpies, 10

identities
    latent, 53-54, 55
    manifest, 53-54, 58
    social, 28, 142
        as chief resource, 199
        in relation to sprees and
            drinking, 156, 160
        and violence, 185
indebtedness
    by attending sprees, 155-56
    to bosses, 145-46, 148
    in relation to violence, 177-78
    scope of, 83
    secondary, 146-47
infant mortality, causes of, 214
Institute of Aboriginal Development
    (IAD), 66, 67-68, 210
integration policy. *See* assimilation
    policy

internal colonialism, 110
invalid port, 46

jobs. *See* employment

Kaidetja. *See* Aborigines, Kaidetja
Kapferer, B., 7
kin naming, 120, 122-23
kinship terms, 147-48
Klockars, C.B., 8

labour
    decline in demand for, 166-67,
        254, 255
    withholding of, 108
land claims, 29
land rights, 19, 20, 28, 36, 228-34
    and Aboriginal culture, 228-34
    and brokers, 231-32
    conditions for, 212
    Frank Hardy's role in, 228-30
    Labor government policy,
        37-38 n 6, 231
    movement, 208-9
    Mt Kelly claims for, 209
    and self-determination policy,
        231
    Woodward Commission, 231
legal aid service, 19-21. *See also*
    Central Australian Aboriginal
    Legal Aid Service
Legislative Assembly, 41
liquor, 11
    categorization of, 160
    as credit, 149
    as mark of affluence, 149,
        158-59, 163-64
    sharing of, 151
    as symbolic capital, 168
    types of, 159-60, 163
    value in Te-exchange cycle, 168,
        168 n 2
Little Flower Mission, 90
locals
    distinction between
        cosmopolitans, 55
    as responsible citizens, 55-56
locus, condition of structural
    involvement, 83

Mafiosi, Sicilian, 141, 172
marriages
    fire-stick, 9, 121
    kangaroo, 9, 121, 122
    proper, 9, 121
    types of, 120

matrifiliation, 124
Mayhew, Angie, 180
Mayhew, Katie, 180, 181, 182
men
    control of children, 165-66
    demands of white society upon,
        126-27
    dependence upon women's
        income, 11
    relations with pastoralists,
        130-31
    reputation of, 134, 137
    role of, 111-13, 117
    types of jobs for, 79-80
middler, 30, 33
mining, 36, 245
missions, 4, 14, 75, 76, 81, 97
    competition with CAALAS, 27
    Hermansburg, 88, 134
    Little Flower Mission, 90
    Santa Teresa, 91
mobility, 83, 84
    among fringe-camps, 84, 99-100
    to control social forces, 84
money
    flow of, 128
    surplus of, 108, 167
mothers. *See* women
Mt Kelly
    bush-burning at, 218
    and cattle industry, 127-29
    concern over racial tension at,
        206-7
    disputes with DNT departments,
        209
    fencing perimeter of, 212
    Housing Association, 210
    as job recruiting ground, 135
    lease application, 210, 211, 212
    personal independence of, 208
    population, 127, 128, 209
    sanitation facilities, 215, 216,
        218
    self-image of, 214, 217
    sewage drain controversy,
        209-11
    standard of living at, 10-11
    and tourists, 212
    violence in, 175
Murphy, Senator Lionel, 46, 51, 52,
    64
mustering camps, 252
"myall blackfellows", 203

National Aboriginal Consultative
    Committee, 18

Native Affairs, 114
Native Affairs Branch, 91, 103 n 2
Newcastle Waters strike, 229
North American Indians, 24, 150

"open-range" technique, use of, 246,
    247, 251
opium, 39
outstation movement, 36-37

Papunya, 206
parents
    demands upon children, 189
    relationships with children, 113
    surrendering children, 118
    violence against, 186
pastoral industry. See cattle
    industry
patterns of avoidance, 143, 145-46
    at Mt Kelly, 213, 214
pensions, 96, 109
    social security, 11, 196
    as source of credit, 151-52
    supporting mothers', 98
    women's control of, 109, 178
Pintubi, 68
police brutality, 59
Prohibited Areas Clause, 90
prostitution, 39
publicans, 69

Racial Discrimination Bill, 50
racial tension crisis, 40-41, 70,
    72 n 1, 206
    causes of, 44, 47, 48, 53
    Cavanaugh's meeting in Alice
        Springs during, 61-70
    consequences of, 70-71
    participants in, 44
    as threat to Aboriginal
        organizations, 53
racists, 55, 57
radicals, 56-57
Rainbow Town, 112
rape, 48, 49
reciprocity,
    domestic, 189, 190, 195
    generalized, 189-91
Redfern, 62
relationships
    domestic, 198
    range of, 82-83
religious customs, 36. See also
    sacred material; sacred places
reserves, establishment of, 39-40

resources
    competition for, 7
    economic and symbolic, 174,
        185
    underuse of, 107
ringers, in cattle industry, 252,
    257 n 2
roadtrains, 254
Roman Catholic Church, 90
Rowley, C.D., 75
rubbishmen, 157

sacred material, 29, 30
    transactions in, 30-31, 32
    and white men, 30-33, 34
sacred places, 29
Sahlins, M., 121
salmonella, 214, 218, 219
Salterson, Emerald, 200
Samuelson, Alfred, 138, 140, 201
Samuelson, William, 132, 138, 140
    relationship with Barry
        Corcoran, 181, 182, 184
    violence against Don Corcoran,
        200-204
Santa Teresa Mission, 91
secrecy, rule of, 29, 30, 31, 32
self-determination policy, 13, 17,
    19-21, 32, 36, 40
    CAALAS support for, 26
    ideology of, 22-24
    implementation of, 40, 41
    and land rights, 231
settlements, government, 4, 77, 81,
    84
    competition with CAALAS, 27
    job opportunities on, 113
    people of, 78
    as ration depots, 79
Sharp, Cameron, 137-38
Sharp, George, 161
    and bush-burning, 207-8, 218
    CAAC officer, 217
    caring for child, 191, 192
    and the DAA, 216, 217, 221
    drinking tastes of, 161, 163
    Helen, 191, 192
    involvement in land rights, 210
    military career of, 196, 198
    Mt Kelly Housing Association
        officer, 193, 208
    Mt Kelly people, 217-18
    parents, 186-99
Sharp, Hope, 191, 193
Sharp, Isabel, 123, 162
    as grandparent, 196

relationship with son George
Sharp, 186-99
taking care of Hope, 193, 194
Sharp, Terry, 123, 162, 218
and George Sharp, 186-99
shigella, 214, 219
Simmell, George, 29
snakes, 220, 221
social life, patterns of, 4
social order
local control of, 51-53
maintenance of, 51
"southern stirrers", 56, 57
squatter settlements. *See* fringe-
camps
stockman, skills of, 136
strategizing, 7-8
structural involvement, multiplex
and simplex, 103 n 1

taxi drivers, 69
Tennant Creek, 34
Thatcher, Helen, 111, 112, 117,
123, 213
and the Sharps, 187, 188
Tjuritja, 90
Todd River fringe-camp, 44, 46-47,
48, 88, 206
"Todd frogs", 160, 162
town plans, 23-24
trachoma, 214, 219
transactional analyses, 7
tribal communities, 23
tribal elders, 28
recruits for land trusts, 29
relations with CAALAS, 35-36
religious importance of, 29
Tungatjira Association, 210

unemployment, 5, 7, 108, 115
United States
black ghettos, 119
restrictions on cattle imports,
130
Unlucky Australians, The, 223
urban housing projects, 77

Vesteys, 35, 230, 236 n 1
violence, 11
between Corcoran and
Samuelson, 178-86
parents and children,
186-99, 191
in cattle industry, 139, 141-42,
143, 147
stockwhipping, 138-39

at centre of social life, 173
Centralian Advocate (newspaper),
45
as discipline training, 147
domestic, 176-78
and exchange of domestic
resources, 177
interpersonal, 176
to keep face, 186, 197, 203
police, 52
psychological explanation of,
174
to restore balance of honour,
204
significance of audience to, 201,
203-4
for social control, 172
subculture thesis of, 170-71
Virgin, Clem, 180, 182-83, 184

Walbiri, 34, 84
walkabout, 125 n 1
wards, 78
at the Bungalow settlement, 116
restricted residence of, 78, 84
Warrabri settlement, 77
Wattie Creek, 35, 36, 223, 230, 232
Wave Hill Station strike, 223
welfare agencies
competition for Aboriginal
support, 12, 15, 17
control over basic resources, 13
history of, 14-17
inter-agency competition, 28, 33
power of, 6, 40
relations with Aborigines, 5-6
Welfare Branch, 8, 10, 12, 75, 110
assimilation policy of, 77-78
control of resources, 79
disbandment of, 17, 25
interference with families,
186-87, 188
limits of, 8
major responsibility of, 111
pastoralists' subsidies from, 78
redistribution of Aborigines by,
76-77
relations with fringe-dwellers,
931-94
supporting of working and
single mothers, 118-19
tactics towards domestic group,
124
Welfare Division of the Northern
Territory Administration, 37 n 4
Welfare Ordinance of 1953, 91

whites, 9
  access to sacred material and
    places, 29
  conflicts and competition
    among, 7
  cooperation with Aborigines, 7
  favoured by Aborigines, 33
  living in fringe-camps, 101-2
Williams, Gladys, 200
  relationship with Barry
    Corcoran, 178-86
women
  controlling domestic economy,
    109, 119
  and drinking, 165-66
  forbidden access to sacred
    material, 29

as head of domestic group, 119
job opportunities for, 79, 80, 95,
  118
as mothers, 108, 118, 119
pensions for, 11, 108, 118
role of, 112-13, 117
Woodward, Justice A.E.
  as broker, 234
  concern for land rights, 18-19,
    28, 38 n 6, 208-9, 212, 232,
    234
Woodward Commission, 231
work. See employment

Yuendumu, 26, 34